Prais~~e~~
The Starre, the M~~oone, the Sunne.~~

"This is a beautiful story. It was a joy to read, a tale of depth and detail. One that will certainly enthral any reader. It's controversial and provocative, which is eminently attractive, and the journey is excitingly powerful."
- **Sir Derek Jacobi,** Tony & BAFTA award-winning actor.

"Roll over, Harry Potter! The Starre, the Moone, the Sunne has all the mystery and suspense of Harry Potter and even more substance, with literary sleuths in a romp up and down and all around the Elizabethan-Shakespearean matrix. Ron Destro's narrator is endowed with consistently ingenious dialect, and Derek Jacobi has a field day in the audiobook exercising his sublime elocutions on the clever word bending. To anyone steeped in the authorship lore, the familiarity of the plethora of names of minor characters is a laugh riot."
- **William Niederkorn,** artist and writer who has written about authorship issues for The Brooklyn Rail and The New York Times.

"When one of the world's leading Shakespeare scholars and teachers pens a novel about who truly conceived and crafted the entire Shakespearean canon, we mere mortals would be well advised to pay heed. When such an astonishingly original tale turns out to be marvellously amusing, deeply passionate, and brilliantly entertaining, then it demands to be read by all. What Ron Destro has gifted the world in The Starre, the Moone, the Sunne is nothing less than the stuff that dreams are made on."
- **Steve Cuden,** co-creator of *Jekyll & Hyde, The Musical*, author of *Beating Broadway* and *Beating Hollywood*, host of StoryBeat.net.

"It's rare to find an historical novel of the seventeenth century that is so vibrant, so Shakespearean in its storytelling, language and humor

— one that feels authentic, yet utterly accessible — as The Starre, the Moone, the Sunne. It's even rarer that the audiobook's reader, Sir Derek Jacobi, is not so much narrating the story as offering a full blown comedic-dramatic performance, sending author Ron Destro's delightful characters and breakneck plot exploding from the earphones. It is a match made in Heaven."

> **- Robin Maxwell,** bestselling author of *The Secret Diary of Anne Boleyn* and *The Wild Irish.*

"Elizabethan scholar and fine comic actor Ron Destro has combined his extraordinary talents to produce this brilliantly written tale of the true genesis of Shakespeare's plays. This novel is poetic, humorous, shockingly original and controversial."

> **- Malcolm McKay**, director, Shakespeare's Globe and the Royal Academy of Dramatic Art.

"The Starre, the Moone, the Sunne is a fulsome tale told by an aged insider to the Elizabethan and Jacobean theater and court, determined to disclose his point of view from his jail cell before his execution. The mystery unfolds with multiple plot lines. Whether one is a Stratfordian or not, there is plenty here to keep the reader engaged, for it is a novel filled with shrewd surprises, wry humor and historical detail."

> **- Michael Kinghorn,** playwright & dramaturg, former Literary Manager of the Guthrie Theater.

"What a wonderful conglomeration of wit, intrigue, mystery, passion and literary magic we have in Ron Destro's new book! It's a great romp through one of history's biggest puzzles, filled with thoughtful insights into the gritty, unpredictable world of Shakespeare's England."

> **- Paul Nicholson**, Executive Director Emeritus, Oregon Shakespeare Festival.

The Starre, the Moone, the Sunne

Ron Destro

Contempo Publishing
Putting your writing dreams in motion

First published in 2023 by Contempo Publishing.
652 Hogans Rd North Tumbulgum NSW 2490.
www.contempopublishing.com
Copyright © Ron Destro 2023.

A catalogue entry for this book is available from the National Library of Australia.
ISBN: 978-0-6458077-1-4 (Paperback)
ISBN: 978-0-6458077-2-1 (E-book)
ISBN: 978-0-6458077-3-8 (Audio book)

Cover design and illustration by Ralph Walker-Smith.
Internal design by Contempo Publishing.
Author photo by Andrew Fingland.

Printed and distributed internationally by Ingram Spark.

In eternal and loving dedication to my sunne, Nicholas,
without whom no starre nor moone
would ever shine.

While this tale is literary fiction, most events depicted about Will Shaksper of Stratford-upon-Avon and about the various noblemen are based on primary source documents.

CHAPTER ONE.
THE LIE.
LONDON, 1624.

I never dreamt this would turn out to be the strange tale of mine own death. I wish 'twas somebody else's, but tales don't always live up to our dreams. They just exist for the telling, and so here it is: mine.

It was a confused muddle in my sleep that night, filled with all the bits and buttles I had discovered over the past fortnight. A mix of notable nobles and beef-witted knaves. The places traveled betwixt Biggleswade and Budlesford. 'Tween Paris and Padua. It was like a fever-dream I dreamt. Young Will pursued by Anne Hathaway, with hair flying this-a-way and that-a-way. The search for a star, and a boy with a borrowed name.

I woke on a dark dawn, glad that dream was over. But I woke to a worse dream. Lying on that stinking jailcell floor. Me, as innocent as a new-born babe from Bingley, thinking thoughts over and again. I thought on the day when my dear friend Nicholas would sure come find me and take me out of this hole. I thought on my precious Peg, whose portly prettiness I longed to embrace. To be held. Even to be knocked 'cross the noggin, for I knew I had yet to win her over with my charms. I thought about dear ole drink, as it had been fifteen torturous days since last I tasted a drop of ale. Or scribbled a line of verse into my book. But what would I scribble if I could? That maybe everything I learnt was a lie?

I also thought on the man who led us all to these our fates. Our dear Poet Willy, who had yet to be revenged. And I fear to say, but must admit 'tis true, I finally thought about quitting hope. And I almost had, when I heard the jailer's key twisting 'round that scratchy latch, as at last he had come for me. At last, I was found!

Behind my big swag-bellied bailer, Nicholas North stood. Uneasy stood, I might add, to paint the full Caravaggio. In all his thirty years, the printer had never faced such a challenge as this. His hand shook at his side, whilst he tried not to draw notice to what mischief he held there. The encouraging glove of his honorable, the very baron hisself, patted his back, near thrusting Nick toward me. Giving him, I suppose, the needed strength to perform his task, as my jailer stepped aside with the mumble, "You've a visitor."

The baron steered my keeper away from the cell, as Nick peered into the dark room where only two narrow beams of sun bounced off my bulk on the floor. There was I. The friend he'd been searching for these past two weeks. Old Arthur Taverner. Looking older, since I was thrown in here, than my threescore years should tell. No doubt appearing as the sorrowful, rounded man of little means, thrust upon hard times so long ago. My rosy nose telling my love of drink. I know that is how I appear. I am not shamed. I am just a man, take me all in all. And 'tis a good thing, too. For the more a man knows how another views him, the more he may refine what good there is within him, and rid what ills should be without him.

At seeing Nick's figure in the threshold, I knew it was he at the first, even in the darkness. For I've always noted in him something quite unmistakable. Not just his tall and comely feature, but something rather special. And being so glad to see such a sight for my sorest eyes, I quick pushed myself up from the dirty stones.

"Nicholas, lad. You've found me!"

I opened wide my arms for the embrace I'd been waiting for these long days and nights. From the friend I knew would sure, in due time, come rescue me.

"At last," I sighed.

But I could see the fret in his eye. For Nick knew that he must follow through with it. Unwilling, he approached me. Unwilling, he embraced me. His body all a-shook with the fear of the unescapable. He looked deep into my cheery face.

"I am sorry, Arthur," he spoke.

And with that, his hand shakily brought up his hidden dagger to my side and pushed it into my sack o' flesh 'til his hand became

2

wet and warm. And then, of a sudden, it became quite cold. Funny how all that does hap. My face must have smiled still, but I know mine eyes looked stunned. My hand met his at my side, and I felt the blood run. With almost a lack of understanding, I could only utter, "I die."

With those my last words spent, my collapse onto the stinking stone floor, which smelled of blood and piss and vinegar, must have summoned my jailer, who rushed in, as Nick, still stunned and standing where he stood, finally released his dagger. 'Sblood! He near hit me again as it bounded by my noggin. The baron stood calm as my watchman grabbed Nick and hurled him against the wall.

The baron seemed pleased.

As for my knowledge of the rest, I now reveal what could only have been learnt after such a mysterious escape from such a life.

★

Later that night, Nick peered through the rusty bars of his own stinking cell. He'd been watching the six workmen in the yard below as they labored to build a scaffold fit to hang a man. It would have been my final resting place, but now 'twould be his. He watched a fellow with a torch light his way 'cross the yard, passing the lane where, toward the end of it, stood the dark playhouse. He marveled at how a place so merry under the sun could look so doomed beneath the moon.

A cold wind hit his face and made him quake. He turned toward the darkness of the walls within, where he could not tell the stones from the lime that gripped them tight. He thought on how all this shall play out. Of the many players in his story who were lost to him now. Who had become mere shadows in a masque formed so many years ago. Formed on that final night of his childhood when he was but nine. On the night of his father's doom.

3

CHAPTER TWO.

'TWAS A ROUGH NIGHT.

TWENTY YEARS EARLIER. 1604.

Nine-year-old Nicholas opened the door that separated the tiny room where he and his dear father lived from the modest print shoppe where Nathaniel North worked. I knew Nathaniel then. A humble printer, kind and tender-hearted, who was a help to me many a time when I lived less prosperous years. Not to say my prosper got any bigger, mind you, but that's the way the saying is said.

Printer North emerged from behind his son, patting him on the head with the affection of a father proud of a boy so clever. A lad so fond of the books Nathaniel printed. Little Nicholas looked up at his hero and his eyes gleamed. They always gleamed in those days.

Nathaniel handed him a new emblem book full of cryptic images and words, and Nick's eyes opened wide. The boy thanked his father and ran into the back room, plumped onto his favorite reading spot beside the hearth, and began to inspect every page of this new-printed treasure. He rubbed his dirt besmutch'd hands onto his shirttail and then careful turned each new page with reverence, as his father crossed into the shoppe to set about the creation of his very new and truly important (but greatly secretive) pamphlet. Had he known how these papers would threaten us all, he might have had a second think about it then. But 'tis too late for that now. None of us could see the dreaded future at that time. And, as they say, 'tis no use crying o'er spilt beer.

Their living chamber was small, but neat-like and always in order. Quite unlike mine own, which we shall come to in good time. The North family, father and son, owned one small bedstead, two chairs, one table inches from the floor, and one portrait of father and mother. It was the only thing young Nick ever knew of this beautiful

4

angel, taken in the birthing of the lad. All in all, it was a place warm and welcoming.

The front room was filled with books and papers. The smell of inks lingered there. On a table lay leafs of paper ready for printing. Next to it was the massive oak press. On the front wall hung a heavy door and window revealing the dark street outside. On the back wall stood shelves of manuscripts and trays of letters. There were big books of folios and small books of quartos. And by the door to the back room was the old fireplace, through which the father, peering 'round a small iron cooking pot, could keep close eye on his son.

Nathaniel approached his letter tray and began. But first a look out the window. Nobody. Good. He could carry on without detection. *Sans interruption*, as is said in far off places I ne'er visited. He lit one candle only and crossed to his press with a handful of letters to arrange onto his frame, but quicker than was his usual fashion. How 'twas he did it so well, I haven't a clue, as each letter was not only writ backways, but was also as tiny as the tongue of a titmouse, which is not a mouse at all, I just discovered, but a bird, so I'll ne'er understand the naming of it.

To make a tricky biscuit all the trickier, Nathaniel knew this pamphlet would needs be printed anonymous. And could only be passed amongst a certain few. For if the new king knew who printed it, 'twould be a coin's toss as to which would be burnt first, the book, or the man who birthed the book. For these were terrible times for telling tales out of court.

He gave another glance to the door as he heard some loud louts amble by. And whilst all this was a concern to him, he took no notice of the man in the shadows watching him from 'cross the street. And knowing what I now know about that miserable man, that Knyvet fellow, I'm half-surprised he could not smell him at the very least. But unfortunate for Nathaniel, he paid no note to that serpent, who had his green eyes locked upon him.

Knyvet had not taken his gaze off Printer North as the man continued to organize his work. But it was only a wink of time 'til Nathaniel could see it. A flicker coming down the lane at a distance. He stopped. It was a torch. They were the king's men!

He quick began to gather his papers. He looked in to see his beloved son and told him to stay put. He closed the door to the back room and took up the pages. If only they had survived. How I could have used them to save myself. The title page had one word writ upon it: *Shake-speare*. He placed the manuscript within a large parchment penned with an emblem. 'Twas a picture drawn by hisself: a star, a moon and a sun. That was Nathaniel's secret mark for this, his last work. He hurriedly scurried to the back wall.

At that very moment, the shadowy Knyvet heard the guards coming and walked over to meet them. And in doing this, he did not observe Printer North remove the loose stone that hung high above the fireplace, hide the papers within, and then quick cover it again. Nathaniel then went to his frame of letters and scattered them onto the floor.

As the guards entered, Nathaniel was ready for arrest. The place was searched, and papers were retrieved. But the secret manuscript was well-hid and never found. Well, not by these guards, leastways. As they took the prisoner away all wrist-shackled, Nicholas peered quiet through the door. Confused and frighted, the lad made a daring decision. And lucky he did, for had he not, he would never have witnessed the signs that would lead him to the answers he would later seek.

He decided to follow his father through the dark streets of London from a safe distance. Down Ely they walked. Past Holborn and Cheapside. Despite the heaviness of his chains, Nathaniel walked quick and silent, thinking only on how his son would fare when all of this was done. Through the Postern Gate, they marched, and still Nick moved his legs as quick and as silent as he could. He did not wish to be discovered, for he thought it might go hard on his dear father if he was seen. But they neither heard nor seen the lad. They were set on one thing alone: get this printer into the Tower quick.

As they approached that daunting dungeon, young Nick took one look at it and was stopped. The heaviness of the Tower completely filled his heart and stayed his feet. And there in darkness he stood, under the Postern Gate, determined to wait the long night for his father's release. A tittle did he know. It was a warm night. And soon it began to rain.

★

Nathaniel North knew the cause of his captivity, but he did not understand the where-ofs nor the why-fors he was taken on that particular night. He was unawares of the imminent plight of the nobleman, who, hours earlier, had been composing his own last work 'cross London at King's Place.

Just outside the city's northern gate in Hackney, King's Place had seen better days. But the name of it shouldn't trip a fellow up, for there was no king living there. 'Twas instead the home of Lord Edward, a man of four-and-fifty. But to look on him, one might think he'd been dragged through more years than that, due to his infirmities and such. He had truly lived the life of ten men, it had been said. But perhaps not the ten he would have chose. And now, the toll of it all was soon to be took.

Like the old lord hisself, King's Place was once elegant. It was furnished with the best velvets and silks, now worn thin. There was a splendor about the place, but it was a faded splendor. Large rooms of Italian furnishings kept as clean as possible with only one servant left. And the Countess Elizabeth. She made certain the place was smart and comfortable for her sickly but ever-loving husband. She was his second bride in life, but this was the one he loved from the start. And she held the same for milord, who, refusing bedrest, was always stubborn at work in his book chamber. Sitting at his writing table, doing what he ofttimes loved and sometimes hated but was always compel'd to do: write.

The room appeared magical. Glistening candles and crystals everywheres a man could see. Like stars they sparked. On the tables and bookshelves. On the draperies and fripperies. The ancient faces of long-dead grandsires frowned down from portraits on the walls, whilst from an easel in the corner rested a beautiful goddess looking up to the deceased sires with a simple smile upon her face. 'Twas a silent conversation eternally spoke. And betwixt a pear-shaped lute at one end, and a dusty ole viol at t'other, was a crowd of books. Books in all tongues. Floor to rafters, books.

At his writing table, he sat. Several pages lay writ, next to the pot o'quills in all feathers. Many a bird was there for the taking, including the old phoenix feathers, which milord never used, but kept on hand for remembrance. But I dare not tell that tale now, for 'tis a sorrowful page from a chapter long-ago writ. Milord was dressed in the finest doublet, now worn a bit rough 'round the sleeve-ends. His scarf of silk was tied tight about his neck. 'Twas not the fashion of the day but his sad necessity that dictated this. His elaborate and somewhat rubbed-away gold-topped walking stick was leant up against the table at the ready, should he need it.

Not well, he desperately scratched out lines on the page, and then crossed them through to hurry replace them anew. He scratched and he wrote. His quivering hand trying desperately to keep pace with the thoughts that raced about his head. And as he tried to steady his fine Sheffield goose quill to the page, he drank his fine Sherborne wine from his goblet, which no doubt made the steadying all the trickier.

His breathing was swift and shallow. And the pain shot through him from the right of his neck down to the poor man's side. As he wrote, images danced 'round in his mind, like lighted candles parading on a bright and dusty stage. But, of a sudden, his head became heavy and fell onto his page. He ceased writing. His goblet overturned, quill still in hand. The red Sherborne bled onto the paper, blotting his new words. It was then approached the two at the back, looking in, unawares that the king's men would soon arrive.

★

King James was having a good laugh. He was a thick little Scotsman with a thick little tongue, which made his laugh all the funnier. Every man 'round him laughed. There was his lord treasurer, Robert Cecil. That strange little hump-back with the blackish eyes. 'Tis no wonder the sovereign called him his *beagle*. *Bunch'd-back toad* was what most named him, behind his bunch'd-back, of

8

course. Cecil was a man devious both in nurture and in nature, with a sidewise curve about him that made a fellow wary. The towering captain of the guard, Titus Addicock, stood present, keeping the new king of England safe.

'Twas all laughs and chucks until a watchman arrived from King's Place. Out of breath, he whispered to Cecil, who then became all serious and carefully approached the king to speak into his royal ear. That was when all the merriment stopped. When the king's face turned white as Gower's ghost. He jumped up, little man that he was, and nearly fell off that big throne of his. He grabbed his codpiece, as was his custom, and then barked at Addicock.

The orders fell fast, and within two shakes of a Scottish swine's tail, the royal chamber was emptied. Addicock was sent to lead a score of men to make the arrests at King's Place, Southampton House, and Nathaniel North's Print Shoppe. Through the panic, the king crossed to look down from his open window, and the guards were swiftly on their way.

The palace gates opened noisily, causing a small man of great letters by name of John Lyly, leaning at the side, to waken from his reverie. Addicock led his impressive guardsmen on. Dressed in sable black, the enormous plumes of their helmets shook the night air as they marched through the streets like mighty piked ravens. Lyly nervously followed them at a distance, as he had been instructed by one Horatio, who knew this night would soon come. At the juncture, Addicock ordered one group of men to march east, another was sent west, and Addicock hisself led the rest straight-ways, which, by my best account, was north. Hearing the words *King's Place*, Lyly knew he had to race there before the ravens could arrive.

Approaching near the place, Lyly spied a watchman standing at Morning Lane, so he knew he must needs traverse the marsh by the mill field in back if he was ever to get to the house before Addicock's men. And as quick as a huffing man of half a century could be, he mushed through muck and brushed through bramble to get hisself to the back entry.

He knocked and knocked and was about to surrender all when he eyed old Adam by the window. Lord Edward's ancient servant held up a bundle of papers. A moment later, the bundle was thrust out the back door, which was fast closed tight again.

Without a word, the faithful Lyly stuck the papers into his doublet and once more mushed through muck and out onto the street. He began to walk swift toward Southampton House. But as he turned onto Nightingale Lane, the small man noticed Addicock and his men approaching. He shoved the papers further under his doublet and held the garment tight, as he had lost his two top buttons earlier in the week, and now regretted his tardiness in replacing the crucial clasps.

Master Lyly neared Southampton House as the baron stood at the magnificent door holding a rather regal black cat. One with a proud white snout and a puffed-up chest. The baron caught sight of Lyly and, with concern, motioned for him to hide in the brambles.

Just then, the third group of guards emerged from the entry with the fair earl of Southampton, who was in the process of pulling on his favorite brown gloves, the ones with the black ribbons. With that done, the baron handed the young lord his stately feline. Despite the strong protests of the baron, a guard politely read the edict, and the earl was gently arrested. A gentler arrest than mine own had been, I can verify. After the men had safely gone, the baron approached Lyly for the papers.

Addicock's men now arrived at King's Place, bringing an old doctor with them.

"You are to enter the house and approach the book chamber only. You shall retrieve what we seek and nothing else, by order of his majesty the king. Is that clear?"

"I shall serve his majesty most well," answered the frightened physician, as he entered the house.

Addicock ordered one of his men to give the doctor a torch to light his way. No sooner had the doctor entered, the large door was slammed shut behind him. The sound of its echo made his heart jump as he turned toward the book chamber door and approached. He slowly entered, finding his patient, Lord Edward, on the floor by the window. His first inclination was to near the poor man, but he knew that doing so might bring more than one danger upon him. He spied the desk and crossed, took an ornate box from atop it, turned to the man on the floor, and whispered a quick prayer as he left.

Within the time it took to pronounce *God have mercy upon our souls*, the door was nailed shut, the doctor was on his way, and Captain Addicock and his men were marching back to the king with the box and all it contained.

'Twas said King James was oft haunted by his dreams. I know not what he dreamt that night, but if what I now understand is true, and there's a bit of justice in this world, he would have been haunted by the memory of a woman wailing at her door. A royal steward snatching a babe from her arms. The rain pouring down. She, useless to help her little one. She, placing a chain from 'round her neck to his. A token of protection. Lightning strikes. Lies become truth. South becomes north.

And as he tossed and tussled in his unsettling slumber, his majesty might then envision the steward returning, handing babe to mother, who weeps all the more of tears and raindrops. And he'd awake with sweats and frets for his crown.

CHAPTER THREE

A BLESSED LIGHT.

Nathaniel's cell was a dark hole, even at dawn. He could hear them gathering outside. A crowd was collecting to witness the execution, not knowing nor caring whose execution 'twas. Such was the entertainment of London when the theatres were closed.

Young Nicholas was there, standing in the distance. Still awaiting his father's return. But the crowd's attention was drawn to the executioner, who busied hisself with his axe.

Inside, the ever-loudening clomping of the guards' boots down the limestone steps told Nathaniel that his keepers were coming. He quickly rose, tossing away the quill given him the night before. The quill he had well-put to use. His confession, though, lay untouched on the floor before him. The men entered and demanded the paper. Nathaniel, careful to guard the hand which concealed his secret, gave it to them with satisfaction, but without signature. They ordered him again to pen his good name, but he refused. Would were I half as brave.

The earl Southampton paced within his neatly furnished cell above. His long flowing hair waved in the very north-east wind of his movement. His cat - I never learnt his name, nor even if he had one, but I suppose he did, as nobles like to name their creatures - crawled along the window ledge, mewing the approach of the king's men. The young lord was amiably escorted from his chamber, on his way to see the king, who ambled restless in the room above.

The crookbacked Cecil escorted Southampton into the king's presence. His sovereign handed him a document, and they spoke. Not long therafterwards, the earl signed the paper, and, afore you could say *Your mother's a son of a Manchester music master* he was released. 'Tis a wonder what the power of a pen can procure.

King James then went to the window to observe the proceedings below.

Nick's eyes were ever-fixed on the gate. And finally, someone emerged. But it was never his beloved father, as he had prayed for. It was Lord Southampton. And his cat. The lord approached his carriage, when out of it popped the head of his new-born son James, being held by the noble baron. Nicholas watched with a bit of envy as father and son (and cat) were reunited. Then the earl got into his carriage and held his son tight, cradling him like the ocean cradles a kingdom. And the carriage began to trot. It passed by Nick, just as the baron looked down at the lad, who thought the face familiar. But how could that be?

Nicholas then returned his attention to the gate. When would his own father be returned? Surely, he would soon appear, feigning displeasure that the young boy had stayed the long, wet night outside. Then, they would happily walk back to the shoppe. Back to home. To a meal and a rest and a return to the only life he had ever known. A meager life, to be sure, but such a happy one. That is what the lad thought on as he waited. But that was not to be, for soon his father did appear, but he was still under guard. And at that, Nicholas knew there was no longer a thing in his life called hope.

As the crowd got loud, the boy moved closer to catch his father's eye. Nathaniel's face was calm, and he gave a warm look to his boy, which gave young Nick the courage for the inevitable. This was the way father and son could always comfort one another. The boy would suffer a fall, and one look from his father told the lad he was not alone, and the boy would smile. That's all it took. A look that said all is not lost. But now, all was sure lost. Now, Nick would sure be alone. There was nothing to be done but be brave, which is not as easy for a lad of nine.

Still a young man, Nathaniel walked strong as he was led to the block, whilst the hungry crowd began to jeer. Up the three creaky steps he climbed, one foot after t'other. But of a sudden, a strange thing occurred. The sun started to peep from the clouds, and as the blessed light shone down from above, Nathaniel beheld the world around him. It was the colors. Almost as if he was witnessing them for the first time. The rich blue of the sacred sky. The pure white puffs of the airy clouds. The lush green of the lawn before him. This is what he thought on, as the deafening roars of the crowd almost hushed to a silence. Of course, they had not hushed. But the magnificent colors. Funny thing to notice at a time like this. Yet he noticed them, nonetheleast.

The executioner barked at Nathaniel to kneel, but he had one more task afore he die. His eyes searched the crowd for his son, as the scared boy pushed through the masses to get to the front. He did not wish to look at what was to come, but an ever-powerful force drove him through the crowd, to be as close to his father as he could be. One last time close.

When Nathaniel eyed him, he held up his hand to the boy. And it was then that Nicholas could see it. On his father's palm was the secret he had kept from the guards. Inked onto his skin were the pictures: a star, a moon, a sun. Nicholas sensed this was a sign. It was his dear father's farewell, but it was also a message. Nathaniel then knelt with great dignity. Nick turned away tearfully. The axe fell and the crowd yelled, "Long live the king!"

His majesty was still standing at his window.

"The heirs lie heavy around us."

He walked away, leaving the delighted crowd to cheer below. They soon dispersed, however, as the executioner's men dragged Nathaniel's headless body from the block, leaving Nicholas to stand there, alone.

CHAPTER FOUR.

VANISHING WHISPERS ON THE WIND.

TWENTY YEARS LATER. 1624.

'Twas dusk as Nick walked toward his home with no reason to think that this was the day that would bring answers to his twenty years of searching. Forced to grow up on his own, it had not taken him long to master his father's profession. And being a friend to Nathaniel North, I would help the lad whene'er I could. I knew the bookseller Millington and asked him to assist young Nick in learning all the inside-ups of the print trade. The lad soon showed promise and was able to put turnips on the table.

But not a day passed that Nick never thought on, nor searched for, those signs. The star and the moon and the sun had haunted each moment of his waking. He would walk down Angel Lane and spy the banner of a star, only to find a wizened merchant selling celestial charts. The figure of a smiling wooden sun would lead him to an old alehouse by that name. He worked by day and searched by night and never did he find it. Never, that is, 'til this fateful eve of his nine-and-twentieth year.

He turned onto Brick Alley near his home and heard the outcries. People running. Shouting. But more than the usual rabble-ribble. Something of doom was in the air. But something else was there, too. As he walked closer, he recognized the shouts.

"Fire! Fire!"

He turned the corner and spied it. Some were running from his shoppe crying *"Fire!"* whilst others were running toward it with pailfuls of water. And there it was. His shoppe, nay his very home, ablazed. A gust of heat hit him in the face as he ran toward it. His neighbors tried to quench the flames as Nick ran into the burning shoppe, desperate to save whate'er he could.

15

He first removed the portrait of his dear parents and secured it safe within his doublet. Funny what a man thinks valuable in times like these. He then grabbed hold of the press, but it was much too hot. Papers flew 'round him metamorphosing into flames, floating upways towards the heavens and crashing downways towards the earth. He grabbed handfuls of books and potfuls of inks, but most were too hot to hold.

The roof began to fall in fiery pieces, just missing his skull. He ran out to get some water, but most pails had been emptied. He attempted to run in again to salvage more books, but, of a sudden, he could move no more. Something powerful was holding him back, and that something was Big Jack Kole, his goodly neighbor blacksmith, who held him strong.

"'Tis a ruin, Nick! The fire's too hot!"

But as fire brings heat, it also brings light. For it was at that very moment that the stones above the old hearth decided to reveal their twenty-year secret. They loose'd from their mortar as if the gnarly limed fingers that had tightly gripped the stones for a century now lay a-dying and a-dissolving in the heat, releasing their terrible strong grasp. The mortar crumbled and the stones tumbled, causing the long-hid papers to emerge and scatter into the fiery wind. The covering parchment flew into the air, and Nicholas caught sight of it. Like a banner, it waved in the night's ether its emblems of a star and a moon and a sun. Nick's heart raced. The hidden papers! Father's secrets!

He just had to get to those secrets. But there was no use struggling with his well-intending friend, who had a grasp on him as tight as Vulcan grips a hammer. And there was no time to explain a story that would take near three chapters in a book to tell. But he had to get to those papers. These vanishing whispers from his long-ago father were now aloft on the wind, dissolving into flames. A moment later, and they would be gone forever, never to speak to him. Yet, Jack's hold was impossible to escape. Nick had no choice. He could see his life's very purpose burning before him, as each corner of each page blackened and turned to ash. He had to act.

With his arms held back by Big Jack, Nick had no other course but to lift a leg and give a quick kick-behind worthy of an angry mule on harvest day. Jack let go with a great yowl, more stunned than hurt, and Nick took that moment to dart bravely back into his collapsing shoppe. The main timbers began to fall in front of him, but he grabbed the emblems, now on fire. He clutched in every which-way, for whatever snitches of papers he could snatch. His hands were burning with these secret words, but he clawed what he could as the heat now became unbearable, and each whisper began to blacken and hush. As the largest beam loosened above, Big Jack got close enough to wrench him out of the building just as each timber tumbled.

Breathing shallow and fast, Nicholas fell to his knees and buried both his saved fragments and his seared fingertips into the cool earth. His blackened hands smoked as he heard the bell. He looked up and saw the constable approaching. He stood unsteady and hid the fragments within his shirt next to his heart. His only hope was that they would not be ravaged by its fierce pounding. Standing there, he awaited the constable's questions.

Few men rambled the lane as the sun rose. Smoldering timbers and stones lay in a heap of what was once Nick's home. He sat in the rubble, having been there all the night, holding the few pieces of parched papers in front of him.

There were the picture emblems, just as he had seen drawn on his father's hand. There was a piece that read *"in this I shall reveal all."* Another claimed, *"My name be buried where my body is,* and *I, once gone, to all the world must die."* But who? *"Lies become truth, south becomes north,"* he read, as if it be writ in a foreign tongue. And the last fragment of this impossible puzzle simply read *"W. Shakespeare."* So, this was the man to find. And this set Nicholas on the journey of his life.

★

On all this he pondered, as he stood looking out of his stinking cell, whilst they had made quite a bit of progress on that dead man's

17

scaffold. And of me he thought, sweet lad. For 'twas I that first came to his aid after his shoppe was in ruins.

★

The Piss and Whistle was crowded that day. Odd, as it is perhaps the awfullest tavern in Cheapside. But if I am to be held to account, I must admit that its true name is The Pig and Whistle. However, most men know it by its more familiar calling. 'Tis a pungent place, and I'd say the food there is fit for a dog, if you don't much care for dogs.

Yet the best reason to frequent this establishment is to view my lovely Peg. And to my good eye, she is a beauty with the fairest face. Now, I know they say *Love is blind. I,* however, am not. So, as my pretty Peg paraded by with an armful of ales, I sat with Nicholas for our talk. A tittle did I suspect that this meeting would change our lives forever. But I do not regret a whit of it. After all, what else is a man to do with a fellow traveler in need?

"So, dear Nick, where will you bed down whilst you contemplate the re-making of your shoppe?"

"I haven't a thought on that yet."

Then my beloved Peg passed. "Two more, Meg. One for me, and one for my new lodger," I quipped to her. 'Sblood, did she turn fast on that.

"You know very well my name is not Meg!"

"Meg... Peg," says I, "I care naught for thy Christian name. But should you finally consent to be my bride, it'll be your wedded name that I'll call ye." I winkled at her, and she feigned disgust.

"What, me a Taverner?" says she, "Now there's a moniker."

"Fit for a monarch," I volleyed back as quick as my wit allowed.

"Fit for a drunkard, more like," she marked, bringing laughter from the lousy louts nearby, and finally bringing more ales.

Not able to resist the nearness of her bulk, I gave her a loving pinch, and she quick hurled about, laying a smart one atop my pate, nearly spilling half the ale I was attempting to pour into it at the time.

18

I answered straight 'way. "I like a bit o 'spirit in me women."

"And more down your gullet," she gibed. She liked to volley back, and I liked her trying.

"Why, in my Italy—" I started.

"And the closest you've ever got to your precious Italy," she stopped me good, "is in the drinking of your sack."

"Is there not some Buxton beef burning 'round the back?" I enquired.

And with that, she trudged off to see what all the smoke was about. Now, this remark was not my attempt to end our battle o' words, for a smoky scent was truly wafting my way. And I have always had a very good nose to sniff out burnt foodstuffs, due to my dear mother being a plentiful maker of it. Not to say my sweet Peg didn't strike me hard with that blow, for 'twas true. My sack took me to Italy. And my books. But never could I sail there. Nor swim there, even, for I am told the sea is deep 'twixt me and Italy.

Our squabbles made Nick smile, and for that I was glad. He'd had a hard time of it, and I was happy I could help.

"You'll stay with me," says I. And afore he could thank me, I assured him 'twas not needed.

But I could see there was more on his mind, and after some poking, he began to tell me of the papers he had found in the fire. I asked to see them.

"This could be a matter of great danger," he warned.

"Your father was a friend to me."

And with that, he took out the burnt fragments and said, "I am determined to solve this puzzle."

"And I shall help you, my boy."

Again, he warned me of the perils, and again I warned him of the bootlessness of opposing my wishes. For once I set my mind to a task, it is as good as attempted. The lad then offered payment for my services.

"I will help you," I said, "and I know the price."

"Name it."

"When you re-open your shoppe, you will print my book."

"Your book?" says he.

"My book," says I.

"What book?" marks he.

"My poems," mark I. "*Poems by Arthur Taverner*."

"Agreed," says he, with a smile full of teeth. Oh, he is a goodly lad. And so, we were now to work.

"What was your father's association with this Master Shakespeare?" I began.

"None that I know," says Nick.

"The play-writer?" I sought clarification.

"And poet."

"Ah, yes, I've read his pentameter. Not bad," I marked, for truly they were not.

"It seems my father was going to print a pamphlet about him. He must've hid this manuscript the night he was taken."

I asked Nick why he thought it was this that the king's men were after, and he told me of his father's sign at death. And I wondered what it all must mean.

"That is what we must discover," Nick resolved.

And so, I too resolved, and promised to take him to Newgate to meet my brother. Although it had been three long years since I myself last saw the man, this seemed our best chance. After all, he was popular and well-learnt. If anyone could uncover the mysteries that lay ahead, it was surely Martin Taverner.

CHAPTER FIVE.

THE QUEST BEGINS.

Not far from my brother's office strode a beautiful lass with black-pearled eyes, trodding the length of the transept of the church we call Paul's. But this beauty – well, she was more than a beauty, for her mind was as full as her smile – had a purpose to her step. She was tallying out numbers in her head, as she so oft liked to do. She'd walk westways and count, then traverse southways and do the like. *But why?* a befuddled onlooker might enquire. *'Twas a habit*, she'd answer, fondly thinking on her dear father, who, afore turning to farming, was termed the Master Mason of Macclesfield. He designed many a few cathedrals in his day and oft told long tales of tall spires to his little lass, who grew enchanted with such mathematicals. How a church was built upon pure quadrates and circles. How walking crost only the diagonal of a chancel could tell her the whole length of a cathedral. Enchanted, she was. And enchanting she also be. But whilst she was busy reckoning floor stones at the church, there was business to conduct at my brother's.

The sign out front read *Martin Taverner, Master at Law* in very fine letters. It was a beautiful sign and a beautiful office, so I had put on my best linsey-woolsey shirt and spent the better part of an hour cleaning my boots so as not to carry any more mud than necessary into it. Nicholas looked unsure.

"You're certain he'll help us?"

"I'd stake my name on it," I answered. Sometimes I do not think. For the next thing I knew, we were standing in front of Martin's desk as he threw the bits of burnt fragments forward and barked something along the order of "Get out, both of you!"

"But brother," I began.

21

Martin rose. "And you'll kindly not remind me of the unfortunate circumstance that binds we two together." Martin had a habit of saying things he oft did not intend. "A twenty-year mystery," he continued. "No legal documentation. Secret writings. Not to mention challenging the king's men. Are you mad?"

"Well," says I, "I see you have a slight doubt on the matter."

"Get out!" was his sole reply. And so out we did get.

I tried to reassure Nick.

"He is a good lawyer, just a terrible brother," I marked. "But fear not, for we shall conquer this ourselves. Were you able to salvage any books of this Master Shakespeare?" I asked.

"I have some," Nick replied. "And can obtain others."

"Good. I'll fly to my digs, and you get the books and come thither." Now we had a stratagem. "Anything you can find, by his hand or about his self. Then, we will talk with this man."

"I do not believe he lives," Nick informed me.

"Then we shall dig up his bones and make them rattle their dirty tale. Now be off."

And with that, Nicholas went one way, and I t'other. I did not know then that my brother was watching us from his window. I did not know then what secret regard he held for me. After all, the cover usually tells the book.

It was a red cover that caught Nick's eye. The new printings were beautifully bound and hundreds of pages fat, stacked up high in the window of Millington's Book Shoppe. The sign read: *The Workes of William Shakespeare. New and Originall: 20s.* Nick noted Master Millington waving him in.

"Nicholas, I was sore to hear of your calamity last even," said the cheerful bookseller.

"Thank you, Master Millington."

"You shall rebuild?"

"As soon as I am able," answered the printer, whose attention turned back toward the new books.

"A beautiful imprint, is it not?"

"Oh, yes." Nick was impressed.

At that moment, three tall-hatted men appeared at the window outside. In the center stood Sir Thomas Knyvet, the knight who looked a thin seventy years and had the air of a serpent still. The very man in the shadows from an earlier part of this tale. He was dressed in cheerless black, which suited him fine. So black, indeed, that it even made the chain 'round his neck shine dull. The two others carried large sacks. And as there was not a cat in sight, suspicions were roused as to the reason for the bags. The smaller of the two men opened the door, and the old knight entered. His followers followed him in, as Millington dropped his smile to the floor.

Nick had a question.

"I wonder, does Master Shakespeare live?"

Millington looked not to Nick, but to old Knyvet, as if searching for the answer to Nick's query in the old man's face.

"Only on the page, I'm afraid," was his eventual answer.

"Had you ever the pleasure of his acquaintance?"

Knyvet was staring back at Millington with a question on his own cragged face.

"No," was the bookseller's unusual short reply. And with that, he took a quick step back and offered, "Your books of Terence will arrive tomorrow. Shall I bring them to you?"

"I'm at Arthur Taverner's," answered Nick. "Can you take them there?"

"At the Shambles? Yes, I know the place."

"And can you find me any quartos by Master Shakespeare? I have a bit of a mystery." And at that, old Knyvet looked to Nick.

"To be sure," came the business-like reply.

Nick returned to the new Shakespeare. "Know you where he lived?" he persisted.

"Stratford," came the worried-like answer, with Millington somewhat disturbed by the presence of this black-clad knight. He opened a copy of his own book and pointed Nick to a passage within it: *And Time dissolves thy Stratford Moniment.*

"Stratford? Up by Hackney?" Nick asked, thinking of the London liberty by that name.

"No," cracked Millington, now beginning to secrete a fair amount of sweating. "A country Stratford. Apparently on the Avon. You see." Millington turned the pages and pointed to where the words *Sweet Swan of Avon* was writ to describe the scribbler.

"I see," said Nick.

And out of nowheres, he heard the loveliest voice.

"A weighty sum for one book." It came soft and familiar behind him.

Nick turned 'round, and it was no other than Valentina Childs. Now grown more beautiful since last he saw her.

"Valentina!" he was happy to see the young lady.

"How goes it, cuz?"

"Good, now that I spy your face."

And with that, she put her hand 'round Nick's arm, and Millington excused hisself to attend to Knyvet. Valentina Childs. Oh, she was a rare beauty with dark hair and darkest pearled eyes, I can tell you. They walked about the shoppe catching up on years gone by. Her sudden presence gave him comfort. A childhood friend, now grown into such a rare creature. He hadn't seen her since her own father, the church mason farmer, died, leaving her all his lands in the north. Such a kind heart. And tutored.

Valentina informed Nick that he needn't search for his coins, as she owned a copy of that very Shakespeare newly-given her by an uncle on a recent trip to London. An uncle living a close distance from the Stratford on the Avon, where she herself had lived for a time. And as the two friends talked, and this goodly woman heard the details of Nick's search for the truth, she gladly offered her assistance. She was, in soothe, a goodly cuz.

Nick moved his eyes from Valentina to the bookseller. "Master Millington," he began.

"I'm sorry," was his answer, without waiting for the question, "but they've all been taken."

Nick looked at the window display.

"The Shakespeares? All of them?"

"I'm regrettable sorry."

And with that, Millington crossed to the window, where the old knight's two men placed all copies of the book into their sacks. Perplexed, Nicholas could see that there was no further business to be conducted at present and escorted Valentina outside.

"Stratford? That's odd," she mused. "You say you're at the Shambles?" Nick nodded. "I shall collect the book and meet you before this hour is done."

Valentina smiled and turned to walk eastways, leaving Nicholas to smile and walk westways. And, as if following an old scent, the ancient knight walked out the door with Millington close behind. Knyvet's green eyes followed Nick down the lane.

"Who is this man?" the serpent demanded.

The Shambles is where I lived when alive. Number Two, to be exact. A tiny triangle of a modest home found at the center of where three of the city's dustiest roads all bang together. On the way to my digs, Nick stopped at every acquaintance he knew and begged to borrow any volumes touching on the name William Shakespeare.

When he and our damsel arrived, the three of us stood in the center of the room. I admit, to the naked eye it may have seemed a tad bedraggled, what with all the books and the bottles and the bed and the inconvenient closeness of the three walls and all. But we had our work to do, and so I scattered the books about the place, at the ready.

"Well, the answer lies before our very eyes," I began the inquisition. "All we need do is find it."

"Perhaps we should start with this," Valentina offered, holding up her copy of that new red-covered folio. "Very peculiar thing, Nick. I laughed when you told me of Master Shakespeare's living in Stratford."

"Stratford?" I interjected. "Up by Hackney? I know a Barnaby Brodnax lives there. Owes me half a groat, the ne'er-do-good."

"No," said the beauty. "A country Stratford, on the Avon. I thought I knew every single soul in that town. But I never heard of a writer there."

"How far a place?" asked I.

"A three days' ride," answered she.

On hearing this, I knew immediate what must be done, and at once.

"Then my good friends," says I, "if we are to find what we seek, there are fardels to fill."

"Stratford?" Nicholas guessed.

"Stratford," I affirmed, as I began to retrieve precious coins from my various hiding places: the shilling under my pillow, the angel above the door, two groats and a ha'penny hid within my book of Dante. I assured them I would discover what I could in London, whilst they must journey to the country. I could even borrow Nick an old trotter from my farrier friend.

I handed Nick the coins. "I was saving these for my impending marriage to Mistress Peg, but that can wait." Valentina looked surprised. "She cannot yet be made to tolerate me," I explained.

Nick refused the coins, but I insisted.

"You shall pay me back with printings of my book."

"You're a writer?" asked the lady.

"A poet," I proclaimed proud.

"Of what do you write?" asked she.

"Of whatever she instructs," answered me.

"Who?" smiled the lass.

I looked about and picked up my bottle of port.

"Here she is," says I. "Inspiration. You take a sip, you think a thought, you drink some more, you write it down." But I could feel the bottle was sorrowful light, and so I tippled her downways and sadly found her empty. "No more poems out of this ole gal," frowned I.

Then it come to me that we'd better ready ourselves.

"The dawning shall arrive quick, my friends, and 'tis a... how many days to this Stratford?" I turned to Valentina.

"Three."

"'Tis a three days' ride that lay ahead," I concluded.

After they left, I drank a tittle of new inspiration, scribbled a bittle of new verse, and then readied the room for the two of us to bed down. Nicholas escorted the lovely Valentina to her inn at the sign of

26

the White Dove on Pleasant Street, where she stayed when in town. 'Twas a handsome place, and there was many a night she was the only lodger in the whole of the inn, which I only mention as this may be a thing a fellow might want to place into the back of his noggin and remember, as it shall seem of greater import later.

I must have been asleep when Nick got back. Soundly snortling in my slumber, dreaming up visions of beauty and spectacles of horror, for that is how my nights are usually trafficked. Nicholas lay on the floor nearby, his head no doubt filled with stories of Romeo running 'round with Juliet, whilst also chasing a bit of ale-keep Rosaline on the sides.

The dawn came early, and the day could be put off no longer. I stood there in front of my hovel as the two of them rode off. A tittle were any of us prepared for what lay ahead. I did not know that Knyvet's men were watching the whole scene from 'cross the road. Nor did I suspect that this was the last I'd ever see of Nicholas 'til that fateful reuniting in my jailcell. I went inside and downed a bit of ale. Had I known then of what was to follow, I'd have grabbed my inspiration and run out of there fast.

CHAPTER SIX.

STRATFORD HO!

At the very moment Nicholas and Valentina rode side-for-side out of the bustling city, in the parlor of the palace, the knight Knyvet stood. His ancient arms fell heavy from the weight of the red-covered Shakespeare, but there was no place to set it down. He knew the king would be furious at this book, and at anyone who stirred the pottage by making enquiries about it and would doubtless reward any man who rid London of them all. Finally, his majesty appeared.

"They must be stopped!" demanded the seething little king.

His majesty turned to address his shrewdest man. The shy and shady Master Digges was the ablest creature for such a sensitive affair. A man strong and swift, once known as the quickest cut-purse in all Damnation Alley, despite the decided disadvantage of lacking two of his best filching fingers.

The road through the country was a well-trod route of ruts, rocks and the accidental wild flower growing along the wayside. The wind was warm, and the sun was bright. Valentina tittered out a ditty on her tuneful flute to pass the time as the two rode on. She sounded a joyous song that she and Nick knew from childhood. I myself do not know which song 'twas, but my shillings are on *Why Doth Not My Goose*. Nick was pleased. He had not known such happiness in a score of years, and the timid lad spoke.

"The last I heard, you were betrothed to marry."

"Marry, I was," marked she, "but marry I did not. It seemed the man liked well my looks, but not my books."

"I am sore to hear that."

"Not I," answered she.

Nicholas looked at her, and she looked right back at him.

After a three days' ride, they arrived in Stratford on the Avon, a sullied market town that appeared all the more sullied in the grey of dusk. They made their way to the outskirts and to Auntie's small cottage. There they were met by the smiling and wonderful face-lined woman herself, who had been as a mother to Valentina during her three years' stay in Warwickshire. And young Kit was there too, eager to again lay eyes on his sorely missed cuz.

They welcomed the travelers into their home, where all hospitality was laid. A hearty supper was et of woodcock and leeks and mulberries collected by young Kit hisself. A boy of early teen, he was exceptionally well-mannered and led the prayer of thanks before the meal. Auntie was sure glad to see her Valentina again, and her wrinkled face, mapped with threescore years of smiles and cares, beamed with happiness. Her small frame belied her strength, and her modest means belied her generosity.

When day was done, Valentina and Auntie shared the bed in the back. Nick was given the chair by the fire, and Kit happily bedded down on a bundle of hay. Uncle was away selling chickens and would return by week's end. It appeared a happy family as night came, and all slept sound.

At cock's crow, after a bit of eggs and cheat-bread were dressed in butter and sage, Auntie and Kit left to tend to the chickens, whilst Valentina took Nick to the court's office in town. I don't know whether they caught sight of Long Tom 'cross the lane, but he certainly had an oogle on them. A tall, thin fellow he was. An expressionless man. One could see just by looking at him that what he lacked in muscle, he more than made up for in wire.

He watched as Nick and Valentina entered the office. He could see them talking with the clerk, a squat man of good cheer by name of Ole Hopkins Hughes. He was always called Ole Hopkins Hughes, even when he was *young* Hopkins Hughes. So, one supposes he was ever a fellow of ancient airs. 'Twas that, or perhaps he was just an easy lad to poke fun on. At either case, Long Tom could see them ask Ole Hopkins a question, and the man just stood there shaking his sorry head.

The two left, having learnt not a thing, and made straight for the parish clerk's on Church Street. Now, I do not remember this clerk's name, nor have I any interesting remarks about it. But this fellow remembered Valentina and was most glad to see her again. For Valentina was the kind of lass that, after you once met her, you were sure sore to ever part company. 'Twas a hot day, and Long Tom was beginning to feel the pearl o' sweat as it ran from the brim of his cap down to the back of his long neck. But he stood there, still and watching, as he had been instructed to do. The beauty asked a question, and the clerk showed them a paper, which they looked on for some time afore saying their *God-be-with-yous*.

Long Tom followed them to Church Street's end where, through the churchyard, they pilgrim'd, coming upon the massive stones of the Holy Trinity. Tom stayed without, as Valentina and Nick went within.

They had a good look 'round. 'Twas cool inside the church. The smell of candles filled the air. It was a clean smell that gave Nicholas comfort. They walked by the colorful windows, Valentina no doubt counting steps as they went. They spied the monuments upon the wall. The figures of the dead who had been buried beneath. The men whose valued positions in the town (or valued coins in their purse) purchased them a burial by the chancel. Then, just past the north door, Nick spied the monument they had been searching for.

"This must be it," he said softly. "It's the only *Shakespeare* here."

"*Shaksper*," she corrected him.

He looked again. 'Twas writ *Shaksper* indeed. But who could fault an ill-learnt carver for not knowing the spelling of such a lettered name as this? It was a simple monument bearing the likeness of a simple fellow. Odd-looking in what the fellow was clutching, for 'twas not a book, nor a quill, nor even the town strumpet, Mistress Whatley. 'Twas a woolsack. Strange, Nick thought, that this monument should portray the family trade. But after all, this was his home. And here the man lived. He bore a thin, dour face with a long

30

frowning mustache drooping over a long frowning mouth. Not the face Nick had expected to see. But it was in truth the face of Master Shaksper.

Valentina stepped back as Nick joined her to read the inscription scratched into the floor:

GOOD FREND FOR JESUS SAKE FORBEARE,
TO DIGG THE DUST ENCLOASÉD HEARE.
BLESE BE THE MAN THAT SPARES THESE STONES,
AND CURST BE HE THAT MOVES MY BONES.

"Odd," marked he.

'Twas indeed odd. Why would a poet of Master Shakespeare's repute scribble such lines onto his everlasting tomb, when he could have writ:

NO LONGER MOURN FOR ME WHEN I AM DEAD
THAN YOU SHALL HEAR THE SURLY SULLEN BELL
GIVE WARNING TO THE WORLD THAT I AM FLED
FROM THIS VILE WORLD WITH VILEST WORMS TO
DWELL.
NAY, IF YOU READ THIS LINE, REMEMBER NOT
THE HAND THAT WRIT IT; FOR I LOVE YOU SO,
THAT I IN YOUR SWEET THOUGHTS WOULD BE
FORGOT,
IF THINKING ON ME THEN SHOULD MAKE YOU WOE.

True, a man would need to have stones the size of all Westminster's floor to chisel those many words upon it, but *CURST BE HE?*

They left the church with more questions than answers and walked down the tree-lined path of Southern Lane approaching the stone archway.

Nick passed under it, with Valentina behind. But the lad heard a noise above and looked to see some stones tumble. Turning quick, he clutched the lass, pushing her away to the ground. The stones stumbled onto them, as he protected her from harm. But as quick as he saw that he was laying atop the young maiden, with a genuine "Pray, I beg forgiveness!" he let go of her and rolled aside as fast as propriety demanded.

"You saved me," she said breathless.

He tried to help the beauty to her feet, but they both could see 'twas of no use. She was pained, and much like a poor drunken fellow arguing a bit of logic with yours truly, she had not a good leg to stand with.

"You're hurt," was all he said, as he carefully took her up like a sack of high-priced Guildford goose feathers and carried her back to Auntie's.

It was then that Long Tom came upon the scene. He bent down to pick up a stumbled stone, holding it in his dirty hand, which made the stone all the dirtier. He watched them slowly amble off, and then he let fall the stone.

As day ended, Auntie wrapped Valentina's leg tight as a Morris dancer's drum. Nicholas looked on and young Kit stood by at the ready, holding his surprise in his hand behind him.

"Now, I'm sure sore if this hurts, dearie, but the doctor says I must wrap you nice and tight," explained Auntie, whose weathered face contorted with such pain that you'd have thought 'twas her own leg that be all twisted and not the young lady's.

It was then that Kit extended his hand to reveal his gift for Valentina.

"I picked these for you," he proudly warbled, holding out a most pitiful excuse for withered red roses.

But Valentina was still in talks with Auntie and heard him not.

"How long?" asked the beauty.

"Orders are not to walk on it for three days," replied the old woman, who then turned to see the surprise in Kit's hand.

"Oh, how beautiful," Valentina lied.

"Beautiful?" Auntie cried. "Now where did you pluck these weeds?" she asked of the boy.

"In your garden," came his innocent reply.

Shamed, she grabbed them afore Valentina's dainty hand could deign touch them.

"Look at these pitiful stalks," she moaned. "Turnips and leeks I can master, but roses, I sure wish I knew." As she gave Valentina a "Sorry, child," the beauty couldn't hide her amusement. Auntie then turned to the boy and led him away.

When they left, Nicholas offered to stay with Valentina 'til she was ready to return. "You shall not. I'll be in good hands. Besides, Master Taverner will be waiting for the return of that borrowed nag. Uncle will be here at week's end, and I'll ride the coach into London with him. I shall find what I can here, and then join you in the city," she promised.

The next morning, Nicholas, all-reluctant, began his ride back to London, which made the journey seem longer by double, now that he had no companion the likes of Valentina. But he was not, in truth, on the road alone. For unbeknownst to the lad, he was being trailed all the way by the mysterious Long Tom, who rode a safe distance behind.

It was when Nick got back to my digs, however, that he recognized just how dangerous this search had become. My door had been a-breached, so he once more entered it to find the place in even more of a shambles than when he left it. My mattress was o'erturned. Papers were scattered every which-where. Near all the books were gone. And most telling of all was the half-empty bottle of ale, which suggested that I must have run out of there in a terrible hurry, for I never leave a task half-finished.

Nick ran without thinking. He shot down the lane with his heart jumping in his throat. He raced past all the bustle. The hurrying rats. The scurrying cats. The innkeeps selling ale from their vats. He found hisself at Newgate practically before he knew that he was running to my brother's. For who else might know of my whereabouts? Who else might care, for that matter? Though, in truth, I'd have wagered against Martin caring. But I've learnt that it is only when one's feet are put to the fire that a man discovers who truly cares enough to stand and make water 'gainst the flames.

33

Nicholas confronted my brother, and my brother answered the call.

"He disappeared the day you left," said Martin. "I learned of it shortly afterward and had the books brought here."

"We found nothing in Stratford," answered a worried Nicholas.

"Nor should you have," marked Martin. "I could have told you that was a trip of folly."

"Then why didn't you?" Nick said boldly.

Martin was taken aback. Nobody had ever questioned him like that. Good for you, dear Nicholas. Good for you. But this bravery also impressed my brother.

"It was a mistake," he finally answered. "And now, we're working on it."

"We?" asked Nick.

Martin paused a bit, then finally uttered, "This way."

He bolted his front door and led Nicholas 'cross the office to a stairway. Looking up the steps, Nick could see a sliver of light spilling out from under a door to the right. He followed my brother up, and Nick could hear men's voices coming from t'other side. Martin took out a key and inserted it into the lock. Of a sudden, all voices ceased.

Martin and Nicholas entered, and the lad took in the scene whilst Martin bolted the door behind them. It was a dark room full of books and bookshelves. There was a large table in the center covered by a bolt of green cloth. A group of well-appointed men stood there in stillness, but for one worried fellow hurriedly scurrying to board-up the row of windows. The room was darker now, and still. Then, Martin turned 'round and gave the assurance.

"It's all right, gentlemen. This is the young man."

There was a general sigh of relief as the men began to breathe again. Light was let in again, and there resumed a flurry. One man uncovered the table to reveal the Shakespeare books taken from my room and ten times more. Others pulled chairs into place, removed books from shelves, and carried papers 'cross the room. All was business again in Martin's private chamber of research.

"You see," Martin began, "you couldn't possibly have found your Master Shakespeare in Stratford because he died eight years ago. Who has that document?" he called out.

His clerk, Simon Simonds, jumped at once. "I have it, sir."

Simonds handed a paper to Martin, who showed it to Nicholas.

"*April, 1616. William Shaksper, gent,*" Martin read aloud. "*Death brought on after a long night in the local alehouse.*"

Nicholas looked to my brother with a puzzled face.

"I intend to find Arthur," Martin said. "And it seems the only way to that end is to solve your mystery. Now, shall we to work?"

Martin showed Nick 'round the room, introducing him to each man who was busied in his own research. You see, Martin often kept such men at hand to solve legal battles he hadn't the time nor the speciality to do on his own. They were always at the ready, whenever the Major needed them, for that's what they called Martin after his former career on the battlefield, afore he took up the law book as his favored weapon.

Here were all the great minds of London: Professor Charles Ogburn, master of English letters. Johnny Rollett, stage player. Jack Loney, the small, bespectacled scholar. And Simon Simonds, well-abled clerk and assistant to Martin Taverner. It was then that Nick understood just how lucky he was to have lawyer Taverner's help. With it, he was sure to find the answers to his father's death, and to the sad disappearance of his friend Arthur.

Martin's methodical mind and his many associates in London proved an endless resource. There was, in truth, no book nor document that he could not obtain. And it seemed the same with learnéd men.

"Gentlemen," Martin began, after all the introductions were introduced. "The first order of business shall be a report on the search for Arthur Taverner. Simonds?"

Simonds stood, referring to his papers. "Yes, Major. After an extensive search of taverns, doctors' digs, and brothels, I beg to report that the whereabouts of Master Taverner continues to elude us."

Martin simply said, "No news shall give us hope, for he's always had the knack of evasion." And that is true, you need only enquire of the bill collector. "We shall continue the search," says my dear brother. "Next, we review the case of William Shakespeare of Stratford-on-the-Avon."

Martin took his seat and motioned for Nicholas to do likeways. Nick looked about for an empty chair and saw one near the bookcase and sat, not noticing the long, thin man standing a few steps away in the dark. A man who had escaped notice earlier, always preferring the secrecy of corners.

Simonds, papers in hand, stood where all could see. "Yes, Major. Master Rollett has provided numerous pages from the Revels. Professor Ogburn and Master Loney have examined texts, both ancient and modern. And I have inspected the Records Office documents."

At this, the old professor cleared his throat a bit, so as to catch the speaker's attention. Once achieved, this caused a nod of the head into the shadows, prompting Simonds to add, "Ah, yes. And Long Tom has obtained a very useful testament."

Everyone turned their heads toward Tom in the corner, prompting Nicholas to do the same. There he was, with a long, sly grin on his face, having just returned from Stratford.

Simonds went on. "We have investigated the records of William Shaksper and find nothing out of the ordinary in his life. His death, however, has intrigued us. And what Long Tom has obtained further verifies our suspicions. Tom?"

Being summoned, Long Tom emerged from the shadows just long enough to hand Simonds some papers. It seems that he too is the sort of man who can obtain any thing and any one. His methods of obtainment, however, were never known for certain, but no one dared enquire. Martin asked what he had uncovered.

"It appears that Master Shaksper dictated his last testament in January of 1616. But in March of that year, just days before his death, describing himself as," and here Simonds read from the document, "*...in perfect health and memory, God be praised,* he revised his will. And thanks to Long Tom, we have a hand copy of that revision." The men in the room were impressed at Long Tom's find. Simonds continued, "And according to the gossip of the local vicar, Shaksper then went to a tavern with Ben Jonson."

"The writer," added Martin.

"And rival," Simonds continued. "That night Masters Shaksper and Jonson had, and I quote," he picked up another paper, "*…a merry meeting and, it seems, drank too hard, for Shaksper died of a fever there contracted.*"

"Is it likely for a man to contract a fever and die from drink, Professor?" asked Martin.

"I hope to God not!" answered Ogburn, picking up his own tankard and swigging it down, causing a hearty laughter from the others.

Simonds continued. "It is just this strange circumstance that has led us to make a list of the man's enemies."

Martin asked to hear them. Nicholas was impressed. He thought his quest would all be over soon. A tittle did he know.

Simonds began, "First is William Wayte."

"Who?" enquired my brother.

"We've found a surety of peace," Simonds said, holding up the writ, "issued against Master Shaksper by one William Wayte. Evidently, Wayte feared for his life. As did anyone who owed the man money," Simonds put it directly, "and that is a rather long list, sir."

Martin was pleased with the progress. "Very well, gentlemen. Tell us more of this Master Shakespeare."

"To be precise, sir," Simonds began, "while the name printed on the plays is *Shakespeare,* the official records of the man have it anywhere from *Shagspere* to *Shaksper*. A common enough name in Warwickshire. It seems the man began as a player with Lord Strange's Men. Then was taken up by his patrons, the earls of Oxford and Southampton."

"From the stories of these lords," Professor Ogburn added, "He made his plays."

"We first hear of Shaksper in London in 1588. It is an important year for the man," said Simonds, "for we find him in court."

"He's at her majesty's court?" Martin asked with surprise.

"Not exactly," came the reply.

CHAPTER SEVEN.

THE STORY OF SHAKSPER.

1588.

"Seven pound, your grace!" screamed the irate Shaksper over the banging staff of the weary justice. "That's what I lent him. Johnny Clayton, I lent you, do you deny it?"

Will bellowed 'cross the clamorous London court of commons. And very common 'twas that day. There were so many crowded louts about that he was standing almost directly atop the very man he was charging. 'Twas not a rat's whisker betwixt them. And they were only three elbows from the exhausted Justice Rush, whose name belied his abilities, as he busied hisself by bootlessly banging his staff of authority.

Next to Will stood his friend and associate, Francis Langley, a cock-eyed sort of fellow that you could just look at and know he'd steal the doublet off your back the minute you turned and heard the noontide wherry whistle blow. Will, standing there a-shouting, was a strong man of mid-twenties. And loud.

"This man here, your grace!" hollers he, pointing to John Clayton, an uneasy baker's apprentice from Biggleswade, who shook every time the judge's staff was shaked. "This motley-minded measle. And he has not paid me a penny of it." Will then turned to Clayton, shouting, "A turd in thy teeth, Clayton!"

As he stopped to take in a breath, the weary judge seized this rare befalling to speak.

"It appears you do not deny this, Master Clayton?"

"N-N-No, your honor," shook the grocer. "'Tis true. But he gives a man the hardest terms that ever you knew."

And afore Will could ready his next soliloquy, the judge banged his banger hard and decided. "Seven pounds to William Shaksper."

"Your honor?" Will enquired, holding up two coins and rubbing them together fierce, as though a fire could be made by the rubbing.

"Ah yes," said the judge. "And twenty shillings cost. Case so ordered," and he slammed his staff again.

Shaksper and Langley yowled with glee, and 'tis possible a few shouts of "You whey-faced puking pignut!" may have been heard above the din as they turned to Clayton, who gave over the coins, which had just been handed to him by a fellow standing near, plunging the poor man even deeper into debt's dirty ditch. And afore one could hear another Shaksper insult generated aloud, they left the crowded court.

As Clayton made his way through the throng, he did it ever so careful, so as not to get jostled by any of those jumping jays. Hands to his face, he protected that one eye. That one hurt eye that had somehow got all blacked-up before the trial. And as he egressed the chamber, seeing Shaksper with Langley waiting outside to the east, he made his way home very careful, via the west.

"I shall kill him, Langley!" muttered Shaksper, as the two charged down the lane.

"You'll do nothing of the sort," calmed Langley, trying hard to keep up with his friend.

"That unmuzzled, rump-fed hugger-mugger!"

"Uh-huh," was all Langley could think to respond.

Just then, a man by name of Wayte turned the corner and was eyed by an angry Shaksper.

"Willy Waite!" he yelled, about to leap after the man, who took one look at Shaksper, twirled about, and bolted fast away, whilst Langley clutched hold of Shaksper to stop his feet.

"No, Will. No."

"That thief owes me money." Will struggled to get loose. "Thou gleeking mother-puttock!" he yelled.

"Do you desire arrest?" Langley asked his fiery friend, and Will began to calm.

"How did I ever get to this stage?"

"Yes, indeed," said Langley, half wondering that hisself. "How indeed?"

★

1586.

The ceaseless screams of the babes could be heard bellowing throughout the crooked Shaksper cottage on Henley Street in Stratford. It was two years prior to Will's performance at the pleas court. As Will's mother busied herself concocting just the right amount of stale urine to use in the cleaning of last week's dirtified garments, brothers Dickie and Gil chased a couple of preciously purloined turkey hens through the house, as younger sibling Ned fetched a pail o' pig shittel to take from the front dungpile to the back dungpile, whilst Will made his way 'round the crowded room laden'd by his bloody butcher's apron all a-drip, pursued by his angry wife Anne Hathaway, with hair flying this-a-way and that-a-way, too busy to fret about her dishevelment.

"I saw you give that Whatley woman the smile!" she shot at her husband. "Why deny it?"

"I deny it," was his clever retort.

"What else have you give her, then?" she persisted. "What else have you promised her?"

But afore Will could re-retort her remarks, his old dad burst through the front door, out of what little breath he had.

"Will, I asked you, gut that pig 'fore noontime."

'Twas then that his mother-in-law came in holding the two crying babes.

"The twins need cleanin' again, children. The twins need cleanin'."

Will struggled to untie his apron as he walked out the house onto Henley, nearly stepping into that pile of pig dung that was getting bigger by the day.

"Where are you going?" bellowed his wife, as she and the entire family emerged out the door.

Finally disentangling hisself from his encumberment, and by that, I mean the apron and not the wife, he threw the thing to the ground (the apron) and began to stride down the lane.

"Where are you bound?" Anne Hatha-wailed.

"I'm going…" he began, not quite knowing how to end his sentence nor his journey. "I'm going…" and then he heard it. Trumpets. Jericho! And that gave him an idea. "I'm going to see the players," he shouted, as he paraded 'round the corner, leaving all of them dumbfounded in the street behind him.

The trumpets sounded loud, and the music sounded lousy. The creaking platform had been full of actors. The Lord Strange's Men, they were. They had just completed their playing, and the crowd that packed the inn-yard was cheering and hollering, banging hands and hats and pots and pans. The players came back onto that make-shift stage for one last jig when, of a sudden, the whole of it began to collapse.

First one plank broke, and then t'other. It had held up for five endless acts of battles and bloodshed but could hold no longer. One bit after t'other rumbled to the ground. One player after t'other tumbled after. The women screamed and the men roared. Children ran 'round like headless Huddersfield chicks. As for the players, many were unhurt, but some were broken.

No one noticed the nobleman in the back, looking on with great concern. 'Twas the young earl Southampton, the one who got hisself gently arrested on the first night of our tale. Here he was, just a boy of teen years, disguised with hooded cloak to appear an ordinary gentleman. But any who knew the earl would recognize him at once by the soft brown gloves with the black ribbons he so oft favored. As he saw Masters Lyly and Burbage were tending to the injured, he hid away into the adjoining inn to await their entry.

An hour later, the inn was crowded with players and laughter, as if the fright of the afternoon had been just another dreaded scene enacted in another dreaded poorly-writ John Webster tragedy long since clapper-clawed and forgot. Young Southampton was seated with company manager John Lyly at the back of the room, just as Lyly, whose nose was so astute that he could tell a dead cod from a deceased carp at a hundred paces, enquired of the owner.

"Innkeep, what is that foul smell?"

The innkeep breathed in a breath. "I sniff nothin' out the ordinary, sir," rebutted the keep.

"I apologize, milord," turned Lyly to the earl.

"'Tis nothing," said Southampton, with that usual smile of his that always made his lessers feel as betters.

Just then, the troop's most acclaimed actor, Richard Burbage, approached.

"Has our great lord yet arrived?"

"I've sent to Bilton," was Lyly's reply, which caused Southampton some concern.

"He's coming here?" asked the lord.

"He is, milord," replied the Lyly.

Burbage then pulled out his well-worn and ever-empty purse. "Are we to be paid this even?" he asked. "I'm a bit short."

"For such a tall figure, Richard, I find you always a bit short." And with that, the player gave a wry but disappointed grin. "We shall be paid in London," continued Lyly, "and don't again trouble milord about it. Now, what about the players?"

"Condell and Heminges are injured, but can play on," stated the actor. "Regarding Kempe," he continued, but then stopped dead in his part and began to wriggle a nostril. "What odor is this?" he enquired and looked about.

"And Kempe?" persisted Lyly.

"Ah, yes. Leg's a bit broke."

"Is he properly attended to?"

"Local surgeon has him. A Doctor Luck."

"His name's *Luck*?" looked Lyly worried.

"*Doctor* Luck," assured Burbage.

"Is the man licensed?"

"No, but he lives close by," reasoned the actor.

"Well, be sure Kempe is in good hands," ordered Lyly. "In the meantime, we'll have to replace him. It's a small part. Is't possible to find any locals of wit?"

And just as Burbage was about to laugh, the two boy-players, young Ethans and George, dressed in the prettiest petticoats a fellow could be wedged into, ran in announcing, "He's here! He's here!"

The players rushed out to greet the arriving earl as young Southampton remained within, wondering if it was better to face the great man direct, or, fearing how he would be met, escape out the back window and through the dungfields beyond.

From out the inn, a fellow could see a good distance down the dry, dirt road. Clouds of white dust rose from the ground, making the twenty racing horses appear like that many Pegasus, pounding their proud hooves into the deceiving earth. Twenty horsemen, dressed in the tawny livery of their lord, galloped toward the crowd, who had gathered there to lay their eyeballs on a true nobleman. Like a glistening cloud they rolled forward, as the score of golden stars on the shoulders of each horseman reflected the late afternoon sun.

"I thought this be the Lord Strange's Boys?" asked one old onlooker.

"'Tis the mighty earl of Oxford, they say," answered a small, excited fellow.

"The great Chamberlain hisself?" asked another, adjusting his hat to a proper position, not really knowing what that position should be.

At last, the horsemen arrived. To the crowd, they were a hundred times more magnificent than the players had been on stage. Some men dismounted to assist the others. The baron, the very man who would someday visit my cell with Nicholas, the one called Horace Vere, bounded off his horse and went to assist his cousin, the great earl, Edward of Oxford, who we likeways met at King's Place at the start of our story. All bowed to the mighty man.

The baron offered Oxford his gold-topped walking stick, as he stood tall to observe the crowd. Some days the pain would cause milord to lean upon the stick to walk. On this day, as on many, he required not the stick, but rested on it like a satisfied Italian duke.

Young Toby, Oxford's page, held his small hands outways, parting the now quieted crowd, to make way for his honorable master. But it was hardly necessary, for, as the lord came through the dumb-struck throng, they all backed away reverent, as if drawn by earthly forces, parting like the sea, as 'twere. Amazed, they stood. For here was he. The great Lord of Oxford. Here, in Stratford.

None had ever eyed such a man in the flesh and bone. A few stared at his glistening ring, which flashed his family sign of the boar. Others marveled at his Italian cloak of fine golden threads. Milord shone a gracious smile, then noticed an ancient fellow in the crowd attempting to descend onto his painful knees to show his respects. Oxford crossed to him swift and assisted.

"Here, father," he said soft, taking a nearby stool to help the frail ancient sit.

"Your humble servant," the man scratched.

"'Tis I who shall serve you," answered milord, to the stupefaction of all who stood there, stupefied. "An ale for the gentleman," he said, tossing a coin to the innkeeper at the door.

"Ye-ye-yes, milord," stammered the keep, who bowed his backside back inside.

Oxford waved to the people, who cheered him loud, and then went inside, followed by Horace, his boy Toby, and all of his faithful men. Those outside just stood there, looking at each other in polite amazement, and then near knocked one another down, rushing up to any unoccupied corner of any unoccupied window to peer into a world they had never known before and would sure never see again.

Lord Edward's eyes surveyed the creaking inn and he smiled. But suddenly his heart shook when he spied young Henry Southampton standing there.

"Great welcome, milords," said Southampton, bowing to all.

"Your ear!" Lord Edward ordered.

Horace joined Lyly and Burbage at the back table for a taste of the local ales, whilst milord took Southampton to a farther corner.

"She would not be pleased to find you here."

"Then let's not tell her," Henry bowed, "milord."

With a smile, Southampton joined the others. Oxford followed, and all rose for him.

"What's that smell?" he asked.

"Stratford-upon-Avon, milord," said Lyly.

And with that, they sat and drank. And soon milord regaled his men with exploits he called true.

"In a fret, all wet, I leapt from my Windsor sickbed, stumbled down dark Datchet Lane, and fell into Frogmore Heath, where you'll ne'er find a frog no more. And suddenly, I heard him gallop toward me! Fearless, I fended him off with bare hands. 'Til I saw his face. Herne the Hunter's face! The villain hanged some hundred years hence!"

It seemed with milord, there was ever a narrow barrier betwixt a telling truth and a fanciful fiction.

Later, the evening found milord walking the yard with Southampton.

"She grieves at your many hours wasted on such sport," warned milord.

"Do you think it so?" enquired the younger.

"It is not within my power to say," replied the elder, placing his arm on the earl's shoulder. "I do, however, entreat you on another matter. Will you visit me this even?"

"Your pleasure is mine, milord." And with that, Southampton smiled and walked away, as Horace approached.

"Do you think it wise to be seen so open with the boy?" he asked.

"'Tis my weakness, cousin," was all Lord Edward could answer.

"When you are together, tongues do wag."

"I know it is not seemly," said milord. "But I fear it is a thing I cannot stop."

45

They moved to Burbage and Heminges, who was feeling better now, thanks to Luck. His bent arm was held in a strip o' strop wrapped 'round his bent neck, making him look a bit like the crookback'd king seeking to sell a kingdom for a horse. They were hearing prospective locals eager to join the company of players.

In particular was one sizable bulk named Godsgift Goode, standing on the re-fortified platform, which stood now at a rather uncertain angle to the ground. Godsgift, pike in hand, recited his verse in the roughest voice, whilst flailing his large arms about as if swatting a swarm of Hungerford humble-bees.

> *Sing a song o' sixpence,*
> *A bag full o' rye,*
> *Four-and-twenty naughty boys,*
> *Baked in a pie.*
> *Baked in a pie, says I,*
> *Baked in a pie.*
> *Four-and-twenty naughty boys*
> *And not a one was I.*

"Master Godsgift Goode, milord," Burbage said slow, as if he was in pain.

"Anyone else besides this twice misnamed man?" the desperate earl asked.

"Happily, milord, 'tis a small part. Carries a pike, mumbles a line, then out on his arse."

"This one will do," said Heminges. "Or there's another. Very anxious to leave town."

"Creditors?" asked Oxford.

"Worse," said Heminges.

The actor nodded to the side where Will Shaksper was standing. He was once more down-weighted by his bloody butcher's apron, with one hand gripping a player's sword and t'other grappling a screaming babe, which made him look a bit like the lead player in the Grimsby guild production of *Titus Andronicus*. He was being yipped and yapped at by his unhappy wife, who was holding the

46

malcontented babe's twin in one of her hands and pointing an accusing finger at him with t'other. There was more noise about them than there had been during the great platform collapse of a few hours earlier.

"Either one shall do," said milord." We'll replace him in London anyway."

"Then I'll take Master Goode, for he owns his own pike," decided Burbage.

Milord turned to walk away as Burbage said to Heminges, "Tell Will Shaksper we won't be able to rescue him."

Hearing this, Lord Edward stopped.

CHAPTER EIGHT.

THE STORY OF HIS PATRONS.

"What is the man's name?"

"Shaksper. Will Shaksper," Burbage answered.

"Will shake spear?" Oxford looked to Horace. "Pleasant Willy!" he smiled. Milord then ordered Burbage to "Hire the spear-shaker."

And so, Burbage told Heminges to give Will the news, and afore Heminges barely got out a word, Shaksper howled and happily handed his still-yapping wife his yet-crying twin, removed his bloody apron, and threw it once more unto the ground. Happy as a pig in Shipston, he was!

Southampton and Horace followed Lord Edward into the inn, as Lyly approached Burbage.

"Who's Pleasant Willy?" Burbage enquired.

"Have you never read Spenser?"

"What plays has he writ?" asked the player.

Back inside, young Toby, ever vigilant, stood by the door with milord's great sword in hand, dreaming on a future when he might handily handle his own sharp bodkin and fight side-for-side alongst the great lord in battle. Course, the time did come for such a fight, and it ended rather badly for the boy, but that's a page for a different chapter.

Toby was the very spit and image of his brother Robin, who milord called *Robin Goodfellow*, due to the pranks he so loved to devise, like tippling over a sleeping Cornwall cow in the fields at midnight or filling his brother's boots with the cow's excrement just afore churchtime. Now, I say these boys were the very spit because they were born on the same day, in the same hour, and atop the same sack o' straw, though Master Robin was a good ten minutes on this earth whilst he awaited young Toby's arrival. A gooseberry cleft in two was not more twin than these.

Toby had a wonderful affection for his beloved Robin, who, being the elder, had been made page to milord afore it was necessary for Toby to succeed him. Robin, too, had dreamt on a future that, he not knowing then, would never find him. 'Tis a great shame so many youths never see their hoped-on tomorrows.

After a lot of drink was drunk, and a bit of food was et, with the favorite of the night being the poached Charlecote deer, Burbage spied milord alone in the yard and seized that befalling to approach him with his new player, Master Shaksper, now at heel.

"You wanted to meet the man, milord," Burbage fancifully removed his hat and bowed.

"Ah, yes. Master Spear-shaker. The innkeep tells us you have a natural wit."

Burbage gestured to the country glover's son to remove his cap out of respect for the earl. It took some doing, but the man finally caught on, and with an awkward gesture that appeared more an attack of the tremor cordis than anything else, he plucked off his bonnet, which caused milord to bite a lip.

"They say I am good with a tall tale, your majesty... uh... your worship."

"Very well," smiled the earl. "Then perhaps we can use you for sundry jobs."

'Twas already planted in milord's mind to maybe keep Will in London, as he took some pity on the man, having spied a bit o' the Anne Hathaway cudgel, and knowing from his own personal story the pain of a life wrongly-wedded. He nodded to young Southampton at t'other end of the yard.

"That is Lord Southampton. He shall be your patron in all you need."

Shaksper said, "I thank your worship."

"And Signore Richard," added milord in his unique way, "you shall take our young spear-shaker under your wing."

"If it please your lordship," Burbage said, for it truly did not please hisself.

"We must go now to Bilton," Oxford turned to go, but then bounded back and tossed Will a coin. "You need buy yourself a pike."

"God reward thee, your worship!" said the new player.

And with a twirl of his gold-topped stick, milord walked away.

"How came he by that stick?" Shaksper asked.

"Don't you know to remove your cap for a lord?" Burbage admonished.

"I never afore met one," replied the novice.

It seemed that Burbage had much work ahead of him, taking this new charge under his wing as milord had ordered, though in truth, the player never wished to perform mother peregrine to this young, peculiar pigeon.

"Let's to it again," the mother falcon began his tutoring. "Remove thy cap."

Shaksper obliged by grabbing the thing with both hands and jerking it off his noggin quick, as if it be shot off by a Frenchman's arrow on a windy day. Burbage stared a-shocked.

"Dost thou jest with me?"

"What?"

"First," the player instructed, as he hisself demonstrated whilst he spake it, "Remove thy cap with thy right hand alone."

Shaksper placed his hat back upon his skull and tried once more. Attempting, as best he could, which was not very best at all, to be an exact and true copy of Burbage's playing. He draggled the cap off his head with his right hand and thrust it down in front of his codpiece. If he had a codpiece. Which he had not.

"'Tis not a codpiece!" roared Burbage. And Shaksper's look told him he most likely did not know what a codpiece was.

"Remove the cap all gentle."

Shaksper did so.

"Lift, don't bedraggle!"

Shaksper re-did so.

"Grasp her by her brim, not her dome."

Shaksper began.

"From the rear, man, from the rear."

And Shaksper obliged.

"Turn."

Shaksper turned.

"The hat, not the Shaksper."

He turned the hat.

"Take with thy right hand."

And Shaksper took it with his left.

Burbage gave a piercing look.

And Shaksper took it with his right.

"Show not the inside of the cap whilst doing so!"

Shaksper quick-turned the thing 'round, so as not to reveal any dandriffe.

"And this be the trick," Burbage warned, as Shaksper now worried. "Swap the cap from right hand to left."

And whilst it took some doing, Will done it.

"Now that your right hand be at liberty, you may use it to give bow."

Whilst swinging his right hand 'round, Shaksper gave a thing, but whatever the thing was, 'twas never a bow. But Burbage thought it best to leave the thing as 'twas, and he called an end to their first lesson, vowing to pick up the bowing matter at another time, after a bit more privacy could be secured, and a few more drinks could be drunk.

Shaksper's eye returned to Lord Edward, still in talks with the others.

"How came he by that stick?"

"Did you never love the wrong woman?" says Burbage.

"Did you never meet my wife?" says Will.

"I shall tell you his story, and you shall act it on the stage. And if you are worthy, you will be his new story-teller. What say you?"

"I shall earn a wage?" asked Will.

Burbage laughed. "You shall, sirrah. You shall earn a most gracious wage."

"The woman he loved?" Shaksper reminded him.

51

"Oh, yes," Burbage said, as he crossed and sat upon the end of the crooked platform. Shaksper followed likeways. "It was a long time ago," Burbage began. Shaksper offered him a swig of his ale to more loose his lips, and Burbage gladly obliged. "He was just a young lad when his noble father died. Discovered in the garden dead. He was brought to London to become ward of the queen, living under the roof of her majesty's chief minister, William Cecil, and soon found himself sought as husband for the man's daughter. Although, at that time, the minister was a mere commoner."

"Like me?" Shaksper interrupted.

"Hardly," Burbage continued. "So that the marriage could take place, the minister was elevated. Her majesty took Sir William and POOF!" scaring Shaksper. "Like in a conjurer's trick, turned him into the powerful Lord Burghley. Surely, you've heard of him."

Shaksper gave a look that told Burbage surely he hadn't, and so Burbage spoke on.

"Li'l Annie Cecil had grown up looking all puppy eyes on young Edward."

"Who's young Edward?" interrupted Shaksper. "I thought we was talking about Milord Oxford."

"That's Milord Oxford's name. Edward," replies Burbage. "He was not, of course, happy about all this. And soon he was married, making him happier all the less."

"I know *that* story," moaned Shaksper.

"But what d'ye think he did before the wedding?" he asked the Stratford man, who truly thought the question warranted a reply and was about to give one, as Burbage barged on. "He first refused the queen. Refused to marry the girl," he said to the shocked Shaksper, who did not think it possible to refuse a queen, though he wished 'twas possible to refuse a marriage. "He ran off to Italy," Burbage continued, "but they fetched him back like a wounded deer. He makes a bargain with her majesty, they say, though they don't say what that bargain be, and he finally weds the lass. The queen then gives him his long-waited travels to the Continent. And you know how the story turns?"

"Indeed, no," answers Will.

"Well, he weds her, but he not beds her, they say."

52

"Who say?"

"Matters not," adds Burbage.

"The stick," urged Will, trying to turn this bull around.

"He's off to Italy," continued Burbage. "But when he returns, he learns his wife had a babe without him."

"Oh, 'zounds!" cried Shaksper.

"Oh, 'zounds, indeed," echoed Burbage. "But there's another story went 'round he bedded his wife by accident."

"How does a thing like that hap?" asked a confused Will.

"Some say he had a long night of drink, then met up with the lady he thought his mistress, but turned out to be—"

"His wife!" Shaksper guessed.

"So they say."

"So, he has no child of his own?"

"Oh, that he does. But not legitimate. He beds down a beauty at court. The queen's own maiden."

"What said the queen?" enquired Will.

"What *yelled* the queen, more like," answered Burbage. "She was none too pleased. For many say that *she* loved milord."

"Oh, 'zounds!"

"So bloody revenge was to follow."

"The queen cut him?"

"Her man did it. Slashed him and left him for dead, he did."

"And that is why…"

"Milord walks with the stick."

"'Zounds!" Will concluded.

And with that, Burbage rose, and Will popped up right next to him.

"Pity," concluded Burbage. "He was the finest dancer at court."

CHAPTER NINE.

WHEN ART ECHOES LIFE.

1624.

Martin looked to Rollett, the only player amongst them. "I don't remember a Shakespeare on the stage here. Did he continue as a player once in London?"

"None that I know ever saw him, Major," Rollett answered on cue. "But Simonds has found a record of a William Shakespeare being a member of the Lord Chamberlain's Men, formed shortly after Lord Strange's death, when many of the players started up with Burbage in Shoreditch."

★

1587.

"*All's Well That Ends Well?*" said Burbage, glancing at the play's name scratched atop his page, as Kempe passed out each man's part to the players assembled on the stage of the theatre that they, most clever, named *The Theatre*, so as, I suppose, to avoid any confusion of a fellow thinking he was by mistake entering Whitehall Palace or Chichester Cathedral.

"Don't we give out the ending with the title, Will?" enquired Heminges.

"Gentlemen," said Will. "The game is not in *what* haps, but in the *way* it haps."

This clever evasion seemed to please the players well.

"Now Heminges, you begin. You are Bertram, a young noble. Your dear father has just died and you are saying good-bye to your mother."

"What'd he die of?" asked Heminges.

"'Tis not in the play."

"There must be a clue."

"'Tis not in the play."

"Well, 'tis certain *you* know."

"'Tis certain I do not."

"How's a man to act it if he don't know how the old fellow died?" asked Heminges, desiring a method to this madness.

So, Shaksper thought on it a bit, and seeing Heminges was having it no other way, and hoping to be done with their first rehearsal by Shrove Tuesday next, which was still but half a year away, he replied, "'Twas in the middle of the Morris dance at the fete at Bermondsey Wednesday last, when of a sudden he got hisself run over by a tap-shackled bull."

This stopped Heminges short. "No one would ever believe such a thing."

"And that is why 'tis not in the play!" Shaksper said, resuming his instruction. "So, Bertram, after the unbelieved and unbespoke tragedy of your father's death, you go to become ward of the king, lucky you. You arrive to learn that his majesty, that is you, Burbage, orders you to marry a commoner, well below your own state. Condell, drop your codpiece and tighten your netherstocks, for you are the love-sicked Helena. The king," explained Shaksper, "in order to make the marriage hap, decides to POOF! grant title to the girl, but Bertram 'scapes to Italy, is returned like a wounded deer, and vows never to live with Helena 'til she be got by him with child. So, the lady tricks him into a tumble with her, whilst all the while he thinks he wrestles under the coverlet with his common drab. After being thought dead, she returns to life full-stomached, he is made to see the errors of his ways, the couple are reunited, and…"

"All is well that ends well!" concluded Burbage.

"Precisely," said Shaksper. "Now, bombast away."

And as the players motioned about the stage, Lyly stood at the back, seeing all this acted in his mind. Yet it was not Heminges' face he saw, but Lord Edward's. He knew the original of this story. He was there. And, of a sudden, a chill ran within him. Knowing how the nobles rather dislike the idea of airing their besmirched breeches in the public square, he wondered, *What shall her majesty think, seeing this story played upon a stage?* And much worse, *What shall she do?*

There was cheers. There was applause. The audience at The Theatre had clappered 'til their hands would drop from more. But Lyly stood worried, seeing the powerful William Cecil, now Lord Burghley, and his crookback'd son, Robert, were both in attendance. After all, was this not the mighty Burghley whose elevation had been echoed on their stage that day?

Will Shaksper too felt a-fret. For now he had an obligation here. With the help of his new-found friend, Langley, he was able to fill a goodly-grown pot of coins through the ancient art of money-lending, a practice perfected by his own father back in Stratford, which abled him to become an important shareholder of this theatre. And seeing the seething Burghley rise at the end of the performance, he quick skirted 'round the back.

'Round the front, however, Lord Edward was not as fortunate, being confronted by the two most powerful men in England.

"This insanity must stop!" barked Burghley.

"'Tis merely a fable," quipped Oxford.

"A fable better left untold," chimed the crookback.

Lord Edward addressed only his father-in-law, without ever a glance toward the younger. "We simply show here until we bring the tale to court," replied the earl.

"Not this tale, milord!" warned Burghley.

"I am no longer your ward, sir! I serve her majesty," reminded the premiere earl of the realm.

"I speak for her majesty," Burghley said.

"I saw your men's *Richard the Third* yesterday," Robert Crookback dared speak. "I never knew him to be a man so evil. Nor so misshapen."

"I do not believe he was," said the lord.

"Then why portray him so?" asked the misshapen Cecil.

"Perhaps it was not King Richard who was being portrayed," said milord, who turned and left, leaving the two Cecils fuming.

56

Lord Edward knew such confrontations could only bring danger, what with the great power her majesty granted these new-made men. Yet, he was one who could not help hisself at times. The hatred he bore both men, so much deserving for what they had done to him and to his children, each in his own turn, had to be unleashed.

Milord rounded the back of the theatre, finding his Stratford paymaster handing out coins to the players. Each man stood and received his share, with Condell last in line. He accepted the five coins thrust into his palm and began to walk away. But Shaksper called him back, and Condell turned over four of his new-got gain back to Shaksper. It was then that Lord Edward had an inspiration.

★

1624.

"Have you the mixture from Dr. Fowl?" demanded the king of his shady man Digges.

"I have, your majesty," answered he, retrieving the packet from his pocket.

"Which shall it be? The canary? The malmsey?" He looked hard at the wines and then came upon one he much liked. "The Rhenish. How say you?"

"Very fine selection, your highness," said Digges, as if they were in preparation of a state banquet rather than a poisoning.

★

1587.

Lovely Lettyce placed her soft hand upon his hard hump.

"Oh, Master Burbage, you were so… so…" she was troubled as she searched for just the right word to express her wonder.

"Wondrous?" Burbage assisted.

"Wondrous. Yes, wondrous," she near swooned.

"Tell me more, fair creature," said he, bathed in the flattery of the lovely lass, who had rushed behind the theatre to bask in the radiance of the man who was London's greatest player.

She completely ignored the rest of the company, who might as well have been a slew of dung-shoveling privy keepers for all the notice they received in the shadow of the great Burbage, who generally left on his hump so as to be better recognized.

"Such a *wondrous* King Richard," giddied Lettyce, getting quite accustomed now to the word *wondrous*. Her pear-shaped face smiled and did in truth smell of pear drops.

During all this, Shaksper and the rest stood by eavesdripping.

"Keep thy dagger sheathed," was Kempe's warning to Burbage, who ignored him quite, whilst the others giggled like a gaggle of Grassington geese. For the hump-clad player and the pear-shaped admirer were in deep colloquy, which could only mean one thing: a quick eventide tumble was being arranged.

"Now, where were we, dear pet?"

"Above the Ram Inn at Newington Butts," smiled Lettyce. "Midnight."

"I shall be there, my Venus," Burbage intoned, as he took her delicate hand and defiled it with his lips.

Midnight. The moon appeared o'er the sign of the Ram. Burbage eyed a clump of flowers in a neighbor's garden and plucked them from the dirt. He looked up at a lighted window and crossed to the door at the side. After a hard knock, and many a moments' wait, Lettyce's man, Willowaugh, opened up. Least, I call him Willowaugh, for I can't right say whether his true name be Master Willow nor Master Waugh, for I heard it bothways told.

"Sir?" spoke the severe old Willow, whose face appeared as though it had never afore been put through the agony of attempting to smile in all its seventy years.

"Tell your mistress Richard the Third awaits," Burbage articulated.

"As you wish, sir," sighed old Waugh, as he closed the door, having no idea who this famed caller was, and equally resenting

58

having to deliver to his mistress such a cock-feeble message. But deliver it he did, and in no time at all, which for him was about eight minutes, he was back down the flight of two-and-twenty steps.

"I come with a message for you, sir," puffed Willow.

"Speak your part, man," ordered the impatient player.

"I am instructed to report that my mistress is otherwise occupied," began the servant, as his eyes rolled up into his head to help him remember and deliver all that he had been instructed to report. "For 'tis well known that William the Conqueror came before Richard the Third."

And with that, Servant Waugh bolted the door tight, leaving outside a most frustrated Richard Burbage. The player stepped away from the door, turned 'round, and searched the heavens for an answer. But the explanation need not have been sought so far into the skies, as the view from the upstairs window told all.

Burbage looked up to see the lovely, unclad Lettyce peering down by candlelight, through yonder window breaking. She was then brushed aside by an equally cladless lad who, by all worst appearances, resembled Will Shaksper. Will looked down on Burbage and beamed a smile full of teeth, as he boarded the window to afford them some privacy, revealing no more of the show to the disgruntled groundling below. Burbage threw his flowery clump to the ground and stormed off to the nearest ale house.

And thus began the wondrous reign of William the Conqueror.

CHAPTER TEN.

SHOCKING DISCOVERIES ALONG THE AVON.

1624.

Martin looked to his men. "What sort of place is this Stratford-on-the-Avon?"

A Stratford ox dropped a loadful of foul-smelling shittel onto the road, as two foul-smelling laborers, half-covered in the stuff themselves, picked it up in their hands and dutifully placed it upon a mountainous heap in front of the humble and crooked cottage where a besottedly wobbling pottle-pot almost wobbled besottedly into it as he staggered down the dusty lane whilst three dirt-bedeck'd urchins, for good reasons none, boisterously bleated like Shropshire sheep, as an old and fisted stable-master cursed and whipped his young and twisted gelding-tasker with a crooked crabtree switch whilst passing four foul-mouthed louts cheating at dice about a walking mile, as the vile vulture flies, from Auntie's lovely and loving home.

Inside that home, the beautiful Valentina lay in bed. Even in sickness, she was the vision of a goddess. She was Pan if Pan be a beautiful woman. She tittered that pipe as cousin Kit sat entranced. At times, he had wanted to join in and sing out, but he knew he had perhaps the awfullest voice in all the Cotswolds, although he knew not what the Cotswolds was. Nor even if he was in them.

"If it please you, cousin," Kit pleaded, "make it sing like the nightingale."

And Valentina happily obliged.

"Ha, ha!" he beamed. "Hear the 'gale?" he called to Auntie, who was preparing to leave for the day.

"I do," said she. "'Tis a beauty. But don't you trouble cousin while I'm away." She then turned to her injured charge. "You just rest there, dearie, and should you need a thing, young Kit will get it you."

"Many thanks, Auntie," said Valentina, receiving a caring kiss on the forehead.

"I'll be back after dark," warned the old woman, as she likeways planted a pucker onto the boy's brow and disappeared out the door.

But no sooner had the latch dropped than Valentina hobbled up as best she could, full-dressed under her coverlet.

"Have you everything we need?" she asked, as if the two had designed some secret device.

"I have, cuz."

"You promise not to tell?"

And then the lad got all serious and spittled onto the three longest fingers of his swearing hand and crossed his heart. "My word, good cuz," he promised.

It was a bright morning as they approached the church, for Valentina wanted once more to examine that Shakespeare monument. But unbeknownst to these two adventurers, dark clouds hung on their horizon. Valentina, who had been leaning on young Kit, stopped to eye the scene. The doors were closed and the entrance guarded by a man she well-recognized. With that crimson nose and smiling cherub's face, it could be no other than sweet Sexton Edmunds. His bald pate shone in the sunlight as he allowed two workmen to enter through the doors, which were quick closed shut again.

"What's this?" asked Valentina.

"It's been closed since you fell hurt," said Kit, as they hobbled ahead to meet their plump friend.

"Mistress Valentina and Master Kit," announced the cherub, his round face lighting up. "Returned are you from London?"

"Only for a time," she replied.

Edmunds then noticed her hibble-hobble.

"You are wounded."

"'Tis nothing," she assured him. "But I wonder if we may enter?"

The sexton dutifully stepped in front of the doors.

"I crave your forgiveness," he sorrowfully said, as he held out his squatty arms and revealed a genuine look of sadness, "but we are in repair at the moment."

"Perhaps just a brief prayer?" persisted Valentina.

"I am given the strictest of orders from the vicar," he answered. And, by way to chisel the full Michelangelo, it should be noted that Vicar Pryce was the type of man that, after his temper was crossed once, it was never to be crossed a second time. "You may return this Sunday next," he suggested, reading the disappointment in Valentina's eyes. "I have the strictest of orders, you see, and am to put up here for the night to ensure as much."

The cheery cherub stepped aside only long enough to allow a Mickel Marcus to ramble in with hammer and pail, whilst his apprentice, Willy Fowler, ambled out for a bucket of ale.

"You'll be here this even?" asked Beauty.

"Most assuredly," assured Saint Edmunds.

"We shall return," she determined.

"But the orders remain," he said reluctant.

"'Tis all one," smiled she, "for we'll come seeking your good counsel and nothing more."

Valentina and Kit hibbled off a good distance and then stopped to discuss this most peculiar turn.

"Did you spy anything when the doors were opened?"

"Nothing."

"Then we shall see tonight."

"But the sexton," worried the boy.

"I know the sexton," Valentina smiled confident. "And I know his one weakness."

The two-penny bottle of Rhine wine was plunked down atop a tree-trunk at the end of the churchyard. It had gone quite dark and stormy in the hours it took them to muster up the wine from the vintner and the courage from wherever courage is kept, in order to enact their daring device. As rain fell on their heads like yesterday's soup, Valentina and Kit struggled to hear each other, whilst the soup-soaked Sexton kept watch at the doors. Valentina eyed the windows.

"You think you can do it?" worried Kit.

"You must distract him in deep discussion while I'm inside."

"I'll try my best," feared the lad, never one to string four words together continuous.

Valentina patted the boy on the head and then made her way to the side of the church, as Kit approached Edmunds with the bottle.

"Sexton Edmunds," shaked the boy.

"Ah, Master Kit," dripped Edmunds.

"My cousin asked me to bear you this," he offered.

The cherub's eyes lit up at the sight of the drink.

"Welcome, my son. Sit, sit."

He offered Kit a dwarfish stool, whilst he hisself leant his short but ample bulk 'gainst the strong oak doors.

"She thought you might be of thirst," said the boy, who could think of none else to say.

"What a thoughtful thought," answered Edmunds, who, at just that moment, heard a THUMP 'round the side.

At this, Kit offered him the bottle.

"'Tis a rough night," said the lad.

"Oh, yes," said Edmunds, as he took a big swig. "Oh, most deliciously yes."

A thunderclap hit, and Edmunds could see the boy was shaking. He offered him the bottle, and Kit, afraid of acting in any way suspect, took it. It was the boy's first taste of the Rhine, and it flowed downstream hard.

Inside the transept, Valentina got to her feet and shook off as much wet as she could shake. She looked 'round the empty darkness and could hardly eye her foot in front of her. She took a taper from that thing that holds up all the tapers and lit it with her stick of pinewood and sulfur. She could now see that the church was newly divided in twain. At a distance, there hung a drape of cloth, much like a ship's sail, masking the entry to the chancel.

Beauty slowly footed her way forward, careful not to fall from the water she dribbled onto the slippery stones below. Heedful, she approached the sail. Mindful, she parted it and entered the chancel that had aforeto been hid from her view. Once there, as her eyes began to harmonize with the blanket o' blackness, she could detect a new-dug hole. Right next to the very grave of Master Shaksper's! But afore she approached this new-dredged ditch, the great man's monument upon the wall called out to her. O' course, by this I speak metaphorical, for the thing was not in truth bellowing forth.

Outside, Kit and the sexton continued, sharing swig after swag from the potent two-penny bottle. All fear had now left the young lad, and he was feeling no pain. Nor any other sensation, neither.

Valentina turned and slow-stepped toward the monument. But giving it good view, she was astonished at what she now observed.

At that very moment, many miles away, Martin asked Nicholas to describe what he remembered of the Shaksper figure. In Stratford, Valentina looked on in amazement; whilst in London, Nick described to my brother's men what he and Valentina had seen.

"The face is long and frowning," Nicholas explained.

But Valentina beheld a new face. A round and smiling face.

"His hands are bare," Nick added.

But Beauty could see he was now holding paper and quill.

"His arms embrace a woolsack," noted Nick.

But Valentina saw no such sack no more. And whilst she gave all her attention to this new-made statue, she quite missed the sound of a door opening behind her. Someone was approaching.

"And this is the eternal tribute to the playwright?" asked Martin, intrigued. For if a man's life is to be forever preserved in stone, what said this monument about William Shakespeare?

And why has it been altered? wondered Valentina.

"Gentlemen," Martin announced, "we have a grave mystery."

Too late to escape, Valentina now heard someone behind her. She turned fast to face him, coming at her from behind the cloth. She clutched her taper hard. And as she saw a figure approach, she let out a yelp, which extinguished her candle, but she hoped not her life. And there he was!

It was Kit. Young Kit. Standing there. A-swaying.

"What is it?" wondered the boy.

"It's you, Kit."

"'Tis I, Kit," his glassy eyes unable to center.

"What of the sexton?"

"Asleep."

"They've changed the figure," she explained.

"But why?"

"I don't know."

"But why?" he repeated, and then she got a good look at him. And understood.

"You're besotted!"

"Oh."

"That drink was for him," she chided.

"I took but a tittle," he excused. He then noticed the hole in the floor. "Is this the grave?"

"It is."

"It is?" he questioned, apparently unable to comprehend an answer if offered only once.

And what of the new tenant? Valentina was curious. Not only to see who lay inside this new hole, but, as it was next to the famed Master Shaksper, she might also see into the resting place of the wondrous man hisself. She got down onto hands and knees and leant over to poke her head into the dark abyss below. But at that very moment, the cloth behind them began to tumble with a thund'ring roar. It caused young Kit to swing 'round and see the stern and solemn figure of Vicar Pryce standing before him.

"Who is it disturbs the souls who seek eternal rest?" the towering cleric commanded.

Kit looked at him. Caught. Then the boy looked 'round confused, for he had quite lost his cuz, who seemed to have vanished into thick air, as they say. He was now alone.

"I am s-sorry, your grace. We've …" and then he artfully corrected hisself, "…*I've* come to seek spiritual guidance."

"Seek it Sunday next!" ordained the minister. "Who let you pass?" he asked the boy, who was now shaking like the tail of a trapped rat.

"None, your grace. None." Kit then began to sway like a tipsy-turvy, and the vicar looked this peculiar boy over, trying to assess his condition.

It was then that the befuddled Edmunds ran in, as confused as the boy be. When the vicar turned to the sexton, Kit took this befalling to turn 'round and look once more for Valentina.

"Your grace," huffed Sexton Edmunds, out of breath.

"We have an intruder," came the accusation.

"I just came in for a prayer."

"You shall find no prayer in here, boy," said the cleric, ominous. "Show him the door, Edmunds."

"Yuh-yes, your grace." Edmunds gave a bit of a bow and gently escorted young Kit out.

The vicar stayed to have a look, and walked 'round the new-dug hole, where, having lost her balance and fallen into the thing, Valentina now huddled all quiet inside, daring not to breathe. The vicar's foot passed overhead, and some of the small stones and dust encloséd there fell onto her pate. She was a-frighted that she would be discovered. But, after a moment passed, satisfied, the mighty figure of the vicar left the church.

To the lady's great relief, there seemed to be no new tenant in the new-dug hole. But that was not exactly true, for, to her horror, she would soon discover she was not the only one alive in that grave.

Unawares of that then, and breathing heavy now, she decided to seize this singular happenstance. After all, she was so close to the great man in the adjoining grave. She reached for her candle and fumbled for her sulfur. Once lit, she slowly turned and held out the flame to the resting place of the great poet. She could see well into it now. But what she saw there, she could neither compass nor comprehend. *What on earth?* thought she. And then she heard a sound. Trembling like a hummingbird, she turned and thrust her taper forward into the darkness. It was then she grasped that she was not alone in that grave. For in the blink of an eye, she saw the blink of an eye! Unable to move, she screamed a frightened but soundless scream.

CHAPTER ELEVEN.

THE DEATH OF A FRIEND AND A MEANINGFUL MISSIVE.

Grim death took me without any warning,
I was well at night and dead in the morning.

Those were the last words of one Thomas Swann, a man Kit was sure thankful for on this night. Still the storm raged, but still it was not, for it stirred and it swilled from the top of the steeple to the graves of the people. And though a part of the night's sky was mysteriously beginning to lighten, this did little to relieve Kit. The rain would be good for the malt in the fields, but it gave no comfort to the lad's spirits, as he sat uneasy atop the gravestone of Master Swann, who had thoughtfully provided a flat surface for just such an occasion. The boy held tight to the stone-top, trying to avoid the sway, which came part from the wind without and part from the wine within.

Of a sudden, he felt a strong spirit tap him from behind, and he jumped of fright, falling into the mud below.

"A rat!" shouted the voice, scaring the muddled lad, who turned to see an impassioned Valentina. "A big, ugly rat!" cried she. "With blinking red eyes and great pointed teeth!" yelled she, as she neared the lad's befuddled face. "Well-nigh scared the life out of me," she exclaimed, whilst Kit was busy trying to keep his own scared life within him. "Kit," she continued, "there is no writer buried inside that hole!"

Kit picked hisself out of the mire and looked to Valentina, who he had never seen in such a state. She took his arm and held onto it tight.

"There is a *new* writer atop the monument," added she, "but no *old* writer within the grave."

"You mean...?" Kit began to catch hold.

68

"The grave is empty!" Valentina concluded. "But for that big rat!"

★

'Twas mid-morning when Nicholas carried his copy of the Shakespeare book to Millington's shoppe, only to find the man on his way out.

"Master Millington," Nick called.

"I'm off for turnip pie."

Urgent-like, Nick took hold of Millington's arm. "I need your help," he pleaded. "Arthur's gone missing."

"I don't intend to join him, Nick," said Millington with a worried brow.

"You deal in many Shakespeare printings," Nick persisted.

"As did your father. And his shoppe burnt down, was it not?"

"I must learn what happened," said the young man.

Millington's eyes o'erlooked the lane, upways and down. So busied with vendors and vagabonds, he did not note the man at the end. The one holding a bible to his face. And after what seemed like a lifetime, Millington finally gave out a long breath and said, "Come in."

Nicholas set down the book and opened it to the Shakespeare face. "Tell me about this man."

"Nick," Millington scoffed, "this is no man, 'tis a jest." And with that, he pointed to the mismatched hair, the over-large'd head, the backways doublet, and the engraven'd line running from the disfigured ear to the rounded chin, making it look like the fellow wears a mask. "There is nothing here that suggests a true man. Nor a writer. No book, no quill, no laurel wreath." Why, all this was true, and I don't know why I myself did not take note of it the first time I laid my eyeball upon it.

Millington then pointed to the words opposite the face, where the scribbler Ben Jonson urges a fellow who seeks Master Shakespeare to seek him, "*not on his picture, but his book.*"

"So, why this image?" asked Nick, his heart beating fast.

Millington thought for a moment, not on what to say, but if he should say anything at all. At the last, the good man crossed behind his table where, from under a deep mountain of Greek encyclopedes, Bedfordshire botany books, and copies of perhaps the awfullest romance story you would ever buy from a bookseller that would never give back your tuppence, should you not like the book, entitled *Guy of Warwick*, for which I should have got my pennies returned because the book was so lousy... But I get away from my thesis here.

From under all of these, Millington removed a small quarto.

"The best I can give you is this," said he, handing the book to Nick.

"*Shake-speare's Sonnets*," said Nick, reading the title.

"Note the hyphen to divide his name," said the bookseller, knowingly. "And why was it quickly removed from all the shoppes?" He then pointed to the two lines at the bottom of the title page, where it is tradition to print the writer's name. "Why no name between the lines?" he noted. 'Tis a pity I had not been there to tell him we were meant to read between them. Then Millington turned to the page of dedication. "You will find your answers here." For here is where Millington hisself discovered the truth. Betwixt this dedication and these poems and a bit o' gossip along the way, he pieced together quite a secret tale.

Nick had never seen this book, though 'twas printed fifteen years earlier. And he had never spied a dedication page laid out so odd. EVERY. LETTER. IN. HIGH. CASE. WITH. A. FULL. STOP. AFTER. EACH. WORD. Not to mention (but I must mention), that all the words were arranged to picture three upways-down triangles.

This was certainly not the usual work of printer Tom Thorpe, thought Nick.

"This book will tell you all that I cannot," Millington concluded, ushering Nicholas to the door. But our Nick would ne'er budge.

"The riddle of the dedication," he urged. "How do I solve it?"

Millington's heart was now racing upways and down within his sweating doublet. After a brief hesitate, he said, "Look to the name and the number."

70

'Twas then he heard a rumble 'round the back.

"We are not safe," he warned, but when he took a look to Nick's eyes, he relented. "Come at the noon hour. I will have more for you then."

Nick thanked his friend and started out the door, but Millington grabbed his arm. "Sometimes the truth lies beneath our very eyes, Nick. You've been searching for a star. After you find it, you must look to the other two. The answer lies in their convergence."

And with those cryptics lodged within Nick's noggin, he left the shoppe hopeful, carrying one old book and one new, leaving behind a perspiring Millington, who crossed to his table and downed a stoup of ale. He then picked up his *Albion's England* and, finding what he sought, tore a special fragment from it. He began to write, still paying no mind to the man down the lane. The man with the bible, whose green eyes lay constant on his Millington rather than on his Matthew or his Mark.

Nick sat at The Piss and Whistle, perhaps the awfullest tavern in Cheapside, too excited to eat more than a crumble of bread nor a tumble of draught, whilst all about him a company of ale-wash't wits noisily stuffed themselves with food and tipple. Seeing ole Peg at work made him think on me.

"Where's your mate?," asked my dear wench, "whose absence of late has caused a terrible calm 'round here."

"He has vanished," came his sad reply.

"How's that?" she said, stopping still. "Have you looked in the Clink?"

Oh, I wish it had been the Clink where I was clank'd. 'Tis the Clink gives a man precious pig's fat slapped onto his bread. 'Tis the Clink that doesn't stink to highest heaven. A sweet place, that Clink, compared to the fetid hole where I was footed.

"He is nowhere to be found these past nine days," said Nick.

Now at this, my dear Peg looked concerned. Genuine concerned, if I may say. That surprised me, too.

"The poor chuck," sighed she.

Nick stood and placed a penny down.

"Master Nicholas?" says she sorrowful, and he turned. "When you find him... say ole Peg is here waiting."

Nick smiled and stepped out the tavern.

To think, the next time I would see my sweet Peg 'twould be her wedding day.

As Nick heard the noontime bells from Paul's, he headed back to Millington's, where his friend had been readying more answers. Oh, if only life was that easy for the lad. As he turned the corner to the shoppe, he saw what he had not expected. 'Twas a gaggle of clattering clacks gathered in front.

He neared and asked a fellow, "What's happened?"

"Fell from the thatch," came the answer.

"Who?" Nick asked.

"Made an awful commotion," offered another.

Nick slowly pushed his way through the tongue-wagglers 'til he saw a body laying twisted in front of the book shoppe.

"Who?" he asked, fearing the worst.

"The bookseller," came the answer.

"No!"

"No doubt had too much drink in him," another ne'er-do-good cried from behind.

Nick crossed to his friend and knelt, looking at the poor man's face. A face he had last seen so troubled, but 'twas now oddly at peace.

Martin and his men stood there, eyeing Shaksper's last will. But answers don't oft jump from the page so easy. A puzzle is made to puzzle, and so Martin re-read the pages with his eyes drawn sharp. And when that did not suffice, he read them again. And he finally recognized it was not the words what were writ on the page that he was after, but the words what were *not* writ on the page.

"What is missing, gentlemen?" Martin asked his men.

No one spoke.

"What should we expect to find here, but do not?"

Just as Nick noticed the bit of *Albion* clutched in Millington's hand, he spied two men making their way through the crowd. He snatched the scrap and ran, not pausing to peruse the page, which in actual fact had no word writ by Millington on it at all, yet 'twas not empty neither. He ne'er stopped running 'til he got up that staircase.

Just as no one was about to answer Martin's question about what was missing from the Shaksper will, which was books, the chamber door burst open with a BANG. Nick, all breathless, ran into the room as each head turned. And lucky for the lad, Martin does not always remember to bolt that door, otherways a knocked noggin would have been his welcome.

"Master North," Martin spoke.

"Millington, the bookseller," Nick finally breathed. "He's been murdered. He was helping me."

This sudden news was a thing unlook'd for but not unforeseen by my brother, causing him to think. He looked at his men and made his decision.

"Gentlemen, we shall resume on Monday. I dismiss you until then and ask that you all be very cautious."

With that, the men put all their work away, and it was not long that only Martin and Nicholas remained. My brother held open the door and looked to Nick, who, scrap still in hand, sat quite lost in his thoughts.

"Coming, lad?"

There was no response.

"Master Nicholas?" he called.

"Oh," said Nick, coming back to this world. "I am sorry, sir." He looked 'round the room and recognized they were alone. "May I stay?"

Martin approached him. "My brother is taken. Your good father gone. And now Master Millington. You know, son, there may be more danger ahead."

Nick knew this. After having learnt at an early age the power of the swift sword of state, he had always tried to live a life away from danger. He was a man who ne'er saw the need for a wrangle when a word would kindlier serve the turn. But now he knew he'd have to face any danger that might come his way. He simply nodded. Martin smiled and crossed to the door.

"Help yourself to the books. There's food and wine below. And bolt the doors."

Martin left. Nicholas rose and did as he was bade.

★

The next day found Valentina standing at the desk of young Master Strittmaster, a sweet-natured clerk, who gently placed before her an arm's length of papers afore going off to collect more. She searched through the documents, whose arrangement it seemed was so disordered that they would have to have been purposefully so misordered, for they could not have got so mixed in any other way. 1602 petitions laid upon 1599 lawsuits folded within 1615 restraints. Kit, however, was seated by the door paying no mind, as he was quite occupied with pressing Valentina's wet handkerchief onto his infirmed forehead, as if it would heal him of his throbbing brain. It did no good at all, but he was always a boy of hope.

After what seemed a half-hour to Beauty, and near half a lifetime to Kit, she had found it! Something that made her eyes even bigger than they already were. A wriggle at the bottom of a page. And then she knew.

"Is that her?" Kit asked, as they stood on Chapel Lane, watching a woman pluck peach-colored roses alongside the largest manor house in town.

"It is," replied Valentina. She then slipped into her pocket a very vital letter she had earlier writ and sealed, and they made their approach. Valentina introduced herself.

"Oh, yes," said the woman, with a pleasant smile on her face. "Your father lives in Deer Wood."

"My uncle," smiled Valentina. "These are beautiful roses."

"Why, thank you," said the woman proud.

The two stood there and conversed, all the whilst Kit looked on wishing he was somewheres else. Anywheres else. They talked of gardens and of neighbors. And of nothing of import. And after what may have been a year or two, Kit noticed Mistress Quiney drop a rose

74

from her small hand, which he kindly picked up and attempted to return.

"Oh, do keep it, young man," she offered. The boy thanked her and happily looked about his clothing for the best hole to receive it. And, as his wool jerkin possessed many holes, this endeavor occupied him for some time.

"It was indeed a pleasure," Valentina finally finished. "We must now be off."

And they began to walk away in the direction of Sheep Street, but the beauty, ready now to enact the stratagem she had devised all along, stopped and turned back to the rose-gardener.

"Oh," said she, ever so natural, removing the sealed letter from her pocket." Perhaps you could help us." Valentina explained that they were to deliver this missive and gave her the mysterious paper, asking, "Do you know the name?"

As Mistress Quiney took it in hand, Kit noticed the look on her face change. All in a sudden, there was an appearance that he could not comprehend. The proud woman looked down at the letter but gave apology and said she could be of no help.

"Matters not," Valentina said. And with Kit by her side, they walked to the corner of Sheep and High. "This is strange," was all she could say, staring at the letter.

"What is?" asked her curious cuz.

"We have undone a great knot, my dear Kit. And pulled a thread that may unravel all." Which caused Kit, for the moment at least, to stop pulling at his own thread, and they walked on.

Auntie fought back tears as she watched Uncle Ned place Valentina's bag onto the coach. "Now you be careful," was her usual plea, as she kissed her husband's ruddy cheek.

"I will, lovie," came his vow.

She then turned to Valentina. "And you be careful, dearie," as she kissed Beauty's cheek.

"Thank you, Auntie," said the lass, as uncle helped her into the coach, with him hopping on afterways.

"And you be careful, too," Auntie said to Kit, as she kissed him fondly on the forehead.

"But I'm not goin' nowheres," he answered, sweet-natured, but a bit befuddled.

"And see to it you don't," was her tender reply.

"Oh, I almost forgot! For you, dear Kit," called Valentina, handing the boy her flute.

"For me?" he exclaimed with a jump. "Oh, thank you, good Valentina! Thank you much!"

The coachman snapped his whip and, with a jolt, they trotted off to London. Kit waved and jumped and shrilled his new-got pipe, as Auntie held the boy tight in her arms, dropping a big tear from a tiny eye.

Nick was at the research room all the week's end. He rarely got a winkle o'sleep as he poured over the scrap he had retrieved from his departed friend, and could make not top nor tail from it, as all that was writ by Millington were the numbers 6.2.4. Now, what could that mean, and why was it writ there? Did the numbers point to a verse in the holy book? Or was it one of those numeric ciphers so oft used by Masters Bacon and Dee, her majesty's men of math and magic?

Nick crossed to the shelves, writ out some scribbles, poured o'er a pamphlet, and returned to that 6.2.4. question, not knowing it was, in fact, not a question at all, but an answer. The day revealed no secrets, but the night still lay ahead. And a tittle did he know that, though the day proved bootless, it would be a night full of boot.

It was Sunday even, and perhaps all the stars were lined aright, for a thing finally did hap. As Nick took a respite from the books and the puzzles, he began to pace along the length of the room. He would likeways peep down from the windows. He paced and he peeped. Peeped and he paced. And on his last go-round, as he looked down to see people jostling through the streets, he saw the man in the gold-lined cloak. But not any man was this, for it be the nobleman! The very nobleman he had seen in the carriage that morning of his dear father's death. One of the many faces that haunted his dreams but could never speak to him. Nick knew not the name of Baron Horace Vere then. That was yet to come.

He ran to the door and darted down the stair. Racing out into the crowds, Nick took off in the direction he had seen Horace and his men travel, but there was no sight of them. He headed toward the river, passing peddlers and eels, with the stink of the stench getting worse as he neared the water. Not a wherry was in sight taking gentlemen aboard, so he turned and ran t'other way. He came upon some men of style and hurried ahead to see if they were they. But they were not.

He stopped and slow turned 'round, squinting his eye on each face he found. He made good view: a woman danced, children played, and a poet lay face-down in the gutter. He walked a bit and beheld nothing out of the usual. A twisted lute-player pluck'd on Crooked Crest, sweethearts squabbled in Lover's Alley, men tended to a fire on Pudding Lane. None of them was Horace Vere.

Defeated, he retreated toward the law office. And as he neared Newgate, he passed a pretty ginger-haired lass. But much like the girl, Nick did not go unnoticed, for there was a pair of surprised greenish eyes fixed upon him. Hung on him like blood hangs on a serpent's fang.

The printer walked on, and his pursuer walked on, too. Nicholas strode faster, and old Knyvet followed as fast as he could. For this was the young man he was after since that day he eyed him at Millington's shoppe, noisily enquiring after Master Shakespeare. The pursuer of one man now became the pursued of the next. Knyvet sought out this printer, just as he had sought out the printer's father so many years before. Such a family of prey. And though the serpent had always succeeded, age had slowed his speed. He huffed as he tried to keep up with his victim. The crowds seemed against him. Knew he not the very world was against him? Yet down this dangerous road they ran.

Within minutes, the race was won. Nicholas bolted the upstairs door and headed back to work. The old serpent walked past the law office and into the lane beyond. He looked left. He turned about. He had lost his scent.

CHAPTER TWELVE.

OF DISTANT SONS.

Nick carefully removed from his pocket the star and moon and sun emblems and placed them reverently atop a leaf of paper. Looking through *The Book of Mythos*, he opened to the page about the moon and grabbed hold of his quill. Under his own moon emblem, he copied from the book the word *Cynthia*. And after examining more text, he writ: *Virgin Moon Goddess*. And he thought a bit.

He looked again, searching for a star, but had no luck. As he went to retrieve another book, only lanes away was old Knyvet, sitting at his own angled table with a crudely-drawn map of the London streets before him. He twisted his dulled old neck-chain with his left hand, whilst picking up his nubby quill in t'other, and with the dirty stubs of his fingers, the serpent dipped quill into ink and drew a small circle 'round the lanes where he had last seen Nicholas. And so, his net was laid. His eyes of green fixed upon the map as if staring long and hard into it would bring him closer to his desired prey.

Nick set down another book bearing the image of a sun. On his paper he writ: *Helios*. And then: *Sunne*. He then noticed a fine scribble on the tabletop in Simonds' hand. The words *Will Shaksper, Stratford* had been scribed, under which was neatly penned: *Anne, wife. Susanna, Daughter. Judith, Daughter. Hamnet, Sonne*. As if by a force of nature, Nick was drawn to this last word, and under his own scribbled *Sunne* he writ: *Sonne. Hamnet. 1596*. Such a critical year for such a sonne as this.

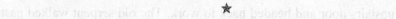

The 1590s.

The players paraded down Curtain Road, keen this day to start their new historical. Every man would receive his part. Motions would be devised. Fights would be thrust and parried. And for the big finish, a song and dance would needs be learnt. All they must do now is enter The Theatre. And on this day, that was the only act forbid them.

A chain stood 'twixt these men and their hopes. With opened mouths, Shaksper, Burbage, Heminges, Kempe, Condell, and the lesser players not worthy of mention, all had eyes fixed upon a parchment that spelt their doom. Words that no actor ever hopes to see writ on the front of his playhouse door. And by that, I do not mean:

NEXT WEEK A NEW COMEDY BY JOHN WEBSTER.

T'other words no actor ever hopes to read are:

CLOSED DUE TO INFECCION OF THE PLAGUE.

"Well, that's it then," cried Heminges.

"What of the play?" announced Burbage.

"How long shall this delay us?" followed Condell.

Funny, not one man spoke any fear 'bout the deadly pestilence whirling 'round them, for their only concern was the putting on of the play, which I think tells a fellow all he needs to know about actors.

"I shall set sail with the Admiral's Men," decided Burbage. "They're preparing a tour to the country. You boys?"

"Back to my cousin's smith shoppe," answered a downcast Kempe.

Looking upon them, Lord Edward spoke a good distance away with Master Lyly and a young man with a striking streak of ginger in his otherways golden hair. 'Twas Munday. And by that, I mean the man and not the day, which may have been a Friday, but I do not know for certain. This Munday was now employed as a second secretary to milord. Tall and striking, he had years earlier been a player in milord's company. Young Anthony Munday he was.

"See to it they're all paid for the remainder of the year," milord told his company manager.

"I'm afraid," said Lyly, "without the clap and the coin of the public, we have no funds."

Milord was deep in thought about this when old Helios peeped 'round a cloud and glistened onto the golden chain hanging about his neck. And once he caught sight of this glimmer, he removed it and held it out for Lyly to take to market.

"Here," was all he said before Lyly had the chance to ask if this was the very gift given milord by her majesty at one of her jousting tournaments.

Burbage then turned to Shaksper. "What'll you, Will? Back to the old wifee?"

This thought shot a great shake down Shaksper's spine. "'Tis not that desperate a time, is it?" said Will, which made Burbage burst out with a laugh.

Will then began to walk away with his head down, deep in the thought of having to return to his dreaded home, when he near collided with Munday and milord.

"You've a son, Will?" asked the noble.

With that, Will stopped and stumbled to remove his cap, making milord smile. "Oh, forgive me, your worship," was by now his usual and awkward reply. And then silence, as he had quite forgot the question questioned of him.

"You've a son?" milord repeated.

"Uh, yes, your worship," finally came the answer. "These nine years now. Name of Hamnet."

"Hamnet. Fine name," said milord.

"After my neighbor, Hamnet Sadler, who's a bit of a cog 'n a cole, but he owns a good name," Will added, with ne'er a reason to.

"Is he a fine boy, your son?"

"Truth be told, haven't right seen enough to tell, your worship," which was indeed true, as Will always preferred the fellows of Hackney to the bellows of Hathaway.

Milord stepped close to him. "Perhaps you should find out," he said, "for a boy needs a father." Milord uttered this, even though he felt a pressing in his heart whenever he spoke of such things.

"You suppose, milord?" pondered Will, deciding whether 'twas better to face his wife or the plague.

"A son is a gift from God, Will," said milord, in a way he never afore spoke to this man.

"You have a son, milord?"

Lord Edward's reaction promptly told Will that it was a question that should not have been asked. But the earl obliged.

"I did. Taken at birth, he was."

Now Shaksper felt a right ass. "Ooh," moaned he, "I am terrible sorry, your worship."

"It was God's wish," said milord. "But he lives on in me. And in all who think of him dear. Go see your boy." And with that, milord handed Will a coin.

Will took it and determined that he would go see his boy.

1624.

The many hours of unfruitful studies finally weighed on Nick, who thought it best to limber his legs and amble the streets with ne'er a destination in mind. But as he walked down desolate Fleet Street, everything was about to change. First, he heard a growl. And next, he stumbled upon Master Botticelli's head.

★

The 1590s.

Tales of sons and fathers are ofttimes tales of joy, if one tumbles into a bit o' luck. But some are tales of loss.

The letters carved into the gravestone were scars that remained chiseled into milord's heart. Like a cicatrix that would not heal. A sad monument for all the world to o'er-read. Milord stood there, reciting the words in his mind. Words he had so oft read:

VISCOUNT BULBECK. ANNO DOMINI 1583.
EARLE OF OXENFORD. SON.

Milord's smile could light a room. But there could also be a sadness about him. He was a man who had truly lived, but this son of his had not. And as he stood there, thoughts ran through his mind of what fathers might tell sons. They flew from his soul in what he knew was a silent missive from his broken heart to the spirit of his lost boy.

When forty winters shall besiege thy brow
And dig deep trenches in thy beauty's field,

Miles away, Will Shaksper strode with his own son Hamnet.

Thy youth's proud livery, so gazed on now,
Will be a tattered weed, of small worth held.

Will handed his boy a new cap, which he excitedly donned.

Then being asked where all thy beauty lies,
Where all the treasure of thy lusty days?

Young Hamnet caught a river pike, whilst his old man took in the line.

To say within thine own deep-sunken eyes
Were an all-eating shame and thriftless praise.

Will played a game of toss with his boy of nine.

How much more praise deserved thy beauty's use
If thou couldst answer, 'This fair child of mine
Shall sum my count, and make my old excuse,'
Proving his beauty by succession thine.

82

Will readied his return to London, but poor Hamnet cried and
would not let go.

This were to be new made when thou art old
And see thy blood warm when thou feel'st it cold.

As Lord Edward looked up and saw the young boy approach,
his heart raced. There, for a second, he imagined his own son nearing,
but he soon grasped that it was his young page Toby. And whilst a bit
of his soul sank, another lifted, as he felt the lad a great comfort to him
in times such as these. And so much like his brother Robin, who
milord would oft think on with a mix of fondness and regret. A good
boy, this Toby. And to think, without such a lad, there would never
have been born a theatre called The Globe.

★

1624.

When Nick stumbled upon Botticelli's Head, it was never a
decapp'd Italianate cut-throat, but the name of an inn near Newgate,
run by a woman called Marianna Magri, whose husband, Joseppi
Miguel Stephano Magri, was brought to London from the town of
Firenze, which many in the world call the *Athens of Italy*, but which
here in England we call *Florence* for some reason that I've not yet
found the answer to.

Nick walked past Botticelli's Head without giving it a
once-'round. But of a sudden, he heard a loud growl from his gut, and,
as if in answer to his hunger, his nose sniffled the strong kick of a
thing he later learnt was called *garlick*. This caused the lad to enter the
inn, where he was given a right royal welcome, for that's how the
Italians always treat a fellow 'til they get to know him.

Inside, he learnt that Master Magri, who was a famed and
learnéd traveler and scholar back in the Athens of Italy, had come to
tutor the earl of Bedford's boy. And that being done, he stayed on with
his bride to serve up oysters to his goodly neighbors in Newgate. And

glad Nick was, for here he could fill his stomach with new foods and his heart with new friends.

Joseppi, I shall simply call the many-named man to save the tip-end of my quill, for some reason, loved to cook. But rather than serve up a good English cow's tongue pie, which could be got for a penny at any inn within the city, Josep was known for his two special dishes. The first was an Italian rooster stuffed with a headless pigeon. However, I suspect he got the rooster not from Italy, but from Greater Ilford (but 'tis a thing I cannot prove). The second dish was a sort of pottage sliced into strings that he named a *vermicelli*. And if I were eating it, I'd be glad I et it in London, for in Italy that name means *little worms*. But 'twas a popular dish, so we may assume people knew not the meaning of it, and it no doubt tasted fair. Nick chose the vermicelli over the rooster that day, preferring a dish more fair than fowl.

After all was et, he bid the Magris his *Dio be with you*, and returned to Martin's office, where, by evening's end, we would find his head upon a book, sleeping and slumbering, as night passed and the dawn quick approached. Soon to be awoke with a terrible jolt.

★

The 1590s.

'Twas the dead of night. The parish was Hackney, the liberty was Shoreditch, and the men were armed. And since every soul in the borough was busy at drink, at sleep, or at strumpet, none of the local inhabitants, at the moment at least, spied the hundredfold of men who, silent as the rats that scurried 'neath their feet, marched in dead quiet toward The Theatre. With mighty weapons in hand and an angry resolve in their hearts, they advanced soundless like a hundred Tarquins.

Will Shaksper was amongst them, though he never liked to walk the streets of Shoreditch at night on account of the name. For all who lived there told the tale when the place was known as Mistress Shore's Ditch, as this was where poor Jane Shore was slain and buried.

And as no one knows for certain where her ditch lay, big Will, even with hatchet in hand, feared to take a step in any direction, lest he place a foot upon her restless grave. These were the thoughts he thought as he joined with the other men that night, who gave him, at the least, a little comfort.

The hundred of them, old and young, came ready for battle. In their great grips, they clutched axes and broadswords, hammers and hatchets. Whatever they could get hold of. They were players and 'prentices, poets and scribblers. But tonight, they be soldiers all. They silently approached by Curtain Road, and like a mass of well-trained recruits on the Bosworth Field, some flanked west and others east. Soon, the unsuspecting Theatre, much like Richard the Third, only a bit taller and much the straighter, was surrounded.

Now, a man may wonder what foreign army had invaded England, entered Shoreditch, and was laying in wait within this playhouse to merit such an attack. And why would a band of players, of whom it may be said the closest they ever got to the battlefield of Agincourt was when they approached a French flag upon a stage in Budlesford, be asked to take up arms in Hackney? Well, patience shall be rewarded, 'tis someplace writ.

Hearts were beating as war drums. Lord Edward gripped his weapon. Horace held high his club. Lyly and Munday looked fierce as warriors. Even Lord Edward's page Toby was to see his first battle, for every hand was needed in this fight.

They stepped into place, cheek to jowl, and surrounded their prey. The Theatre itself, silhouetted 'gainst the moonlit sky, looked as alone as these men felt. Each eye turned toward Lord Edward to give signal. However, he was of a different mind. He thought the man who had inspired this siege should be the one to lead it. And so, he turned to his young boy and said, "Sir Toby, attack when ready."

CHAPTER THIRTEEN.

THE DEMISE OF A THEATRE, THE DEATH OF A SON.

I suppose if a fellow was looking for the cause of the Great Shoreditch Battle, he might find the seeds of it were hatched a year earlier, when the plague paid a terrible visit. Whilst some souls sought to flee the crowded city, others dared not leave their homes for fear of catching it. Although no man truly knows how 'tis caught. And even the lowliest of God's creatures could never escape their fates, for in Eastcheap, you couldn't hurl a dead cat without hitting a dead cat.

The poor and the rich perfumed their chambers, and still they died. They wielded lancets and leeches, and still they died. Whether 'twas God's wish or foreign ships brought it to us, we were left with only prayers and bolted doors to fight it. Lavender and sage, wormwood and smoke. Ashes. Ashes. We all fell down.

But the worst of it was the parting of the people. Folk were frighted to get near one another for fear they'd catch it. Those on the empty streets were near alone, where the few who braved them cloaked their faces to hide the fear on their faces. But what is a man if he cannot touch another being? Nor embrace a cuz, nor kiss a loving lip. Hold onto a dying grandsire's hand. Nor hug a newborn babe tight. This was the true sadness. The loneliness that a fellow could see in the separate rooms of the world. To go without the touch of another for so long is a terrible thing. I know.

To heap insult onto the injured, the Pest stole not only lives but livelihoods. For the inns were empty, the shoppes barren, and the playhouses closed. So how was a barmaid like my dear Peg to get coin whilst there were no loud louts to lure? How could an innkeep keep up whilst all others kept out? And how might a man like Giles Allen endure?

Allen was a man of trade. He found his calling in the buying of lands, on the top of which other men could build their fortunes. He had leased his Shoreditch plot to the Burbages, who built their playhouse there.

But many things threatened to close the playhouse doors. There was the plague. There was bad plays, writ by fellows the likes of John Webster and perhaps that lout what writ *Guy of Warwick*, if he ever writ a play. There was dangerous dramas, as some writers, such as that Marlowe fellow, scribbled stories that much displeased the queen. 'Twixt all those troubles, Giles Allen began to fear. So, it came as a sizable blow when he summoned Burbage.

"Never renew our lease?" cried the player.

"You must understand, Burbage," answered Allen, "I must make way for a more profitable endeavor. With the Curtain and the Rose now open, I'd get more traffic here if I ran a pig market."

"Pig market!" squealed Burbage. "My family have invested a fortune in these timbers alone," he bellowed.

"I shall do it!" asserted Allen, not afraid of a threat made by a player whose only fisticuff experience was upon a stage in Bicklesby.

Burbage stormed off to seek an ear of sympathy at the Boar's Head, where Lord Edward and Master Lyly tippled a tap of sack.

"There must be some remedy," said milord, tossing a tennis ball to his young Toby, who stood 'cross the room.

"Milord," said a soft-spoke Burbage, unaccustomed to being soft-spoke, "I have asked my lawyer, who says there is no hope. I have asked my mercer, my friar, and my farrier. I am out of men to ask." And out of despair, he even turned to Toby. "What say *you*, Master Toby?"

Toby was not expecting to be spoke to, nor was Burbage expecting to be answered, but the boy did oblige.

"Pity 'tis not a cockerel pen," said the lad, who then received long, befuddled looks from all.

"What means you, lad?" finally asked Lord Edward.

The boy approached. "Well, milord, when I was young..." and he stopped to think on how best to conduct his first grown conversation. And isn't it always an owl hoot when these young boys start off with a "when I was young," as if they are now old and decrept, sans teeth, sans eyes, sans face, sans everything? He continued. "My brother Robin and me built a cockerel pen at the end of our land in the Colne. And our neighbor," the boy scowled as if it had just happed this Thursday last, "mean old Master Mugge, said he meant to tear down our pen the very next morning as 'twas too much in abut of his own sheep-grazing."

The men all looked at the boy without an idea of how this telling would turn, but turn it soon did. "So, Robin came up with a device. We rose when all had gone to bed, crept out under the moon, and took apart that cockerel pen, bit by bit, and re-built it on t'other side of our field." He took a breath, all prides and smiles. "I was just saying, pity 'tis not a cockerel pen."

And that is when Burbage looked to Lyly, and Lyly looked to milord, and milord, who had none else to look to, and who would never countenance the likes of Giles Allen turning their Theatre into a pig market, looked to Burbage and said, "Why not?"

★

The lad took a deep breath, and every man raised his weapon. After just enough time for all present to bid one final farewell to the place they held dear, Toby raised his hammer high and gave the silent signal to attack. And attack they did, rushing bravely onto and into the building, tearing her limb from wooden limb.

It would now be apparent to any onlooker emerging onto Curtain Road, having by this time drunk his drink, slept his sleep, or trumpeted his strumpet, that the victim of this attack was not any standing army within, but the stumbling structure without. Burbage raised his axe to the great oak door, and what had seemed one solid portal fell to five single planks within that many o' minutes. Condell and Heminges hammered and sledged 'gainst stage floor right, as Burford and Bows slammed and fledged 'gainst stage floor left. Will Shaksper's hatchet tore timbers into parts whilst Dick Waggman's latchet banded timbers into carts. Dudley and Dickinson tore down hither as Crick and Cole carried them thither. Milham and Maycock

88

and Malim cut wood, as Babbage and Nix and Brazil just stood. Geoffrey Falstone pried walls from their wattle whilst Dickie Rowe compiled dowels in a bottle. Percy Ward potttled, James MacGrath swaddled, Rafe Smith noddled, and Robin Dettelbolt doddled. All around them, wood was felled as if the great Forrest of Essex were all a-fire.

"Heave ho!" hailed Master Anders whilst "Heave high!" marked Ander's son. Woodruff Engwell danced a ditty, whilst Marcus Alexander sang right pretty. And as timbers tumbled like Joshua's wall, the two strongest, Masters Turner and Clarke, carried heavy oaks to the edge of the road.

Slow but sure, the men who once raised this sacred building now razed this sacred building. Lord Edward peered into the hallowed and hollowed half-structure, now illumined by the single pale moon shining down onto where the stage had been, whose old boards were being ripped like brittle bones from an agéd skeleton. It was on these boards that battles were fought and kingdoms won. Lovers were wooed and singers sung. Joy and enlightenment had daily showered all who paid their penny. And now, the very life of the building was being taken, timber by tamper, and stacked along the roadside.

Horace oversaw the piling up of the new-hewn logs onto the carts, which would take the guts of The Theatre, that was no more, rest her soul, to the other side of the river.

When all dismantling was done, and afore the march begun, the players assembled for one final call on Curtain Road. Each took out his ale, having one last look at where The Theatre had been, and would most like, they mused, become the site of a place they would christen *Giles Prickington's Pig Market*. Each raised an arm in cheer, and all drank a good sad drink.

Burbage, who stood aside Toby, handed his jack to the boy, who, encouraged by the moment, took a good swig of the ale that the locals call *Mad Dog*, and it came back barking, for it caused a strong wind to erupt from the back of the boy's throat like Vesuvius upon ole Pompey. Well sir, Toby's belch turned a sad song into a merry, and all the lads laughed. That is how they begun their journey to the Bankside.

With wagons timber-filled, they trudged their loads through the fields. First into Finsbury, then out Bonner, cutting 'round the marshes of the Moors, and then trampling the streets of the city and down to the eager ferryboats. The sky was growing lighter and the river was as glass, as their boats did glide 'cross to the other side. The lads sang songs to set sail, whilst their windy sails sang the songs back to them.

Once on the south bank, the procession stayed a noisy one, where Mackie McKay, I think 'twas, led the chorus of *Sigh No More*, though I prefer the ever popular *A Wench, A Whale, and a Pint of Ale*.

Our Shoreditch soldiers soon arrived at the south side of Maiden's Lane and collected where Burbage thought best to set up his new playhouse, not a rat's scurry from London's deepest prison and cheapest brothel. As they all stood upon the spot that would become home to their next theatre, The Globe, as they'd call it, Lord Edward looked upon his young page. And proud as a peacock he was of his cockerel pen lad.

It didn't take long for these men to construct their new playhouse out of the old. 'Twas Thomas and Samuel Brend who were given charge of rebuilding. And whilst Tom wished a structure-maker to build it the same as 'twas in Shoreditch, Sam wanted a maker to add a bit of the new. And soon they completed the main stage, inner stage, tiring house, and open yard. Of course, the yard they needed not to build for God had got there afore them.

On their first day back to work, merriment filled the new-built Globe. Burbage was far the noisiest, imitating the barnyard fowl he had observed whilst late in the country. He looked sure peculiar, too, as he paraded 'round sounding like a half-plucked chick, whilst at the same time dressed in the cloak and crown of King John. Lord Edward spoke with Lyly at the back. Heminges and Kempe playfully tossed daggers, whilst, in safer pastime, Shaksper volleyed balls with the boy-players. All spirits were as they should be until Francis Langley walked through the door.

His face was all-serious, and Burbage was the first to notice him.

"Langley!" he clucked, strutting his way to him.

Langley simply told him. He could hardly be heard above the din, and so Burbage had to put his ear to Langley's mouth, and then Burbage hisself was still. He called on Shaksper, and all could see there was trouble. Waves of silence spread as Burbage told Shaksper, who near fell to the floor.

"See to it," asked milord, sending Lyly straight way.

The men were heading out the door as Lyly reported back to the earl.

"Word from the country. Will's son is dead."

And Lord Edward's heart heaved.

Shaksper placed his pack 'cross the horse as milord and his men stood by in silence. After he rode off, the others slowly turned 'round to re-enter the court of King John. Lyly handed Lord Edward the coins.

"He would not take them."

And milord watched the sole rider disappear.

Each moment on that stage revealed its own secrets. The men strut and bellow, speaking as if imitating others, but each man knows he is, if truth be told, telling tales from deep within his own soul. For that is why a man becomes a player, I suppose. True, the writer spills many of his own secrets there, but players, too. Want to know the true heart of a player? Then watch him *on* the stage and not *off* of it. For that is where he may truly be hisself. Lord Edward thought on this as he stood at the back, seeing his men play kings and cardinals and grieving mothers, yet all the while speaking of their own hearts' achings.

"*I have heard you say,*" cried the actor playing Constance to the player who was the Cardinal, "*that we shall see and know our friends in heaven. If that be true, I shall see my boy again.*"

"*You hold too heinous a respect of grief,*" replied the Cardinal.

"*Grief,*" she cried, over the death of her poor son.

91

Grief fills the room up of my absent child.
Lies in his bed, walks up and down with me.
Puts on his pretty looks, repeats his words.
Remembers me of all his gracious parts.
Stuffs out his vacant garments with his form.
Then have I reason to be fond of grief.

Lord Edward knew the rest, but could bear no more and left them, as Constance continued.

O Lord, my boy, my Arthur, my fair son.
My life, my joy, my food, my all the world.
My widow's comfort, and my sorrow's cure!

★

The grim procession moved slow through the streets. The boy's uncles held high the wooden box. Inside lie young Hamnet, barely eleven years. His tiny hands placed loose over his cherished new-given cap. The mourners walked the bitter road through town and on toward the churchyard. Anne and Will followed at the end of this sad train. Saddened that the end had come so soon for someone he had just begun to know. Wishing it was he instead whose time had come.

They walked and they prayed. Quiet, they prayed. But then all seemed to stop. The mourners halted. Those in front had just turned the corner to the churchyard and ceased the procession. Will looked up to see what was the cause. He walked 'round them and to the front. When he turned the corner, he could see that his family were all stooping low, and this he could not comprehend. He then looked up to see his master, Lord Edward, seated high upon his steed, dressed in sable black.

Will walked before the Lord Great Chamberlain, removed his cap, and bowed. He rose, and milord, respectful, and quite unknown for a lord, took off his own hat, astonishing the tearful crowd. He, together with his horse, bowed to Will with sadness, and bid them proceed. The stunned and grateful mourners advanced through the churchyard to young Hamnet's grave. As they approached, their eyes teared more in disbelief. For, at the humble spot where they were to lay young Hamnet down, was a mound of rues and rosemarys. As tall as a man, they stood. A monument to his new-found son. His sorrow's cure. And Will turned back to Lord Edward, but he was gone.

CHAPTER FOURTEEN.

THE TRUTH LIES ON THE PAGE.

1624.

The banging wrenched Nick from his sleep. His face bolted up from his pillowed page. His heart jumped as he saw daylight fill the room.

He raced down the stairs. The clanging had ceased, but the pounding in his chest continued strong. Nick looked 'round for a weapon of protection. He chose the large iron candlestick from the table and approached the door slow. He raised the candlestick high and opened fast.

"Valentina!" he yelled.

"I received the note you left with my landlady," said she. "What is this place?"

"Come in," he urged, as he began to breathe again. She entered and he locked the door behind them, putting down his weapon at the last. "I will explain. How be your hobble?"

"But a hibble, dear friend."

"Come," he led her up the stair, "I will tell all."

And all he did tell, as they sat in the secret room and shared what each had learnt. Nick held Valentina's mysterious wax-sealed missive in his hand.

"So, you gave her this?" he marked, "and she knew nothing?"

"Not a thing," Valentina answered.

"Why this means..." he thought, but needn't say it.

Nick grabbed the red-covered Shakespeare and they set out to walk the streets. A tittle did they dream that this was the day they would untie their knots. And with the help of old Arthur, to boot. Thus, they conversed as they strolled. *What of his unprinted manuscripts? He mentions them not in his will. Why was the monument changed? And the grave empty?*

And finally, they came 'round to the key of this whole riddle. "You think we'll see old Arthur again?" worried sweet Valentina.

"We shall find him," assured Nick.

They were about to return to Martin's when Valentina had the good sense to remark, "Pity you did not find anything in Arthur's papers."

This stopped the lad.

"What is it?" asked she.

"I didn't look," said he, recognizing that he very well should have looked.

They wasted no minutes in flying to my digs. And as my papers were already well-tossed about the place, they had an easy time locating them. But the trick was in knowing which paper was of what help.

"Creditors. Tavern bills. Nothing of use," said Nick, little knowing that lightning was soon to strike. Valentina was lost within some other of my pages.

"This must be the poetry he wants you to print."

"Perhaps we shouldn't read that now."

"Oh, no," marks she, "for to find the man, we must read his works." Now, here sings one smart sparrow, as far as I can tell. "Listen to this," quoth'd the sparrow, as she chirped my heartstrings:

> To my dear Peg,
> For I do beg,
> To hold your hand in mine.
> We'll live as two,
> Forget our woe,
> And our true love we'll find.

"'Tis no Chaucer," said she.

Now, I shall forget that remark because it comes from one who has not yet lived long enough to appreciate mature love poesy.

"And he rhymed *two* with *woe*," she admonished, being obvious unfamiliar with my style. She then took up another Taverner original, *Love lingers like a lilting lily*, and wrongly accused me of overusing the same alphabeticals over and again, which I definitely don't do, lest necessary.

Nicholas grabbed up my most recent work.

"Oh, not another!" said the pretty admonisher, herself not aware that a bolt of enlightenment was on its way from the heavens and aimed at the very two of them.

"But this one is entitled *Nicholas and Valentina*," said he. Now, that one she wanted to hear.

> *Two souls, whose youth and friendship, now take seed*
> *In me, a new friend helping them in need,*
> *But whilst they think I help with clues obtuse,*
> *Tis I who're helped by them, who've made me of use.*

Nick gently placed my poem onto the table, and they both seemed pleased. Then Valentina struck upon what they had been searching for, without knowing 'twas indeed what they had been searching for. The heavenly bolt let loose.

"This one is rather good," said she.

> *Even as at Arles, where rests the Rhone awhile,*
> *Or as at Pola, on Quarnaro's gulf,*
> *That shelters Italy and bathes its shores,*
> *The tombs diversify the countryside.*
> *And from each tomb there rose such piteous groans,*
> *As only souls in torment could produce.*

This seemed to impress the young printer.

"Arthur wrote that?" he asked.

"Good, yes?"

"Wonderful good."

"Of course not," Valentina answered." Dante," said she.

"Dante?" asked he.

"Dante Alighieri," showed she, holding the paper to his face.

"Comical. Very comical." He had been gulled. "Let us go," he said, a bit red-cheek'd, whilst the lady was pleased.

"You don't know Dante?" she persisted.

"Of course I know Dante," said he, as he approached the door.

"You think Arthur could have written that?" she teased.

"Shall we go? There's nothing here," said Nick, little-knowing.

"You think Arthur has been to Italy? To Quarnaro's gulf?" she would not let go.

"I think it not likely," he said, "but I—" and *'ZOUNDS!* it hit him. The lightning struck. A heavenly gift of enlightenment knocked square onto Nick's noggin.

"What is it?" asked Valentina, seeing the light in the lad's eyes. "Nick?" she called, but he was already out the door, shouting, "Of course! Now it's all clear!"

But to Valentina, it wasn't. "What is?" To Valentina, 'twas still dim. "Nick!" she called, as she tried hard to hobble after. "My leg!" said she, but he was already well ahead of her.

When she rounded the corner, he was standing there all grins.

"Where are we going?" says she.

"Fancy some little worms?"

CHAPTER FIFTEEN.

A POET-APE EXPOSED.

"Any news about Long Tom?" began Martin. "No one has heard nor seen the man these three days?"

"No, sir," came the reply.

And now Martin became concerned. "Gentlemen," he took a breath. "Let us all take care in our inquiries."

He then returned them to their work, so as to get their minds off the troubles such a search was starting to bring.

"Simonds, what was the first printed play of Master Shakespeare's?"

Simonds grabbed a paper. "That would be *Titus Andronicus*, Major."

"And how was the Shakespeare name writ?" asked my brother.

"No name, sir," the clerk explained.

"No name?"

"None of his first printings had a name attached, sir," the clerk replied.

"That's odd," mused the Major. "How many quartos were printed anonymously?"

"I've found twenty-nine, sir," said Simonds. "*Romeo and Juliet, Henry the Fifth, Richard the Third*." Simonds looked up. "I can go on."

"Thank you, no," Martin answered. "If this man traveled here to London to become a famed writer, why then should he not add his name to his plays?"

It was then that Nicholas burst into the room. The sudden explosion alarmed the researchers and nearly woke the professor.

"I beg your pardon, Major," apologized Nick. "But I want to introduce you to–" and he turned 'round to find that he was singing solo.

"Yes, Nicholas?" said my surprised brother.

The lad continued, hoping the hobbling Valentina would soon make it up the steps. "Sir, I believe we have found the answer."

"We?"

'Twas then the lovely lady entered. All of the men dropped what they were doing (and some, what they were holding) to eye the bedazzling beauty behind him.

"This is my dear friend, Valentina Childs, who lived for a time near Stratford on the Avon."

As the gentlemen rose, Simonds poked the professor, waking the old man, who got up just in time to watch the rest of them sit.

"Then, by all means," Martin said, for some reason adjusting his crooked shirt collar, as he stepped aside to give the young man audience. All eyes (that were not lock'd upon Valentina) were now set on Nicholas.

"Gentlemen, we have been following the wrong man."

The researchers looked puzzled. "To find the man, we must read his works. He has been to Italy. We know this," said the excited lad, "for it is in here," he held up a playbook. "In fair Verona." He held another. "And Padua." And another. "And Venice." Nicholas looked at the men, who were now at full attention. "How did a man who never sailed south of Southwark know that there are flint streets in Venice? Sycamore trees at Verona's west gate? Or about the traditions of soul-cakes and dishes of doves? Who told him of the mosaic on the floor of Sienna Cathedral depicting the seven ages of man?"

"*First the babe*," came a small voice from the back of the room. The voice of a hesitant Master Loney.

"Know you of the cathedral, Master Loney?" asked my brother.

"I know the play," answered the little man. "*All the world's a stage,*" he said soft, and hesitantly stood. "*And one man in his time plays many parts, his acts being seven ages. First the babe, mewling and puking in the nurse's arms."*

Sensing all eyeballs upon him, Loney looked down and, almost with apology, admitted, "I've read them all," and then he shrunk back into the woodwork.

A surprising fellow, that Loney. Here was a man who finished top of his class at Oxford, they say. Despite the fact that, at every week's end, instead of being at book, he occupied his hours serving as what they call a cook's swain, whate'er that may be.

Each man in the room now thought on how a fellow who never crossed the creek of Cockermouth knew so many small particulars about a country so far away.

"But how do we know these details about Italy are in fact accurate?" enquired my brother, knowing none of them either had been to Italy.

"I have a friend from Florence," he answered. "A traveler and a scholar."

"Professor Magri?" perked up the professor.

"Yes, you've heard of him?" Nick asked excitedly.

"I've eaten his vermicelli," smiled the man.

"We've just spoken to him, and he's verified all is true, down to the last, minute detail," continued Nick. "Gentlemen, the writer Shakespeare has also known-well the court. The man from Stratford has not. We have gone there, Valentina and I, and found a man who never once attended a school, never traveled, was a money-lender, a merchant. Whose monument has been made anew. But there is more," he added, as he took out the mysterious sealed letter. "This, Valentina handed to the man's daughter."

Nicholas gave the missive to Martin, who then passed it to Simonds, who gave it to the professor, and so it made its way 'round the room. Each man puzzled as he read it. Nicholas looked to Valentina, who explained.

"I gave this to Master Shaksper's daughter, Judith, and asked if she knew the person whose name appears there. She replied that she could be of no help."

100

Master Rollett was the last to receive the letter and looked on it curious. For on the outside was writ: *For the Benefitte of Judith Shaksper Quiney.*

"Gentlemen," said Nicholas, "the daughter of 'William Shakespeare' cannot read." The room fell silent. "The clerk's records show that his children, his wife, his father, his mother, all signed with marks. None could read nor write. Would not our greatest poet teach his own children to know his works?"

"No one in Stratford that I could find ever received a correspondence from him," said Valentina.

'Twas then Professor Ogburn had the hyphen stuck in his brain.

"The conclusion cannot be avoided," said Nicholas. "The man himself could not read nor write. Which is why his will was signed with three scrawls, all spelled differently. He was unable to sign his own name. And that explains why there are no books mentioned. He bequeathed no books because he owned none to give. I believe his name was used," continued Nick, "by the true writer, who employed Master Shaksper."

"That would explain the hyphen," said Ogburn.

"Professor?" Martin invited him to speak.

"The writer's name is often printed as William Shake-hyphen-Speare. And as no true name is written thus, it must point to a false name."

Martin thought about this, and then turned to his men. "Who are the other hyphenated writers that remain unknown to us?"

"Martin Mar-prelate," said Simonds. "Cuthbert Curry-knave, Tom Tell-truth."

"A spear-shaker," added Rollett, "could be a jouster. Are they not called Shake-a-Spears?"

"Or a follower of Minerva," added the professor. "Protector of the arts. Depicted shaking a spear."

"Professor, know you Minerva's motto, inscribed on her shield?" asked Martin, knowing full-well the professor full-did.

"*Obscuris vera involvens,*" answered the expert of such obscure information.

"*Truth enveloped in obscurity,*" translated Martin for the young ones in the room. "Can you find us Peachum's *Minerva Britanna*?"

And with that, the professor went to the shelves. Martin then urged Nicholas to pray continue.

"The true author must have used this player, if indeed he was a player, as a name only. He has been places and seen things foreign to this actor." He then turned to each man. "Have you not read the plays, gentlemen? They portray a world belied by this Stratford man's life. And what of his death? When the poet Spenser died," Nicholas posed, "he was buried in the abbey near Chaucer. Do you gentlemen remember? The streets were lined with mourners. When Beaumont died, there was similar tribute paid."

And true 'twas, for come to think on it, I recall that miserable day. The streets were so impeded it took me a full three hours to get from The Measly Magpie to The Shaking Woodpecker.

"And yet," Nick went on, "who here remembers when William Shakespeare died?" No one spoke, for none could remember. "It's been only eight years. No mourners. No procession. No burial with the other poets. Nothing, for the best." Nicholas then held up his new book. "I did not understand it 'til now, but I believe this book tells us that the writer Shakespeare was dead by 1609." He read them the title, "*Shake-speare's Sonnets.*"

"I've never seen such a book!" Ogburn approached, eager to examine this rarity.

"There were not many printed," said Nick. "They disappeared quickly, and there were no new editions."

"'Tis strange," said Ogburn, thinking of the near twenty reprintings of Shakespeare's other poems of *Adonis* and *Lucrece*.

"In this 1609 dedication," explained Nicholas, "the author is referred to as *our ever-living poet.*"

"Ever-living?" echoed the astounded professor.

"Words fit only for one who had already shed this mortal coil," said Nick.

102

"So we have it by 1609 that the writer Shakespeare appears quite dead," added Martin, "while our country fellow lived until 1616. So much for the Stratford case."

Ogburn, who opened the Shakespeare folio, seemed befuddled. "So, why does this new work point us in the wrong direction, with Ben Jonson telling us the writer is a *swan of Avon* with a *Stratford moniment*?"

"If the true writer had been given a mask, misdirection would be required," answered Martin. "For some reason, like with the other concealed writers, we must not know his true identity."

"Perhaps Master Jonson can tell us," suggested Valentina, who was enjoying the company of these learnéd men.

"Ben Jonson's exploits," warned Martin, "have resulted in two imprisonments, a branding, and a near execution. I fear he will talk to no one. Let me see that Peachum," Martin asked, as the professor handed him the book. "You see here," he pointed out to all who gathered 'round, "Peachum printed this book of puzzling emblems and anagrams in honor of the noblemen at her majesty's court. These books of hidden secrets were quite popular during her reign."

"*Minerva Britanna*," Nick called out the title, as they all stared at the frontispiece.

"She is the spear-shaker," my brother reminded. "So, who is this writer pictured on the cover, hiding behind this curtain? Who is England's spear-shaker?"

They all looked at the picture, which shows, clear as a summer's day in Knutsford, the arm of a hidden scribbler reaching 'round a theatre curtain, writing on a scroll.

"Who is this invisible writer?" Martin posed.

"What is it he is writing?" asked Valentina.

"*Mente Videbori*," said Martin.

"*By the mind's eye, I shall be seen*," explained Ogburn.

"But who is he?" Nick urged.

"Professor," Martin handed the book to Ogburn. "Perhaps you can work on that."

And the professor crossed to his seat with this most-important task at hand.

"It seems that, whomever he is, he is not our man from the Avon," Martin concluded. He went on to suggest that the plays might lead them in the right direction. As the works portray the life of the nobles, he reasoned, it might make good sense to search for a nobleman. One who read Latin, Greek, Italian and French. "If a noble," Martin reasoned, "then he would never publish under his own name for fear of disgrace."

"Especially if penning for the stage," Ogburn added.

"Master Simonds," Martin had a thought. "Find me Vicar's *Manual of Rhetoric*. Remarks on Shakespeare. Master Rollett, the John Davies poem." And with their orders given, each marched to the bookshelves and soon-thereaft returned.

"Thomas Vicar, sir," said Simonds.

"What does he say?"

"About the outstanding recent authors, he writes, *To these I believe should be added that famous poet who takes his name from shaking and spear.*"

"*Takes* his name," Martin repeated. "So, if he *takes* his name, it is not a *given* name. Master Rollett, what is the Davies poem?"

"*To our English Terence, Mr. Will Shake-speare*, sir."

"A rather odd thing to call him. Professor, who was Terence?"

"A Roman slave, Major."

"He wrote *Hecyra*, did he?"

"Most scholars now believe him to have been a cover for the true play-writer, his noble patron Scipio," answered the professor.

"A servant pretending to be a writer. A cover for a nobleman. So, Davies is calling Shakespeare a cover!" said the Major, putting a fine point on an already well-sharped sword.

"Davies also claims *the stage doth stain pure gentle blood*," added Rollett.

"*Gentle* blood?" questioned Martin. "He's calling him a nobleman." His attention then turned toward the picture.

"Who has the engraving?" Martin asked. Simonds brought out the portrait, and my dear brother asked Nicholas to examine it. "Do you know this face?"

Nick's heart raced, for 'twas just hours since he had seen Horace Vere in the flesh. And now, the second face of his silent dreams appeared before him.

"It is one of the noblemen I saw that morning my father was taken!" answered Nick.

"1604, it was?" Martin pursued.

"24th June, 1604," answered Nicholas. "Who is this man?" he needed to know.

"Professor?" Martin said.

"Henry, third earl of Southampton," Ogburn answered. "The only man to whom the writer Shakespeare ever dedicated any works."

"Very intimate dedications," revealed Martin. "So not likely written by a commoner to an earl. When is the first appearance of the name *William Shakespeare,* professor?"

"1593," he answered. "*Venus and Adonis.*"

"Although the name appears not on the title page, where we'd expect to find it," added Simonds, "but at the end of the dedication to Lord Southampton."

"So, he was not eager to use the name," concluded Martin.

"And the next year," Ogburn continued, "came *Lucrece*. Also dedicated to Southampton. Both fully-developed works," the professor pointed out.

"So we may assume," said Martin," that whoever wrote these, and signed the name *Shakespeare* to them, had written before. Master Rollett, when is the first play published with the Shake-speare name?"

"1598, Major" said the actor. "*The Tragedie of King Richard the Third* as by *William Shake-hyphen-speare.*" Rollett then turned to Simonds all-proud, "I played it two-and-twenty years ago in Swinford."

"With or without the hyphen?" asked Simonds, confusing the player.

"Gentlemen," Martin began, and then quick corrected hisself, "and good lady," he added, with a bow of his head and another touch to his crooked collar, "it would seem the way to finding this writer Shake-speare is to search for one whose works first appeared anonymous, or written under another name. One who stopped using that name before he began to attach the sign of *Shake-speare* to fully-matured works. The good research of Master Nicholas and Mistress Valentina has shown us the way. Now," he said to them all, "go find the contenders."

And with that, each was sent to find the man hidden behind Minerva's curtain. Dear Martin left to search for me, his bothersome brother. Simonds examined that huge-headed portrait of Shakespeare. Loney looked to the encomiums (whatever that is). And the professor, Nick, and Valentina eyed-over the new-got book of sonnets.

'Twas the dedication page that had them so befuddled. The page that his friend Millington hadn't the chance to explain on that fateful day of his death.

TO. THE. ONLIE. BEGETTER. OF.
THESE. INSUING. SONNETS.
MR. W.H. ALL. HAPPINESSE.
AND. THAT. ETERNITIE.
PROMISED.
BY.
OUR. EVER-LIVING. POET.
WISHETH.
THE. WELL-WISHING.
ADVENTURER. IN.
SETTING.
FORTH.

There 'twas. The strange lettering: all high-cased. The full stops at the ends of each word. All shaped like three pyramids o'erturned.

"There's something here," said Nick, "This is what Millington was hinting at. 'Look to the number,' he said."

"The number?" asked Valentina. "Well, if it is here, then we shall find it."

106

Ogburn wished them well and walked to his chair to attend to his Peachum puzzle, if any puzzle was there to be solved (and any *was* there, I can assure a fellow). Nicholas turned to Valentina, who seemed spellbound by these upside-round triangles. If anyone was to discover their meaning, he knew it would be the daughter of the Master Mason of Macclesfield, for her brain was as bounteous as her beauty was beauteous. After a while, the professor, troubled by his inability to solve the Peachum, suggested they pause for the midday dinner.

Just then, the door burst open loud, and Long Tom fell into the room, breathing hard. As his friends ran to help him, they could see he had been beat bad. His left eye was bloodied and closed shut, whilst half his face appeared a full size larger than t'other.

"What has happened, my boy?" asked the professor.

"Get a chair," said another.

"Are you alright?"

"I was seized upon," said he.

"By whom?"

"Don't know."

They sat him down, and a doctor was sent for. One with a license. Valentina tended his face with her handkerchief.

"You shall be fine," she assured.

This is a bloody business, Nick thought, as he boarded the windows and bolted the door.

CHAPTER SIXTEEN.

THEY CALL ME HORATIO.

The professor stayed behind to tend to Long Tom. And after all tending was tendered, his curiosity to read the new sonnets quite overtook him. Given the events of the morning, he was captured by lines that read:

> *My name be buried where my body is,*
> *And live no more to shame nor me nor you.*

As if the poet with the buried name was telling him all along that his name was not Shake-speare. Ogburn then sought clues that might reveal the man's true identity, and he just may have tumbled upon one when he read:

> *Why write I still all one, ever the same,*
> *And keep invention in a noted weed,*
> *That every word doth almost tell my name,*
> *Showing their birth, and where they did proceed?*

Every word doth almost tell my name. These words he writ on a paper and sat fixed upon them, endeavoring to decipher how *every word* doth tell the poet's name. Almost.

Outside, Nick joined Valentina.

"Will you come dine with uncle and me?" she asked, as Nicholas adjusted his eyes to the sun. "Our landlady is preparing a small feast."

"I would like to," he said in earnest, "but there is something I must do." Valentina shot him a worried look. "I shall be fine," he assured her, "but I will see you to your inn."

"I, too, shall be fine," said the fearless beauty, "and will see you this midday."

They parted ways, and Nick headed down Thistle. Whilst Simonds paraded up Alban's. Whilst Knyvet slithered through River Walk, fingering his map. Nick approached a bookbinder friend. Simonds arrived at Field's print shoppe and opened his book of Shakespeare. Knyvet walked past Field's and eyed the book. Knowing the name *Southampton,* the binder pointed Nick in the right direction. Simonds thanked old Field and left the shoppe. Knyvet followed Simonds down the lane. Nicholas walked up the path to Southampton House. Simonds returned to Martin's office. Knyvet smiled and stood outside. He had at last found the lair of his quarry.

Nick rapt on the magnificent door until a servant opened. After a word, the man disappeared. Funny how 'tis when one is waiting on another, and something may cause an eye to wander to a thing when there is never a reason to. I do not mean as in the unfortunate situation like when I am standing alongside my dear Peg at the Piss and Whistle, and then the beautiful ale-keep Agnes walks by with an armful of ales, and my good eye wanders off to admire the fine pulchritude, by which I mean the ales and not the Agnes. 'Tis what I explain to my angry Peg, at any rate. But then I find myself in a fine Penistone pickle! And why should she care anyways, since she claims I am a base-court clod that interests her not? Ah, good maidens, I shall never understand! But I fear my mind has wandered off to the Midlands here.

My meaning was to say that, for good reasons none, whilst Nick stood waiting, his eye traveled up to the impressive Southampton family crest carved in stone above the door. A massive cross with four magnificent falcons. 'Twas a beautiful thing, which caused his heart to pull a bit and he knew not why. After another moment, the door again opened and Nick's heart now leapt, for he was face to face with the baron.

"Your lordship," Nicholas bowed.

"I was expecting you," came the unexpected reply.

"We have met?" Nick asked.

"You were but a babe," said the soft-spoke noble.

"Milord, I've come to enquire after Lord Southampton," Nick boldly pushed.

"Yes, I know," came another surprising turn. "He is presently fighting in the Low Countries." He paused, and then said something that made Nick's heart jump higher. "You are interested in the story of your father."

"Yes, milord!"

"It is a story best not pursued," warned Horace.

"But I must know it," pursued Nick.

"There are dangers about, and now new troubles."

Nick knew not 'twas a fire burnt hot in Cripplegate last even, and so he pushed on unawares.

"I am in it inch-thick, milord."

"Ah yes, knee-deep," Horace answered, as if this were the coded greeting of a Walsingham spy. "You will not quit?"

"I am sorry, milord," came the reply, "but I cannot."

Admiring this young man's persistence, and certainly expecting no less from him, as Lord Horace had known firsthand the same determination in the printer's father, he searched the front gardens with a keen eye, making certain there were no serpents lying in the grass.

"Very well," he finally answered. "Meet me this even at the Boar's Head Inn. At nine, can you?"

"I will, milord."

"You'll have your answers then," promised the noble, who always knew this day would come.

"Thank you, milord," Nicholas bowed. And just as he was about to walk away, he turned back. "Ah, who shall I ask for, milord?"

The baron smiled a gentle smile. "They call me Horatio."

Nicholas beamed and walked past the neat-trimmed hedges that replaced the brambles which long years ago had hid a hiding John Lyly. He found his way back to Thistle Street, now feeling closer than ever to solving the mystery of his life. The servant reappeared at the door and asked Horatio if he could be of service.

"Send to Cuddy," said the baron. "Ask him to enquire of our prisoner, Arthur Taverner."

CHAPTER SEVENTEEN.

A TRUE POET REVEALED.

Outside of Martin's, four children played that game we all favored in our youth. One urchin, 'twas always the dirtiest, took a stick and scratched squares and triangles into the earth. Or if a stick was too far to fetch, he'd do it with his filthy finger. Another, as a rule the smartest, etched out numerals into each box. Then a third, the loudest, called out the numbers like a town crier. He'd yell "Three!" and they'd all answer," One! Two! Three!" as the fourth, the smallest, would hop his way 'round the triangles on one foot like a headless Italian pigeon 'til he either reached his number or fell flat on his arse trying. The small ones would always fall flat on their arses.

From within the research room, you could not see these jumping jays yelp out their numbers, as the window-boards were closed tight, but you could sure hear those noisy creatures. Valentina stood at the table's end nearest the windows examining that sonnet dedication. The one with the full stops and all.

With a stick of Dover chalk in her white hand, she decided to copy the dedication onto the side of the tallest of the shelf boards next to her. She chalked out the page word for word, making it look just like in the book.

Professor Ogburn sat nearby. Befuddled by his new-copied *Every word doth almost tell my name*, he finally set it down and picked up another bit of verse. All the others were busy at work, but for Master Rollett, who had stepped outside, being occupied with a new-purchased trinket. Inside, Simonds went about the room pouring gratis glasses of Rhenish (p'raps the most popular wine that year).

"All is well, son?" Martin asked Long Tom, who sat bandaged and fed.

"'Tis but a cat-scratch, Major."

Then Martin raised his glass to all. "Gentlemen… and lady, a drink in thanks for Long Tom's return to health."

"To your health!" all thank'd and drank'd, and then brother became quite serious.

"Our business here must be discreet. Keep your eyes open and your mouths closed. When you arrive, come like an old puzzle, by misdirection. And when you go, walk like new poetry, in couplets. Be safe," warned he. And then they all returned to work.

Nicholas crossed to the professor, who held a poem.

"*To Master William Shake-speare*," Nick read the title. "Who wrote this?"

"A Master Nameless, I'm afraid."

Nick read the first lines:

Shake-speare, we must be silent in thy praise,
Cause our encomiums will but blast thy bays.

"Why must we be silent?" Nick reflected, hoping for a bit of enlightenment, whilst 'cross the room, Valentina was awaiting a lightning bolt of her own.

The beauty picked up the chalkstick, but then took her attention away from the dedication page as she oped the window-board a touch and looked down at the noisy children shouting their numbering game below. The sun would soon set, and these hopping poppets would play elsewheres, thought she, foolishly wishing her distraction away. A tittle did she know that she needed those poppets desperately. She needed them for her answer. For bolts from Zeus' chariot were heading a-swift and a-sured toward Valentina.

It was when she saw those triangles dug by the children in the dirt. As she brought her chalkstick closer to the plank upon which she had writ her dedication, she stared at the young lass hopping onto triangle number one, and Valentina traced a line 'round the first triangle of her dedication. She then followed with more lines of chalk, enclosing the next triangle of words. And then the third. She began to stare at that new-formed image, as the children called out their numbers. But of a sudden, 'twas not the poppets' voices she heard, but her dear father's. *Count it out, dear girl. Count it out!* And she did. And sparks from Zeus alit her brain and 'ZOUNDS! Valentina had discovered the secret.

"The numbers!" she shouted. "The numbers!"

With this, Nick, the professor, Martin, and Simonds crossed to her, joined by Loney behind, and even Long Tom rose.

"It's a cipher. You see, three triangles," she pointed to them. "If you were to lay out twelve lines of dedication in three triangles," she queried, "would you not make them four lines each? But here, the first triangle is made of six lines. The second is only two. And the third triangle has four lines. This divergence points us to the numbers. A possible cipher: six, two, four."

"*6.2.4!*" exclaimed Nick, as he pulled out the scrap that had been clutched in Millington's dead hand. "Those are the numbers Millington wrote!"

Martin and his men stared at the marks she had made on the bookcase. And true 'twas. Why, even a blind blooter from Beackonsfield Bush could see it, for the first pyramid of six lines read:

TO. THE. ONLIE. BEGETTER. OF.
THESE. INSUING. SONNETS.
MR. W.H. ALL. HAPPINESSE.
AND. THAT. ETERNITIE.
PROMISED.
BY.

The two-lined triangle stated:

OUR. EVER-LIVING. POET.
WISHETH.

And the last triangle with four lines of text revealed:

THE. WELL-WISHING.
ADVENTURER. IN.
SETTING.

113

"Now, what does placing a full stop after each word tell us?" she asked.

"They separate the words," contemplated the professor, who suddenly understood, "which allows us to count them!"

"So," she continued, "if our cipher is six-two-four, let us count off every sixth word, then second word, then fourth. If there is any meaning here at all, it can be no accident." She took the point of her chalkstick and excitedly tapped each word as she counted.

"One, two, three, four, five, six." She shouted the sixth word, "*THESE!*" and circled it. She continued.

"One, two. *SONNETS!*" she cried, and likeways enclosed it.

"One, two, three four. *ALL!* One, two, three, four, five, six. *BY!*"

And just as she had spoke, "*THESE SONNETS ALL BY...*" Master Rollett, who had just entered the room unawares of what was occurring, took this unopportune time to squeeze unopportunely betwixt the lady and her shelf of words, holding a new spyglass in hand, with a polite, "Terribly sorry," and "Excuse me, please."

"*Whom*?" Nicholas was about to burst. "These sonnets all by *whom*?" he cried.

As soon as the gent was out of her way, she resumed with stick to shelf.

"One, two. *EVER!*" she circled. "One, two, three, four. *THE!*" And she next enclosed her final word. "One, two, three, four, five, six. *FORTH!*" Valentina then read all of the circled text. "*THESE SONNETS ALL BY EVER THE FORTH!* It makes no sense," she frowned, nearly throwing water onto lightning.

"Perhaps it does," answered Nick, who scribbled on paper the word *EVER* and handed it to her, asking, "The name of Shakespeare's company?"

"The Chamberlain's Men," answered Simonds.

And with this, the young lad ran to the back shelves in desperate search, nearly banging into Rollett at the end of the room, who was standing by the window in deep preoccupation, holding the new spyglass to his eye, like a sailor perched atop the *Golden Hind*. But this over-aged swashbuckle looked down onto a different sort of treasure, for on the street below he eyed, ever so accidental, young Ginger. For that was what he named her as he gaped. She was standing 'cross the lane and was sure the loveliest ginger-haired beauty in all of Newgate. He knew not her true name was Kate. Why, of course 'twas. For I never met a Kate in my life that wasn't a beauty. Nor a Agnes, even. I wonder why that is? But I fear my horse is trotting fast off the track here.

Nick found his book, and within it, his answer. Smiling like the hungry cat that just et the tiny tit bird, which *is* a bird, he crossed back to Valentina.

"Who is it?" she asked.

"Patron of The Chamberlain's Men. The given name of the Lord Great Chamberlain of England." And with that, he put his hands upon hers, which were still holding the paper he had give her, and he tore it right in half, "Edward Vere!" announced he, separating the *E* from the *VER*.

Excited they were. All but Master Rollett, of course, who was still in scientific study.

"E. Ver!" says the lad. "These sonnets all by E. Vere!"

"Our E. Ver living poet!" says the lass. "But the fourth?" Valentina persisted.

"He was the *seventeenth* earl of Oxford," frowned Simonds.

Martin thought a bit. "Who has the *Proclamation of Accession and Succession* for our good King James?"

They all looked to Simonds, who crossed to a book of records and retrieved the document. He placed it in front of Martin on the table, and all the learnéd leaned in.

"Well," brother stepped away satisfied. "There you have it."

"What do we have, sir?" asked Simonds, still not having it.

"All official documents of the realm are signed in order of precedence in the Privy Council. Whose signature is first?"

Simonds bent to read. "The Archbishop of Canterbury."

"Who was second to sign?"

"Looks to be Lord Keeper Egerton."

"Third?"

"'Tis Baron Buckhurst."

"And who is the fourth?" They all took in a deep breath, in wait and in hope.

"Edward Vere!"

They all exhaled in elation.

"As Lord Great Chamberlain and first among the nobility," Martin explained, "Edward de Vere was the fourth ranking member of the council. The very fourth man in all of England."

"Edward de Vere," Nick repeated slow and sure.

"Six-two-four," said Martin, taking up the scrap bearing the very same numerals. "The number of letters in his name."

"June 24th. The night he died," added Valentina.

"The night my father was taken."

"That's six-two-four," said Valentina.

"Edward de Vere was William Shakespeare," said Nicholas, and the men cheered.

A cheer which grabbed the attention of the afore preoccupied Master Rollett, who then thought it best to join the others.

"Did I miss something?" asked Rollett.

"Oh, nothing of import," said Martin. "We've simply discovered the true identity of the writer William Shakespeare."

"Oh," said the player rather absent-minded. "What's that?" he finally shouted.

And after he was brought aboard this new ship, Rollett said, "Why that explains this," holding high his spyglass.

"Yes, I do wish you would explain that," said Martin, half wondering hisself.

"I mean *this*," corrected the confused man, throwing down his spyglass hand and raising up his other, which clenched a paper. "Ben Jonson," he clarified.

"We shall get to Ben Jonson," said the Major. "But first, if we are to claim that the earl of Oxford, Edward Vere, by way of honor titled *de* Vere, was the true writer, we need to know of his reputation for writing, if any. Who can tell us something?"

116

Martin looked 'round the room and, of a sudden, heard the flutter of pages flipping and spied a small arm raise at the back of the chamber.

"Master Loney?"

The scholar began to make his way through the group, carrying a stack of books that was perhaps half his own height again.

"Beg pardon, Major," he began almost inaudible, even to hisself. He placed the books next to Ogburn's paper, on which was writ the yet unsolved Peachum's "*MENTE VIDEBORI.*"

"William Webbe," continued Loney, "in his *Discourse of English Poetry*, calls Lord Edward..." and here he read from one of his books, "*The most excellent among the rest of lords and gentlemen with poetic skills at her majesty's court.*"

"Is he mentioned by Meres?" asked Martin, knowing that Loney would no doubt happen to have that quotation at his fingertops as well.

"I happen to have that," Loney said, putting down one book and taking up t'other. "And yes, the Lord of Oxford is named *best for comedy.*"

"Thank you, Master Loney."

The diminutive scholar stood still, as if wishing to say more.

"Master Loney?" Martin answered the look.

"'Tis the Puttenham, sir," he said meekly, holding up the book.

"What says he?"

Loney was pleased, and he read it aloud. "He says some courtiers write well but suppress it *or else suffered it to be published without their own names to it, as it were a discredit for a gentleman to seem learnéd and to show himself amorous of any good art,*" and the little man looked up to see if the rest were still giving ear, which they were, and so he continued. "And some noblemen *have written excellently well, as it would appear if their doings could be found out and made public with the rest, of which number is first that noble gentleman Edward, earl of Oxford.*" And he stopped and wanted to smile.

"The book?" my brother enquired.

117

"*The Art of English Poesy*, sir, 1589. Published with no name, but it has Puttenham's style written all over it."

"Very good," Martin commended him.

As Loney took up his book-mountain and was about to slink back into obscurity, he noticed the professor's Peachum on the table and quietly mumbled, almost to hisself more than to any man present, "*Tibi nom de Vere*," and he began to cross away, but was stopped by Martin.

"I beg your pardon?"

"The Peachum text identifying Britain's spear-shaker, sir." He pointed to the words *MENTE VIDEBORI*. "If you rearrange the letters, they spell *TIBI NOM DE VERE. Thy name is de Vere.*"

Martin and the others stood there with mouths open.

"Why, of course!" shouted the elated professor. "*Thy name is de Vere*. Of course!"

"So, Peachum seemed to think that Britain's spear-shaker was de Vere," said Martin.

The professor then looked down to his sonnet puzzle. *Every word doth almost tell my name*. Elated, he placed his quill below it and took the *E* from the start of *Every word* and the *d* from the finish and grabbed the *wor* from the midst and scribbled *Edwor*. He then dropped the *y* from his *very* and revealed the name *Edwor ver*. And he smiled wide. For *Every word* did indeed *almost* tell his name!

"But what of this *swan of Avon* remark?" Martin looked to Simonds. "What is the complete phrase Jonson writes?"

"Um…" Simonds ran his fingers through his well-looked-over scribbles 'til he hit upon it. "*Sweet Swan of Avon. What a sight it were to see thee in our waters yet appear and make those flights upon the banks of Thames that so did take Eliza and our James.*"

"On the Thames?" Martin noted. "Master Rollett, where would the monarch see courtly shows on the Thames?"

"At the royal palace, Major. Hampton Court," said the player.

"Never at a public theatre?"

"Oh, never, Major."

Which led Martin to ask the professor to seek out Camden's description of the palace. And whilst that was afoot, my brother turned back to Rollett.

"Now, that Jonson."

"Yes, sir," said Rollett, standing straight. "Jonson writes on how the works of their best writer was being claimed by another:

Poor Poet-Ape, that would be thought our chief,
Whose works are even the frippery of wit,
From brokerage is become so bold a thief,
As we, the robbed, leave rage, and pity it."

Rollett stepped back, and Martin pursued. "Brokerage? Who was the Lord Chamberlain's play broker?"

"I believe," offered Simonds, "it was Master Shaksper, sir."

"So, Jonson is complaining that a play broker is pretending to be the chief poet of the day." He then turned to his men, half-bemused. "Did every man in London know this Shake-speare was a cover but us?" Professor Ogburn approached with his book of Camden. "Professor?"

"Camden calls Hampton Court Palace *a stately place for rare and glorious show.*"

"Well, that helps us not," Martin appeared a bit disappointed. But the professor looked at him with the satisfied smile of the cat what et the rat. "Is there more?" Martin asked him.

"There's more," said he happily, as he read on. "*Hampton Court, which in times past, by name of Avon men knew it.*"

"Avon!" Martin lit up. "So, the sweet swan of Avon is the sweet poet of Hampton Court Palace!" He then turned to Simonds. "Where did Edward de Vere live? Where is King's Place located?"

The curious name of King's Place struck Valentina. *Why would a lord live at a king's place?* she wondered, not knowing that she herself would soon be dining there.

"Hackney, sir," answered Simonds.

"Hackney," Martin repeated. "Where the theatres stand. Master Rollett, what is the name of the liberty just outside the city to the west of Bonner Field?"

"Why, Hackney, sir," said Rollett.

"And to the east of Bonner Field?"

"Stratford."

"Stratford!" echoed Martin.

And so it was. It seemed that both the Stratford and the Avon mentions found printed in the Shakespeare book pointed a finger to both men. A clever fellow, that Ben Jonson.

"Master Rollett, who employed Jonson to write these comments in the Shakespeare folio?" asked the Major, knowing they must now be near the end.

"Ben Jonson is in the employ of the Herbert brothers, Lords Pembroke and Montgomery."

"They are the two nobles to whom the book is dedicated," added Simonds.

"And so, they put up the funds," concluded Martin. And this made him glad, as he happed to know the many ins and outs of who was wed to which in the world of the court. "Does anyone know to whom Philip Herbert is married?"

"I know," answered the professor. "To Countess Susan Vere. Lord Oxford's—"

"Daughter," Martin jumped in. "So it was Edward Vere's own family who saw to it that the Shakespeare works will live on forever."

"For E. Ver, sir," smiled Simonds.

They were all so enthused within the room, they hadn't noticed that the world outside had darkened. The children had long scurried hurriedly, and a serpent now stood at their door.

"Excuse me, sir," came the familiar voice from the back of the room.

"Yes, Master Loney," Martin said, without even looking up to see who spake it.

"I wonder if this Latin encomium from Gabriel Harvey," said the small man, as he slow approached, "might be pertinent? He addressed Lord Oxford before queen and court."

"And what said he?" asked Martin.

"Well, to put it in English, he speaks of Edward Vere's *splendid fame, with Minerva concealed in thy right hand,*" quoth Loney. "And he concludes by saying to Lord Edward, *Your eyes flash fire, your will shakes spears.*"

"Yes," said my brother flat, "that would seem pertinent. Thank you."

And that seemed to button up the doublet all nice and tidy.

"A pity none of us holds acquaintance with Master Jonson," spoke the professor. "For 'tis certain his own library houses the Shakespeare manuscripts."

"Not no more," stood Long Tom at the back.

"What's that?" asked Martin.

"A fire burnt hot in Cripplegate last even. Jonson's papers are none but dust now."

"They burnt down his home?"

Of a sudden, there was a thundrous SMASH of glass. It sounded as though it came from the front window below, which as bad fortune would have it was the only glazed window in the office. Martin cautious-like made his way to the door.

"Everyone hold," were his orders, as he quietly unbolted it and removed hisself from sight. The chamber below seemed darker than he had ever known it. He slowly descended the stair, listening for any who could be hid within. At the foot of the steps he stopped, breathing hard. He then crossed toward the window, and his boot crushed a bit of glass below it.

Through the window that was no more, he could see no one on the lane. He had never seen no one on the lane, and this gave him pause. In the midst of the shattered glass, lay a rock. He then walked up the stair and bolted the door tight.

Martin stood at one end of the room, and his men gathered at the other. He pondered a bit, and then decided. "I had hoped none in London knew of our work here," he said, "but I fear that our secrecy cannot be maintained. Therefore," his heart dropped, "I am concluding our inquiry, and thanking you all for your good services."

No one moved.

"I ask that you now leave Nicholas and me to find a resolution on our own."

Nick was relieved that he had not been dismissed, for, even if his meeting with Horatio that night might bring him closer to his father's secrets, he still desired to help Martin find his brothersome bother.

"You shall find remuneration in the morning," Martin added. But no one stirred. "Do you hear? There may be grave danger ahead."

Martin observed a timid hand rise from the back and by now he knew it to be Loney's.

"Master Loney," he said softly.

"Respectfully, sir," said the man, as he slowly stepped forward. "I... I am anxious to resume work." And he crossed to his chair and sat. "Begging your pardon."

A second later, Professor Ogburn walked over to where young Loney sat and took the chair next to him, defiantly opening a book on the table before him. Simonds smiled and did likeways, followed by Rollett and Long Tom and Valentina and Nicholas. The Major now felt like a Frenchman on a bad day at Agincourt and understood that he was quite outflanked.

"Three days," Martin said finally, "to a full report on Edward de Vere, earl of Oxford. We must learn of his life, and of his fate, if we are ever to discover that of Arthur's and Nathaniel North's."

After the broken glass was gathered, and the window well-boarded, they all went their several ways. Master Loney took his usual stroll on the grassy grounds of Paul's Churchyard. Rollett went wenching dockside. Long Tom disappeared down Magpie Alley. And Martin and Simonds joined the professor at Mistress Margaret's Mistake, the aptly named tavern run by Mistress Margaret's idiot son. Nicholas escorted Valentina to the sign of the White Dove. He could not stay, for he had his secret meeting with the baron. So, when Valentina bid him farewell, she had no idea that the lad would never again return to the Taverner law office.

CHAPTER EIGHTEEN.

BRAWL AT THE BOAR'S HEAD.

The Boar's Head Inn, perhaps the finest tavern in Whitechapel, was deceivingly tranquil from the outsides. A tittle could Nick have guessed what sudden violence awaited him within. He approached expecting the sort of serenity that one might find at such a fine establishment. But the moment he opened the door, two enraged brutes, full of sounds and furies signifying everything, thrust two sword-points to his face. Terrified, Nicholas stood as still as he could stand.

Now, there are many a wise thing I learnt in my threescore years of life on this sceptered isle. I learnt that "Man is never undone 'til he be hanged." I learnt that "An old cloak makes a new jerkin." And I learnt that England is called "a sceptered isle." But most important, I discovered from my book-trafficking friends that suspenseful digressions make for a better tale.

So, if I may be allowed a momentary meander, I'd remind a fellow that even a schoolboy with a head full o' milk 'n mush knows that, while daggers are always best avoided at a London tavern, there be another form of attack, not of the sword, but of the word. For aren't words ofttimes used as daggers? To wound and to maim? Do they not oft prove more lasting? Consider the ditty I oft heard recited at The Sniveling Sibling after crookback Cecil lost his battle with life.

Here lies little Crookback
Who justly was reckon'd
Richard the Third and Judas the Second,
In life they agreed,
But death they did alter,

Great pity the pox prevented the halter.

I say no need for a hangman's halter when words such as these can so well execute a man. And what of those slanderous songs sung 'bout our virgin queen at the Bull and Spectacles by Newington Butts?

> *She that many years refused to wed*
> *And boasted what virginity was worth,*
> *Even she, I say, hath lost her maidenhead*
> *And daughters three to all the world brought forth.*
> *Which I'll declare on Church and on Church-steeple*
> *Are bastards bred, right children of the people.*

So, the rapier wit might be mightier than the rapier itself, for dagger wounds can heal, but the scars left in print live on forever. Thus, one may find a moral in our own tale, if one was of a mind to look for such a truth.

But back at the Boar's Head, this was a night for Nicholas, and we left him at the point-ends of two long swords. The weapons had been drawn amidst shouts of anger. The villain on his right yelled, "Ho, you rat-catcher!" whilst the rat-catcher to his left screamed," At you, villain!"

Nick quick jumped out of the way as one Lancelot Lloyd charged a Migsett Miller. Lancelot slashed the Miller a big gash, and to Nick's surprise, blood streamed out his side. Now, this might be a sight one would expect to find at less reputable establishments, such as the Bucket O' Blood on Bath Row, where I did see one Peter Puckett thrust ole Thomas Tingle from the thatched roof onto the horse trough below, breaking both the horse and the Tingle. Or at the Hung, Drawn & Quartered off Cutthroat Lane, where self-claimed reborn-messiah Willy Hackett attacked schoolmaster Rosicrucian Barber after an insult was thrown by the Barber, upon which the Messiah flung the fellow to the floor and proceeded to bite off the dangle o' the poor man's ear before eating it! Now, I must admit, digestible food was always in short supply at the Hung & Drawn, and their usual fare was no Barnoldswick banquet since burnt butt-fish was always their especiality, but I'd have rather et a bit o' burnt butt than a Barber's dangle!

Here at the Boar's Head, Nick never knew a man to have so much blood in him. But the strange thing was, it ne'er slowed the wounded villain down. It just seemed to please him not. The bleeding brute, without a care, raised his own weapon high and, with a yell that could sure be heard all the way to the Bucket O' Blood, attempted to attack the rat-catcher. But instead of a hit, he caught up his sword-tip in the draperies over the wall. All tangled as he was, and bleeding onto his high-cost buskins, he seemed not to fret a whit. He even stopped his disentangling long enough to grab a nearby ale and swig it down.

In the mean of time, t'other fellow approached from behind and, rather than stab his disadvantaged enemy (as I would have done), he instead dropped his own sword, preferring to take a swig from his own cup. And they be all smiles and chucks. He even helped the first to loose his sword from the draperies! 'Twas then Nick grasped that these fighters were no fighters at all, but mere players, for he spied a corner where other actors were working out their parts. And so, he placed his heart back within his doublet and looked 'round the place.

Nick had never afore visited such a clean and well-lit inn. There must have been two hundred candles afire. The serving wenches seemed fine enough to walk the daylight with. And the gentlemen, whilst still a boisterous bunch, seemed like they could, in sooth, be actual gentlemen.

At the far end of the room, Nick spied Horatio, who waved the lad over. He sat at the table, piled with platters of goats and saucers of vinegar. They ate and they drank and the noble spoke. Nick hung onto every word. How fortunate he was to find his answers in Baron Horatio, the beloved cousin of Lord Edward Vere hisself.

It was here that night that Nick finally learnt most of the true story of the poet he had so admired. And why this knowledge had led to so many deaths. Why his father had been taken. And wherefore I myself had vanished. I say he learnt *most* because, as I have found, in mine own life (and mine own death), things are not always as they seem, and unlike the peacock, the full tail is seldom spread.

Nick was likeways told of his task. He would have no choice but to come to my cell the next dawn. To fulfill the final scene of our story. His only wish that night, as Lord Horace gave instruction, was that it could be done of quick, for he liked not the task at hand. And that whatever might hap to him, would hap to him swift. He stayed for the while, to learn what must be learnt, and then he left that place, knowing where to find me the next morning.

CHAPTER NINETEEN.

THE INVISIBLE KNIGHT IS BORN.

When curiosity gets the best of a person, there are ever two outcomes. One is that a fellow may fall deeper into danger. T'other is that a bit of light may be lit. So, as the sun dawned the next morning, Valentina marked out her course. After a breakfast of eggs and currants, and a pleasant stroll with Uncle Ned before he headed back home to Warwickshire, she left her digs at the White Dove and walked east, making her way onto the old roads of Hackney. There she came upon the seemingly given-up King's Place, all dark within and wild without.

She stood, wondering what stories these walls could tell, if in fact walls had a desire to converse. But after hearing not a word from them, she was about to traverse back down Morning Lane and return to her inn when her heart told her to approach. As one who always used her head and never her heart to direct her feet, she did not know why, but she found herself moving toward the door. She knocked, expecting no answer at all.

Ready to turn away, to her surprise, the door did open a tittle, and an ancient head peered out. Valentina eyed the withered and smiling face of a creature who must have been a century old, at the very least.

"Why, God b'uy you, my sweetie," was the old lady's greeting, as if she had known the lass all her living.

Taken by such friendliness, the beauty smiled and said, "God b'uy you, Madam. I wonder, is this the home they call King's Place?"

The old woman's eyes sparkled. "Why, I haven't heard it called that in ages. Come in."

And Valentina did.

"You've arrived at a most fitting time," beamed the old lady. "For now 'tis dinner, and is years since I've had a young face to feed."

Before Valentina could say a thing, she was seated at a long table in a vast room lit by a mere three candles, sharing the widow's Wednesday-brewed pottage, which was topped with enough grizzle to choke a Colchester cat. The room was so dark, she could barely see what she et, which in my book is called a blessing. It was then the beauty learnt who this congenial woman was.

Widow Eliza Sears had been cook to many a noble in years past. And what she lacked in cookery skills, she more than made up for in gossip. She appeared a frail woman, but looks are a deceiving thing. She was, as they say, full of vinegar. Not as much as what she poured into her soup, but that is besides the mark. Her eyes twinkled every time she opened her mouth, which made her companionship all the more to enjoy. And a funny sight 'twas, too, for she had a full smile that was but half full of teeth, which attested to her love of pomegranates and sugars.

"Did you cook for the Lord of Oxford?" Beauty enquired.

"Why, I cooked for all the nobles, I did. Including the great Lord Edward," she began. "At that time, I was working for my Mistress Mary, afore her child was born," her voice softened. "Just afore all the troubles started. How's that mutton fat?"

"Oh, 'tis good," Valentina lied. She begged her continue, and the old widow did, needing no urging.

"Her husband, the old Southampton, had been arrested. She could not visit him. And thanks to God, her dear friend Edward, the great Lord Edward, was there."

"Tell me about him."

"He was a friend to both my Mistress Mary and later to her son, Henry Southampton. Some say more than that, may they bite their bitter tongues. But so close was milord to Mary, her husband in the Tower and all. They was friends from childrenhood."

Her bright eyes searched the cypress above, as if seeing this story played out in the rafters.

"Young Edward Oxenford," she grinned. "And little Mary Montague."

128

★

The 1560s.

Edward was a mere lad of twelve as he sat, quill in hand, beside the serious Arthur Golding. It was late morning at Castle Hedingham in the lush north Essex country. The day of her majesty's visit, and the lad had dashed off a poem for her. He was good at writing poems, since he had ole Uncle Arthur, the famed religious translator, to give him tutelage.

Edward was sure glad to be home, where he could spend a day with his beloved father, earl John. The lad had sorely missed the kindly earl since, from the age of four onways, he had lived with others. First with his tutor, Sir Thomas Smith, that many call *the Flower of Cambridge*, but who I shall call Sir Thomas. Then at eight, the lad had been shipped off to Cambridge itself for more studies.

Back home on this special day, Edward excitedly handed his uncle his scribbles, which were inspected with great care. Golding liked the poem well, though his face rarely managed to reveal his likings nor his dislikings. But a small smile did finally crack upon the corner of the ice, and the boy hoped his work was met with approval.

"What think you, dear nuncle?" Edward asked, all eager for some praise.

"It is very good," said Golding, who then became serious. "Just one small matter." He pointed to the bottom of the page where was writ *Edward, Viscount Bulbeck*.

"That is my name," said the lad.

"Matthew six, my boy. *I follow the counsel of Christ...*" he began, hoping his young charge would know where that river flowed. And his nephew answered the call quite admirable.

"Which exhorteth men to do their good deeds—"

"—*secretly*," his tutor concluded. "Your poem is a great gift to our queen. When you give it her, you must not give it her with your name."

"But when I give it her," the clever lad reasoned, "she will know it is *I* who give it her."

Caught, Golding paused. "A man of gentle birth, dear boy, cannot attach his own name to his works. For what is it we value among all else?" he posed.

"One's good name, nuncle," said the boy.

"Dear Edward," Golding almost smiled, "your poems are beautiful gifts. Made all the more beautiful when given in secret rather than in boast. Remember, you shall someday follow your great father as the noblest earl of the realm."

And true that was, for his father's line went as far back as William the Conqueror, and I don't mean the naked one in the window above the Ram Inn.

His uncle continued. "You shall be the queen's Great Chamberlain."

"And brave knight," the boy enthused.

"Be her invisible knight, dear boy," advised the old man. "Unknown and unseen. The greater to protect her majesty."

"Invisible knight?" repeated the boy. Why, this idea captured his imaginings. "I shall do it!" he decided. And with that, he took pen to page and scratched out his name. "May I use another name, nuncle?"

"Why, of course," said Golding.

The thought of using a new name intrigued the lad. On the desk before him were a handful of translations he had previous writ-out. For his uncle had spent years teaching him to render from the Latin and the Greek. And whilst he tried his best to get his student to rework the books of Ignatius and Clement and all the holy rest, the boy inclined more toward the lusty poets. You know boys these days! So, reluctant as his uncle was to let him touch such texts, the teacher was of a mind that somesuch was better than nonesuch.

In a fit of inspiration, young Edward eagerly grabbed hold of one of the long manuscripts he had just completed, and on the cover page the boy scratched out his true name and wrote a new one next to it. He handed it to his tutor.

130

"*Arthur Golding,*" said the now flush-faced Arthur Golding. "Why, that's *my* name."

"A secret gift to you, as well," reasoned the boy.

"But—"

"Looks good on my translation."

"Oh?" Golding's face fell to the floor. The thought of such lustful stories attached to his own pious moniker made his stomach pull.

The excited lad jumped up and asked, "Is her majesty's tournament to begin?"

"Did you not hear?" answered Golding. "Your poor cousin Northampton was thrown from his horse, and there is no defender for the crown."

The boy's heart leapt at this. "Oh, but there is, dear nuncle! There is!"

And with that, my young lord raced out of the room, leaving behind a bewildered Arthur Golding, who turned to a page in that licentious Latin he had just been handed. And his face grimaced. *Why did it have to be the Ovid?* fretted he. *Oh, why?*

Widow Sears went on with her remembrances, which Valentina found not only a help to her cause, but a pleasing divertissement to be sure. She was even getting accustomed to the grizzle.

"My sweet Mary was there with him on that dark day that was to forever change the boy's life," she proceeded. "The day he was to become earl in his own right. Our beautiful queen was there, rest her blessed soul." Here, the old lady took the corner of a worn napkin from the tabletop and dabbled 'round her welling eyes. So many years since, and still folk dabbled for our good queen.

"Her trusted minister, Sir William Cecil, and her handsome consort, Lord Robert Dudley," but the widow quickly clarified. "I can't say for certain he was her consort, mind you. But they did do a lot of consorting together, if you follow my nut path." And she gave a winkle of an eye, thinking about Dudley. The mighty earl that stole our good queen's heart, in the addition to many other things, many say. "It was the day that young Edward began his famous feud with that Philip Sidney. Long afore their war of words," said she, "came their war on the fields."

The castle grounds had been arranged for a jousting tournament, for there was nothing her majesty loved better. At the center, sat the afore-talked-of queen and dignities. Her majesty Elizabeth, dressed in violet velvet, was a beauty in her youth (and none dared say she wasn't a beauty in her old age, neither). The crowned queen of England, Ireland and France - though why that France bit was stuck in there I haven't a guess, for I thought her grandsire lost it long ago. Alongside her majesty was the young mistress Mary, a pretty lass of about Edward's age, sitting next to her mother, Lady Montague. There were lesser courtiers about, whose names I have neither the memory nor the inclination to tell, and a troop of musicians played nearby.

The madrigals of Morley were the ditties of the day. *Come Lovers Follow Me* was quick followed by *Come Sorrow Come*, which I believe the writers of today call a fitting irony. And after all fiddles were faddled, Uncle Golding, new-made master of the joust, approached the field dressed in an elaborate cloak.

"Your gracious majesty!" Golding bowed and bellowed, as if he was awkwardly *O, for a muse of fire*-ing from atop the stage at The Globe. "Most noble lords. At this, the first of her majesty's jousts, we bid you welcome in honor of our glorious Gloriana." And at the mention of her royal highness, the dignified crowd screamed like wild jackdaws at the Bucket O' Blood. "We shall now have contest: three of five breaks. As brave challenger," Golding caterwauled above the din as he faced his right, "I give you young Master Philip Sidney!"

As they cheered, young Sidney emerged from his tent of silken silver. He was dressed in armor of the same shine, and his horse, a beauty of a Barbary named Pegasus, was likeways covered in matching mail. The young lad held high his shield in his left hand. He trotted to the front of the crowd, raised his visor up, and sitting high in his saddle, bowed low his head.

"And now," Master Golding continued, "I present to you the brave and...uh," he stopped and gave a worried glance to his left where his noble brother-in-law, the sixteenth earl John, stood confident in front of the golden tent at t'other end of the field, "...nameless defender of her majesty!"

More cheers as the mystery defender, who they knew not at the time, but we know now to be Lord Edward, appeared from his tent in armor of glistening gold, with visor down. He sat atop his steed, by both breed and name called Capilet, likeways dressed in golden guard.

"Who is it?" asked one lord in the gallery, receiving no reply.

The defender approached the spot next to Sidney, and both he and Capilet bowed in one to her majesty, as low as could be done without toppling head over ass. Or should I say head over horse? 'Twas a sign of the great control the young lad held on the reins, and the great love he bore for his sovereign.

"To your places!" cried Uncle Golding, as they turned their steeds 'round and trotted to opposing ends of the field, where their servants awaited, spears in hand. Each warrior was situated on his own side of the center barrier.

"Spears up!" came the command.

And with that, Edward's servant Adam handed his young master a spear, whilst down the field, young Philip was attended by a fellow named Buckles, though his name is of no import, as he features not prominent in our story. Sidney then lowered his visor, as this was a dangerous business, and procuring a pike in the eyeball was worse than punching a pig in a poke.

"And begin!" announced Golding, as he ran as far from the danger as his scholarly legs could scurry him.

Both lads began to race 'cross the field toward t'other with remarkable speed, and the crowd began their chant.

"Shake-a-Spear! Shake-a-Spear! Break-a-Spear! Break-a-Spear!"

They repeated this ditty over and again, as enthusiasm filled the royal air. Excited, young Edward sat high in his saddle, looking to the crowd, eyeing the queen. It must be admitted that the boy was flaunting hisself a bit. And this caused him to be a very large mark for his rival Philip, who was now only a few feet distant, and getting nearer with every half-second. Sidney lunged at Edward's shield and broke the top of his tip onto it. The crowd was cheering afore Edward knew what had hit.

"First break for the challenger!" Golding announced. "To your places!" he instructed.

The two lads returned to their positions, with Edward having a tittle of the wind knocked out of him, surprised at how fast the flutter flew.

After a moment to collect themselves, "Spears up!" was heard, and each young man received a new weapon. Then the order came, "And begin!"

And begin they did again, and ride they rode again. But with no alteration in his approach, young Edward was once more traveling tall, and young Philip took anew the advantage. As the boisterous crowd chanted their chant, young Philip raced his spear tip toward Edward's shield and broke off another goodly piece.

"Two breaks!" called out Golding. "Three breaks to win!" he said, shooting a worried glance to his unnerved nephew. "To your places!" was the call.

This time, the shaken Edward returned to his spot and then rounded the far side of his tent, pulling up his visor to speak with his dear father and his kindhearted cousin, the Duke of Norfolk, who both awaited him, whilst a worried Adam ran to fetch the boy a beer.

"You're too big a mark, son," said earl John.

"Think small, lad," advised Norfolk.

"Small, yes. Invisible!" said the lad, remembering the visions that whirligig'd about his brain earlier that day. He lowered his visor and turned to eye the field. *I shall be her invisible knight!* thought he, now more excited than ever.

"Spears up!" shouted Golding. "And begin!"

And the crowd once more chanted their cheer.

"Shake-a-Spear! Shake-a-Spear! Break-a-Spear! Break-a-Spear!"

The two courageous opponents raced toward each other. But this time, young Edward sat small in his saddle. Invisible. He looked not to the spectators. He looked not to his sovereign. He looked solely to Sidney's shield. He eyed-in only on the shield.

At first, young Philip could see defender and horse coming. But, of a sudden, all became a blur. There was, of an instance, no defender, no horse. There was only a golden gust. And BANG! He had been hit. Before he knew it, he had been hit.

"What was that?" said Sidney.

"I am invisible," whispered Edward.

The crowd cheered, as it is always a joy when the dog under becomes the dog atop. All huzzah'd. All but Lord Dudley, who had envy for any who received attention but hisself. And I should add that he was also uncle to young Philip.

With Edward's spear broke off on Sidney's shield, the words rang out.

"Two and one. Places! Spears up!"

Each lad was given a new spear.

"And begin!"

The two combatants raced toward the center. Again, Edward was invisible. And again, he was invincible.

"We are at two and two!" proudly belched Golding, after Edward broke off another tip onto Sidney's shield. "This final break shall determine the victor. To your places!"

Each opponent got into position. The crowd became for once silent.

Uncle Arthur, who could feel his heart pounding, faced the queen. "For the win. For her majesty. Spears up!"

Each lad was handed a spear.

"And begin!"

This was the moment that all who were waiting long had long-awaited. It was a contest that queen and court would never forget. From one end, came the challenger to the realm. From t'other, raced the unknown defender of the queen. Her Majesty's Invisible Knight, as he was destined to become, hurried his silent spear toward Sidney's shield. 'Twas all he eyed. He got nearer and aimed at nothing else. And this time, when he smashed into it, bashing off half his spear-shaft, the violent impact forced Philip off his horse and onto the ground. It was only after Edward heard the crowd's gasps that he recognized his rival had been downed.

Then all fell into a fearful hush.

Edward jumped off his steed and raced to his friend, lying motionless in the dirt. He raised Philip's visor, and gently patted him, cheek by jowl, calling his name. After a tittle, Sidney, all befuddled and befused, came 'round. He took the hand of her majesty's mysterious defender and was pulled onto his unsteady boots. The crowd began to cheer wild, and all was now well with Edward, who could breathe again. Golding approached the two and pulled them forward, presenting each to her now-relieved highness.

"The challenger!" he shouted, raising Sidney's arm to the clapper-claws of the onlookers. Then the proud uncle lifted Edward's arm, announcing, "The victor!" And all rose and roused a yell you could hear clear to Macclesfield. As their rowdiness eventually subsided, our fairest queen stood.

"Young man," said she. "Bear us your face."

Edward, ever smitten with the beauty of her highness, slowly approached her and bowed deep. "I would like to oblige your gracious majesty," says he aloud, "but I serve for your glory, my Gloriana, and not mine own. I most humbly beg your pardon."

Off to the side, the boy's father beamed with a pride fathers have when they grasp their sons have grown into men.

The queen removed a glittering gold and diamond chain from 'round her precious nape and motioned for the helmeted lad to come forth. Excited, he approached, and she handed him the glistening gift, which he took to his visor as if to kiss it. He bowed, and before one could say *Hail to her majesty*, the boy was— well, in actual fact, 'twas about the time it took to say that old school verse we learnt declaring *May thy pigs be set upon by ravens and torn asunder leaving only bespeckled bone and curdled fat on which the rats may feast* — before one could say that, the boy jumped upon Capilet and galloped away. The queen was left smiling, Dudley was left irked, and earl John was left right proud.

CHAPTER TWENTY.

A TALE FROM A TO B.

"Mistress Sears, you said that this was the day the young boy would become earl?"

"'Tis true, child." And never one to disappoint an attentive ear, the old widow continued. "'Twas later, in the gardens. Young Edward read his poem to the queen, and of a sudden, there was a scream. They soon learnt that his father, earl John, had been found dead. Of what, I never knew. The Countess Oxenford, Edward's mother, was took inside. Her majesty sent that William Cecil to discover the cause. And the poor boy's twelve-year-old heart must have broke."

Sir William returned, wrenching the poetry from Edward's hand. "No more time for this, my boy. You are now earl of Oxford. You are now ward of the crown and must come with us."

As he left the lad standing there, young Mary approached and took the broken boy's hand.

Albeit he was now ward of the crown, Lord Edward would never live in any of her majesty's fanciful homes as a fellow might expect. Even though she possessed the keys to many a palace, including Whitehall, larger even than the pope's in Rome (which I am sure much displeased the pope), she had not a single room for the lad, who would now call Cecil House his home 'til he be one-and-twenty.

'Twas not long after his arrival, with bare enough time to unpack his horse and remove his inky cloak, that he heard the terrible news about his mother.

The first blow struck a month after earl John's death, when he learnt of her quick remarrying. The second blow hit when he discovered the man she had wed was well-below his own father's state. Well, truth be told, there was none in England who could rise near the state of a Vere. But this lowly man had been Dudley's horse master, if one can think it!

The final blow blew when he learnt the man's name: *Tyrell*. Now, this be not the same Tyrell who the crooked King Richard asked to do him the favor of liberating him from the poor little princes in the Tower (and by *liberating*, I mean introducing them to the wrong end of a heavy cudgel), as that would put this Tyrell's age at twenty years past a hundred. But sharing the same name, and perhaps the same blood, as a multiple prince-cudgeler (a man from Gipping, no least!), could never endear such a stepfather to such a son. A stepfather that was no more like to earl John than I am to Hecuba. Not to mention the quick attempt to usurp his dear father's place within his mother's heart and hearth. And so, with that, Edward's mother passed out of the young boy's life, for some reason. There were no long letters. No warm visits. And in a few years, she herself was dead. Poor lad.

At Cecil House, perhaps of most interest to young Edward was the library, which was the largest in Christendom. Not for the distance 'tween the walls, though 'twas indeed a long walk betwixt *A* to *Z*, but for the many texts contained, holding near two-thousand books.

This *A* to *Z* reminds me of a jest I told at the Nasty Plate in Bankside to an ill-nurtured dolt by name of Allen of Nilson on Pendle Hill. We were in deep colloquy about Sir Francis Drake and his navigational skills. So, I says to the dolt, "The intent of any good voyage is to get from *A* to *B* without falling into the *sea!*" Now I think 'tis a funny, but my lousy adversary ne'er would laugh, clearly not understanding how the mind of a true wit works. Or perhaps he ne'er quite reached the third letter in his hornbook.

Cecil's magnificent library held all the books in all the tongues. Latin, French, Greek, and a bit o' Old English, as Lord Edward liked "to rest long beside Ole Chaucer," he would say when his eyes grew tired. 'Twere many chambers filled with books, new and ancient, and tutors that could be described likeways.

138

At dawn, whilst most of us still lay atop the straw dreaming of ale-wenches, milord would start with a dance master at seven. He would pavane a bit, then galliard awhile. And if all went well, and no legs were broke, he would courant off to breakfast.

At eight o' the clock, 'twas time for young Edward to master the language they mumble in France. Then at nine, he'd study the tongue of wherever 'tis they mumble Latin. And when the tenth hour came 'round and milord ran out of languages to mumble, you would find him at his desk and dust-box writing and drawing.

His midday dinner was a crowded affair, since, in the addition to Sir William, his wife Mildred, his son Robert (later to be known as crookback), and his daughter Annie (later to be known as sorrowful), there would daily be congested 'round the table the gentleman usher, the deputy usher, the yeoman usher, the ewery yeoman, the gentlemen waiters, the carver, and the sewer, the last being the fellow what tastes and serves the dishes, and not the waters what took what remained atop the dishes and carried them off to the river.

After dinner, milord would needs open the cosmography books. What they were and why he would needs open them, I've not a clue. But afterways, it would be more of his Latin and more of his French. And when time could be found, he would practice with horse, hawk and bodkin, as all complete courtiers must.

Final to this would be common prayer and on to supper, where, if I was a guest, I might suggest a well-cooked quarter of Malmesbury mutton with a butt of malmsey to follow. But if it be a fish day, 'twould be a different kettle entirely. And thanks to Sir William, near every day o' the week was a fish day, what with him asking the Parliament to add Wednesdays to the meatless Fridays and Saturdays. A veritable fishmonger, that Sir William!

The food abounded and all got their fill, 'cept maybe for young Robert, who always requested of his father the rarely-made treacle tart. Though I truly suspect the crooked lad would have been happier with a treacle'd smile and a sweet embrace from stern ole William. But, as was his nature, the father forever deprived the boy of all three.

The continued education of Edward seemed to be an important duty of the queen's chief minister, now made master of her wards. And that is an employ he took serious (and for which he was well-compens'd, I hear). Which is why Edward's days were so well-trafficked in long studies. And if such studies was not enough, and I myself am bedraggled just by thinking on it, the famed cartographer, the honorable Lawrence Nowell hisself (though I never heard of him, nor know why he was so honorable), would come 'round to tutor the boy. But a fellow should not be fooled by the title, for he was not there to teach the young lad how to construct a cart. A cartographer, I am rightly informed, is a maker of maps. But this man had more than maps up his smock sleeve, for he also taught the lad ancient history, ancient peoples, ancient rocks, ancient tongues, and ancient laws. Seems he was not over-educated in new things, but perhaps this was all Sir William's purse could purchase for the boy's education at the time.

Master Nowell also owned many a rare book, and so he and his young charge would oft be found o'er-viewing copies of such antique tomes as the *Exeter Book*, full of four-hundred year-old poetry (which I ne'er read), *Saxo Grammaticus*, telling the story of some sad Prince Amleth from Denmark who mopes about a bit (which I ne'er read), and even his own self-writ *Vocabularium*, the fattest dictionary of all the Anglo-Saxaphonic words what he knew (which I ne'er read, but 'twas on my list, as I meant to read it, but ne'er got 'round to it).

Soon studies with Nowell ended, and not because the boy had a head full o' milk 'n mush as my poor teachers used to say of me, and not due to a rebellious nature, from which I likeways suffered afore I wised 'round. But in young Edward's boots, his tutor came to see that what he had to offer the young lord was already well-surpassed in him.

Afore he left, however, he did give the boy a rare manuscript that was so scarce, 'twas the only copy in all the world, they say. Though why a young Essex lad would want to read an ancient poem about a Danish king who hires a Geatish warrior to kill a Grendely monster is beyond my comprehension. 'Tis called *Beer Wolf*, if my memory serves. Perhaps this is why old Cecil got hisself rid of this

Nowell fellow, filling milord's head with useless tales of kings of Denmark and moping princes and murders and revenges and such.

To say all of this bookwork reminds me of mine own education would be as far from the truth as I am from Catherine, Countess Palatine of Kleeburg. Fortunate was I to obtain a modicum of learning, just this side of three years, from Master John Smith o' Bampton at the petty school at Mary le Bow's. Now, I know the name John Smith o' Bampton is a disappointing one for a schoolmaster, as they usually have names the likes of Master Bantickle Prickling of Stickleback, but as my tale is true (mostly), I must name names where they lay.

Whilst my brother Martin excelled in the trivium, I exceeded in the trivial. And I admit, but shamed I should be, that there was many a day I'd sacrifice flourishing in the classroom for floating in the Thames. If truth be told, I should have got a university honor in that art, for that's how good was I at swimming!

Back at Cecil House, many hours in a day young Edward would be followed about by little Annie Cecil, six years his junior, who doted on the lad as if he was Adonis in a doublet. This, of course, irritated Edward, who wanted nothing least than a noisome little sister at his heels. There was also the crooked Robert, who was later to become his majesty's treasurer. This little hump-back wailed about the place, sneering and jeering at milord with no rhyme nor reason. Usually on the way, I'd wager, to the library to pick up his copy of the latest book by Master Machiavel.

Despite all this, milord prospered. After his studies at the great Cambridge University was complete, he was given a place at Oxford, which I hear is a right fair school on its own. And to finish his rounding, he spent the last of his school days at Grey's Inn, which might sound like an alehouse to the common clod, but I assure you, law books were all one could find served up at this bar, for the inns of court were schools for those training in the legal profession. However, on any day o' the week, a man could find as many play performances as pleas in this place.

'Twas here milord renewed his love of the theatre, reminding him of the days when, as a child, he would be paraded 'round the

141

castle on the backs of his father's players, who laughed and sang and danced 'til dawn. For, alas, those were his days of yore, and he knew them well.

Growing towards manhood, whenever Edward could, he would sneak away to visit Mary Montague, who still held his heart. Which I think broke when he later learnt what that Dudley done to her.

But time turned 'round, and boys turned to men. Their playthings left behind, they looked to broadswords and battles. 'Twas time for Edward to join his troops, led by the great Sussex. Standing by his horse, the lad said his sorrowful farewell to fair Mary. The lass began to tear, and Edward gently lifted a drop of it from her pale cheek.

"Now, I am the richest man who lives, to receive so many watery pearls," he said, smooth as a sheared Shropshire sheep. I would I had the words to say similar ditties to my sweet Peg when I caused her eye many a time to water.

"You take my breath away," said she.

"Then I give you mine," answered he, as he kissed her gentle on the mouth. Smooth, indeed.

The horns sounded, and young Edward, Lord Sussex, and the rest of the budding warriors rode off, as his young love looked on with the broken heart of youth. Milord was sent off to fight the rebellion in the north, whilst back home our queen's man Dudley plotted his own designs for the girl.

"My poor little Mary," sighed Widow Sears. "She knew not what was to come."

As the old woman continued, Valentina's eye became distracted by a movement seen through the window-boards. In the neglected gardens in back, she could spy a man approaching the house. He appeared to be of about seventy and wore a humble frock. The sunlight above lit onto his silver hair. But what caught her eye was a striking streak of ginger in his locks.

142

CHAPTER TWENTY-ONE.

THE BOY NOW SENT TO BE A MAN.

"Anthony Munday," said the widow, as she did the introducing. "She's in search of a friend," the ancient woman explained to the old writer and secretary, "and thinks she may find him within the story of your great acquaintance."

Always a fellow captured by a pretty face and a bit of interest shown in him, Master Munday reflected on those days long past.

★

1571.

'Twas not the bloody battles that would haunt Edward for the rest of his days, but what he witnessed on that cold January afternoon atop Garrowby Hill.

It may be hard to remember now, but those of us with a bit of silver under our caps can recall the rebellion of the northern earls, who were bent on restoring the church of Rome and plotting with a paper from the pope to kill our blessed majesty! Perhaps he was still vexed his palace was smaller than hers.

However, when word came that the powerful Sussex was riding toward them, many retreated to Scotland, cowards that they were. And of the captured numbers held tight by Sussex, her majesty commanded they be dealt with, a tittle anticipating the effect had upon young men the likes of Edward. It came the day the exhausted lad was leaving a body-strewn field, and a soldier approached with the news. Troubled, milord jumped upon his steed and charged off. He approached Garrowby Hill to view the vale below. And seeing the scene he saw, he fell to his knees. This was a picture that would haunt him.

Gradually, his anger grew. Determined, he bolted up, grabbed a standard bearing the queen's colors, and jumped onto his steed, racing off with flag in hand.

Edward's horse charged ahead. Holding his weapon high, he raced toward his opponent and violently smashed the man's shield. In haste, he dashed away, as queen and court once more cheered their Invisible Knight, again victorious against the now-grown Philip Sidney.

Afterwards, gloomy Luton lutes filled the air of the great chamber at Whitehall. Sullen Dublin-dweller John Dowland was the darling of the music-loving court at the time. Played that day were such heart-crushers as *Burst Forth My Tears* and *I Saw My Lady Weep*.

'Tis enough to say that, if this be a funeral procession, 'twould be amply accompanied. However, this, in the stead, was meant to be a happy celebration. And to my taste, I would have much preferred *Charlotte ye Harlot*, which better befits my ear.

Nonewithstanding the musical calamity, the post-tournament celebration was in full regale. The chamber was filled with well-wishing peers and non-peers. *Nonpareil*, as they say in places I wish not to visit. Two men who were most assuredly without peer stood at room's end. Servants they were, one tall and full o' bones, and t'other squat and full o' beer. But ask not which was what, for I've not a memory for unimportant details. Master Mickel Mutt held a tray of wines, whilst his accomplice, Mister Geoffrey Boyle, clutched a trencher of pippin pies.

Mister Boyle reached over to Mutt's offerings and grabbed hisself a silver goblet of Gascon that was meant for a more-noted guest than he and downed it.

"My dear Master Mutt," he began.

"My good Mister Boyle," came Mutt's reply, as he reached for his own goblet of goodness.

"Where be our honored guest, the young Lord of Oxford?" he enquired, looking about the roomful of nobs.

"Nay, not young no more," answered Mutt. "Today he be a man of one-and-twenty."

"Is this the cause we taste the best wines this day?" asked Boyle, sipping his sweetness.

"I prefer the cheaper," said Mutt. "Better suits my palate."

And then he saw Lord Edward, dressed in his new red velvet cloak, cross the floor.

"Ah, here comes the man."

Upon eyeing the guest of honor, the musicians ceased the tear-filled tunes, dropping their mournful lutes for triumphant trumpets, displacing Dowland for Byrd. They touted loud *The Earl of Oxford's March*. A right bright and cheery, which caused all in attendance to celebrate milord's entrance into the world of adulthood by clapping their hands together in his honor. Lord Edward graciously bowed and began to march rhythmically 'round the room, for, after all, 'twas *his* march. Always one to present a fine exhibition, if he could make a man laugh by his antics, 'twas all the better.

They continued to clapper in measure as milord was joined by his marching men. The young and hopping John Lyly, the old and hapless Thomas Churchyard, the drunken Tom Nashe, the scribbler Ed Spenser, and the joyous teen-year'd Anthony Munday. When the march was done, and the claps o' the crowd completed, Lyly draggled milord to a table where his dear companions were there assembling. Only such a valued friend could draggle a noble so.

"Hail the victor!" shouted Nashe, holding up his jack of mead.

"Birthday cheers for milord!" barked Churchyard.

"How does my worthy opponent?" Edward asked, not having seen Sidney since the bout.

"Shall live another day," came the reply from behind him, as Philip appeared on cue, accompanied by his own man, George Gascoigne, the middlin' writer from the Midlands.

Sidney was never known for keeping good company, and Gascoigne was no exemption. The chitter 'round the chatter was that he was a notorious ruffian, an insulting slanderer, and a forever-indebted atheist. And he was from Cardington, no least! They also say he killed a man for no good reason. He would later be crowned by the queen.

"Cheers for Philip Sidney!" shouted milord, ever the generous victor. And cheers did answer. "A better rival never was."

"With spear or with pen, milord?" pushed Philip.

Now, this was a point of contention, for Lord Edward was commander of a band of poets known as the Euphuists (whatever that did connote). And Sir Philip captain'd the Romanticists.

"Long live the Euphuists!" yelled Lyly proud.

"Long live the Romanticists!" came Gascoigne's counter.

"Please, Gascoigne," whined Churchyard. "Call you those roaming hexameters pleasant?"

"More pleasing than your Greek and Roman rhymes," said the rival.

"Your rules of Petrarch were meant to be broke, my dear Gascoigne," yelled Lyly.

"As are necks!" shouted Gascoigne. And Lyly took a step back.

"Hey-ho, a challenge," rose the besotted Nashe, sensing that the heavy gauntlet had been heaved. "But what shall be the game?" Nashe yelled, "Eh, Spenser? What shall it be?"

Why did he ask? For it was always rhyming.

"Milord," asked young Munday, looking admiringly to his hero. "Dost thou accept?"

Oxford looked 'round his table and liked nothing more than to please his men. "So long as there's drink enough, there shall be words enough. Let's to it."

And with that, each cheered, filled his cup, and encircled the table to loudly contest the contest. Lord Edward sat at one end and Sidney at t'other. This friendly feud did not escape the watchful eyes of the servants 'cross the room.

"Another match," muttered Mutt.

"I'll pledge a coin on milord of Oxford," said Boyle, as he shot some spittle into his palm.

146

"I'll take that bet," said Mutt, who spittled into his own and shook with Boyle.

"The game is rhyming," says Spenser.

"And you shall judge, hey-ho!" cries Nashe.

"He who loses will buy the morrow's meal," says Sidney.

"Let us begin," says Oxford.

"But what topic?" asks Sidney.

"Let's see what's in store," marks Spenser.

"None too easy," pleads Sidney.

"You are poets," answers Spenser.

"Shepherds of the arts," chimes Nashe.

"You shall speak of love and holy days and…"

"And sheeps!" peeps Nashe.

"Yes. And sheeps," laughs Spenser, just to make it troublesome. He then turned to address each poet with a new name, for, as we now know, poets never use their originals. *Poet Perigot,* he addressed Sidney, and *Pleasant Willy,* he named Oxford.

"We are at the ready, *Good Colin,*" shot back milord, tip for tap.

"And begin!" shouted Spenser.

"Hey-ho!" Nashe heaved his mead as they began, with Sidney first and Oxford on the reply.

"*To fell upon a holy eve,*" challenges Sidney.

"*Hey-ho holiday!*" answers Oxford, attempting to both set his rhyme and mock his Nashe at the very same time.

"*When holy fathers wont to shrieve.*"

"*Now ginneth this roundelay.*"

"*Sitting upon a hill so high.*"

"*Hey-ho the high hill.*"

"*The while my flock did feed thereby.*"

"*The while the shepherd self did spill.*"

"*I saw the bouncing Bellibone.*"

"*Hey-ho Bonibell.*"

"*Tripping over the dale alone.*"

"*She can trip it very well.*"

"*The glance into my heart did glide.*"

"Hey-ho the glider."
"Therewith my soul was sharply gryde."
"Such wounds soon waxen wider."
"So learned I love on a holy eve."
"Hey-ho holiday."
"That ever since my heart did grieve."
"Now endeth our roundelay!"

With boisterous cheers and pats o' the backs, the two rhymers were heartily hailed. And barely heard above the roar was Sir Philip's question to Spenser.

"Who has the victory?"

"A sicker round never heard I none!" was Nashe's judgement.

"I deem each has gained!" answered Spenser.

More cheers, and Lord Edward rose with cup in hand. "To Sir Philip Sidney, a most worthy rival."

"Here, here!" the response rose up as the drinks drank down.

"Now, let's to the tables for a bit of peacock," came milord's usual generosity. And as each man made his way back to the store of food and tipple, Lord Edward could feel a tug on his velvet.

"You've just returned from the north?" asked Philip.

"Yesternight," came milord's reply, wishing not to think on it more. "What of your fight in the Low Countries, Philip?"

"Parma took Antwerp. We gained Flushing. Their arms were strong, but in the end, we were the stronger. I hear you met with many numbers."

Lord Edward's mind once again returned to atop that hill, a memory that ever troubled him. "There's not much can be told. I intend, however, to ask her majesty for Command of the Horse in Holland."

"Oh?" Sidney said.

"Have you not heard, milord?" mumbled Gascoigne, with a mouthful o' peacock. "Sir Philip has the post."

"Is't true?"

Sidney answered true, for amongst their life-long rivalries, in military pursuits Sidney seemed always the victor. 'Til the end, of course, but that's a tale to come. Otherways, milord could claim winner in all other contests, in verse, in joust, and in jest, to be sure.

'Tis *The Great Battle o' the Tennis Balls* comes to mind. It seems one day milord had been at his tennis, and Sir Philip barged onto the royal court claiming his time had come to play. And thus began the quarrel. Yet in the reality, it was never about tennis balls at all, but a proposed marriage 'twixt her majesty and a French prince, which milord favored (in public) knowing full-well 'twas never going to hap (in private). But Sir Philip favored not the match, public nor private, being nephew to Lord Dudley and all. And as the French emissaries happed be standing in the upper galleries overlooking the tennis at the time, I'd not put it past milord that this was more a show about a marriage match than a tennis match.

Adding to the discomfiture betwixt the two men, 'twas said milord had previous called out Sir Philip for being a bit of a poetry pilferer, which Sir Philip did not want going 'round, as 'tis hard enough to sell a book without such disparagements. As a poet myself, I know 'twould sting like the dickens to be accused of stealing another scribbler's work when there are only so many words to choose from out of the pile, and 'tis quite easy for an accidental phrase or two to be pilf'd. For even in the best of times and in the worst of times, refraining from calling out a man as a word-thief 'twould be a far, far better thing to do.

Thus, a bit of a battle o' words did ensue on the court, and some tennis balls did hit some heads, and it all ended with milord calling Sir Philip "A puppy!" which we all know to be a son-of-a-cur. So, not to outdo Masters Hall nor Holinshed, this be my historical chronicle of *The Great Battle o' the Tennis Balls*.

But back to the celebration, Sidney verified all.

"I leave next week with Christopher Hatton my lieutenant."

"Hatton!" milord could not believe his ears – nor his eyes, as he looked 'cross the room to the man who was laughing his horse-faced laugh with Dudley. The horse-face was dressed in his usual ill-fitting goose-turd-green doublet and a feathered cap much too tall for his feathered head, making him a cross betwixt a mad baker from Barking and an o'er-weening constable from Clopton.

"Appears he's dressed for battle a-ready."

Nashe approach the earl.

"What shall you do with your funds, milord, now you get them?" he enquired, not fully understanding 'bout the affairs of nobles.

"I shall supply a fleet of ships, travel the Continent, and fund you miserable thread-bare writers," said milord, apparently also ignorant on such matters, and his men cheered.

"And a troop of players, to boot!" finished Oxford.

"Yours shall be best, milord," added Lyly.

"Ours, good Johnny. Ours."

As they spoke, the fifteen-year-old Anne Cecil mustered the courage to approach.

"Who's she, who's she?" dribbled Boyle, drinking up another vessel.

"Why, that's Mistress Cecil," said Mutt.

"The minister's daughter?"

"Look at her," noted Mutt. "Doting on the great lord."

"I'm told 'tis Sir Philip who she dotes with," blabbed Boyle.

"Who told you so?"

"Master Hesterfield."

"Which Master Hesterfield?"

"There's only one Master Hesterfield."

"You mean Master *Willard* Hesterfield?"

"That's the one."

"Well, what about him?"

"Master Hesterfield told me about Sir Philip."

"What about Sir Philip?

"Are you not listening, man?"

"I'm perplexed at the moment."

"Master Hesterfield told me that Mistress Cecil dotes with Sir Philip."

"Master *Willard* Hesterfield told you so?"

"That's the one."

"Her majesty's palsy-handed 'pothecary?"

"There's no other Master Willard Hesterfield, and there's no other of her majesty's palsy-handed 'pothecaries, is there?"

"Well."

"You see?" He nodded to Dudley, who was approaching Sir William. "They negotiate her marriage now."

"I never knew," said Mutt.

"Why should you know?" answered Boyle.

"Did not Lord Dudley beat his man this day?" asked Mutt.

"What man?" asked Boyle.

"Master Gooch," answered Mutt.

"Milord's lute-tuner?" asked Boyle.

"Milord's lute-tuner," answered Mutt.

"What was the cause?" asked Boyle.

"He bowed not deep enough to milord," said Mutt.

"I say!" said Boyle.

"Boxed his ear," said Mutt.

"The good one?" asked Boyle.

"The good one," answered Mutt. "They say Lord Oxford shall marry the queen."

"Who say that?" perked up Boyle.

"Mistress Green told me so."

"Which—"

"Mistress *Nan* Green."

"The queen's single-eyed launder woman?"

"None other."

"She told you such talk? Between the nobles?"

"Better still," smiled Mutt. "She told me such talk between the sheets."

"Ah. But I heard Lord Dudley holds her heart."

"And I hear Lord Edward holds her other parts."

And with that, they cackled like a gaggle of drink-drowned launder women.

"Sir Hatton, too, wishes to marry the queen," said Mutt.

"But you said afore Lord Oxford shall wed her."

"They all desire it."

"Why, of course," continued Boyle. "Would not *you*?"

151

"What?" said Mutt. "And lose my cabinet post?"

"What cabinet post?" asked Boyle.

"Steward of the wine cabinet," answered Mutt, as he downed another goblet.

"You may be right of Hatton. Look how fiery he looks on Lord Edward. They say he too is a poet."

"Oh, for shame."

"Why waste these men on such trivialities, good Mickel Mutt?"

"The trouble with the world, dear Geoffrey Boyle. Men never know their place."

And with that, each man took a new swig from a new cup.

Mistress Anne looked all lovesick into Edward's eyes.

"Many happy blessings, milord, on this your special day," said she.

"Why thank you, Annie," was his short reply.

And as she, with no more words to spend, crossed back to her father, Master Nashe saddled up to milord's ear.

"She's sweet on you, milord."

"'Tis *my* master she pines for!" said Gascoigne.

"'Tis *mine*!" argued Nashe.

"She is promised to Sir Philip," said Gascoigne.

Oxford turned to Sidney. "Is't so, my friend?"

"My uncle and her father do but talk of the matter." Sidney gave a slender grin and stepped away.

Lord Edward turned to Lyly. "You intercepted the letter as I asked?"

"I did, milord."

"What was it Hatton asked Dyer?"

"How he might win her majesty's heart from your favor to his. Hatton wishes to make you look bad in the eyes of her majesty."

"So, that's his game. And Dyer's reply?"

"*Reserve affection to him,* he advised, *for Oxford's boar tusk may both raze and tear.*"

Sidney rejoined them, as Mistress Anne again walked past.

"Your lily, Sir Philip."

"Does not milord find her fragrant?" asked Philip.

"As a sister," came the answer. "For the fairest flower I find still grows in the gardens of Lord Montague."

And with that, fell the smiles of his friends.

"What is it?" Lord Edward read their looks.

"Do you not know?" Sidney asked, turning to the others. "Has no one told him?"

Oxford looked to his men. Reluctant, it was John Lyly who braved the news.

"When you were in the north, milord. We thought you heard."

"Heard what?"

Churchyard looked to Lyly, and then they took milord by the arm and walked him to the chamber entrance. His heart sank as he saw a throng of well-wishers surrounding the fair Mary Montague, holding the arm of her new husband, the second earl of Southampton.

"Southampton," Edward whispered.

"They wed no sooner than you were sent away, milord."

And milord stood there with his heart broke, as Dudley and young Tom Knyvet stood watching.

"Surprise!" Knyvet's yellow grin widened.

"So much for a powerful alliance," said Dudley.

"Who was it saw to this?" asked milord to Lyly.

"You see them now gathered," he said, nodding to Dudley and Knyvet, standing next the buffoonish Hatton.

"Dudley, Hatton," said milord, who then drew his eye toward the serpent. "Who is the snake?"

"Name of Knyvet. Uncle to Mistress Vavasor," Lyly replied, looking beyond the snake to the circle of the queen's ladies-in-wait.

Oxford's eyes were quick drawn to the dark beauty standing at the center. "That Venus who waits on the queen?" he asked.

"'Tis she."

Yet milord's attention turned back toward his fair Mary, trying now to make the best of a thing that was truly the worst.

"What needs a man of wooing, wedding and repenting anyway?" he said, knowing these words to be untrue. "I had but one constant love in all my life, and it is not she."

"Then who, milord?" asked Lyly, for this was news to him.

"Matters not. For the heart I speak of was long ago stolen by a gypsy," said milord in his cryptic way. Why do all these lords employ the cryptic, I wonder?

'Twas then Dudley's servant approached his master. And he bowed. Deep bowed, I might add, having no doubt heard about Master Gooch, the broken lute-tuner.

"Has he been dispatched?" Dudley enquired.

"He's in the yard below, milord."

"Good," was all he answered, as he sent his man to approach Lord Edward.

"You've matched the girl," murmured Knyvet, "but how, milord, do you intend to match the earl?"

"That, my dear Knyvet, has been arranged." And Dudley watched as his man had a word with Lord Edward and then started toward the entry with milord at his heels. "Behold," Dudley announced, "the boy now sent to be a man."

As Edward and the servant approached Dudley and the serpent, Dudley raised his glass. "Birthday cheer, milord." But his awkward smile suggested quite a different intent. He then escorted Lord Edward the rest of the way to the stair.

"'Zounds, no!" said Master Mutt, a bit too loud.

Mister Boyle turned fast.

"What means you, Master Mutt? What means you?"

Seeing Lord Edward ascend up safely, rather than descend down roughly, Mutt then breathed a sigh of relief and took a good swig of whatever was closest.

"For a moment I thought Lord Edward be in danger."

"In danger? But why?"

"I spied Lord Dudley grimace milord. He then took him to the stair and had his hand upon his back."

"What danger is there in that, man?"

"Have you not heard, good Boyle?"

"No, tell me, fine Mutt."

"You know Lord Dudley has a sweet eye for her majesty."

"Tell me a thing I do not know."

"Well, his Lady Amy, his loving bride, has of recent met with a terrible tragedy."

"Do tell. I did not hear."

"Why should you hear?"

"Hear what, Mutt?"

"It appears she was of late found dead. Pushed down a stair. And not one stair neither, but a score o' stair. A flight."

"Of stair?"

"Not of geese, dear Boyle."

"Pray continue."

"They say the Dudley done the deed."

"Who say?"

"They all say."

"And why would they all say? They are always all saying and there's rarely a reason. Couldn't a young lady simply fall down a stair without their all saying?" enquired Boyle. "What proof have you to spread such gossip, my good Mutt? 'Tis easy to fall down a stair, flight or otherways. I fall down them quite frequently."

"They were heard to squabble," Mutt added.

"So?"

"She possessed bruises."

"Still…" hesitated Boyle.

"And her poor neck was broke."

Boyle looked to Mutt, and then to Dudley, in laughs with Knyvet. After a breath, Boyle muttered softly, "Better take care, Lord Edward."

CHAPTER TWENTY-TWO.

DEBTS TO PAY.

Within the queen's chamber, milord stood before the master of the wards, Sir William, who sat at an ornate desk with his ornate account book. And, as if Mary Montague's secret marriage was not shock enough for the lad on this, his special day, a new indignity was about to be thrust upon him. For Robert Dudley had in truth crippled him for the rest of his life, with ne'er the need of a stair to do it.

"But what of all my father's estates?" he asked the ill-eased minister.

"There is little left, I fear," answered William.

"But Lord Robert was entrusted all," milord declared, not understanding then how much hatred was bore him by Robert Dudley, who had been given the governing of milord's estates, 'spite the fact that he was a secret enemy to milord's dear father. "Has he not cared for them as he should?" enquired the young earl.

"It seems, milord, his head is not for business."

"While he plots to sit the rest of him upon her majesty's throne!" spoke Edward, who ofttimes said what many knew, but dared not say loud.

"There are many debts to pay the crown," old Cecil continued.

'Twas then something like the light of dawn finally shone upon milord. "Was his intent to bankrupt me?"

At just that moment, saving the poor minister from denying the truth, he looked down the great passage.

"Her majesty comes," said he, as he rose all respectful.

"But so much gone," was all Edward could say.

"This was none of my doing, Lord Edward," spoke Sir William soft into milord's ear. "Please believe me."

But milord did not know what he could believe. Sir William bowed and went, leaving Edward alone with our beauteous queen. And to young Edward, she was indeed beauteous. Her hair of crimson curled about her delicate ivory face. The rose red of her lips glistened, and her brown eyes pierced. She looked on Edward with affection. She could always rely on this young lord to tell his true mind and reveal to her what might be useful. She enjoyed the lad's jousting skills, marveled at his private poetry, and, when not dancing with Hatton (whose best features were his dancing legs, it seemed), loved couranting with Edward above all others whenever the sounds of Dowland's lousy lutes played. But 'twas his eyes that most captured her, for they were that rare mix of green and tawny brown which always sparked like stars.

"Your majesty," Edward bowed and began. "I humbly request Command of the Horse in Holland."

"Sir Philip Sidney has the post," she answered.

"I beg you reconsider," said milord. "Never has an earl of Oxford failed to serve the crown."

The queen smiled. "Your time shall come, Edward. We know well of your eagerness, but now send Sir Philip."

"With Christopher Mutton!" Milord's heart raced at the very thought.

"His name is Hatton," she corrected.

"Still a sheep that bites at the heels of Sidney," he steamed. "Sir Philip's skills are known, but what can this Hatton do?"

"His bravery is proved," defended her majesty.

"In fashion, I grant!" volleyed milord.

"He is daring," she challenged.

"On the dance floor."

"Many seek his advancement."

"Yes. Up to some scaffold, there to lose his cap."

Her majesty tried to keep her smile from showing.

"He is an accomplished wit."

"Now, there you've gone too far, madam."

"Envy, Edward?"

"Of him, there is no cause."

"His poems can stir a heart."

"A stomach, perhaps." And he could stand this no longer. "His poems?"

"Both he and his man, Gascoigne, top our list for Royal Poet," said she, with the straightest face she could muster.

"What!" he boiled.

"Fear not, dear Edward," she laughed. "For your name rests beside them."

Edward picked up a pike beside the door and offered the handle to the queen.

"Here. Finish me now."

And her majesty wiped a tear from the corner of her eye.

"Royal Poet? Why, if poems be flowers, these men cultivate weeds. With such a post as this, my men, who are more deserving in their sleep, could be well cared for."

His pleas were sincere, for he truly admired none so much as the writers he gave support to. Though he had not much to give, his purse being small, and made all the smaller now he learnt his fortunes were not as great as when his dear father left them.

"Then rest assured, my beautiful boar," said his sovereign, "we shall consider all. But now, on this special day, we must entreat you on another matter. As ward of the crown, your marriage choice has been made. Should you refuse, the penalty is five thousand, which you can ill-afford to pay. So, we do hope you will accept our choice, for this match would make us especially pleased."

And whilst this talk happed in the upper chambers, down below, Masters Mutt and Boyle, blurry-eyed as they be, observed Sir Philip approach a bevy of beauties, amongst the which, the beautiest were the love-sick'd Anne Cecil, the dark Nan Vavasor, and the fair Mary Montague-now-Southampton.

"A shilling says he'll ask Mistress Mary for a dance," said Mutt.

"My money's on Mistress Anne," wagered Boyle, as they spittled, clinked and drinked. However, Sidney took a different approach and neared Sir Christopher.

"He's going to ask Hatton!" said a muddled Mutt.

158

But soon Sir Philip turned direction and by indirection found Mistress Anne. He spoke a word into her dainty ear, and the two pavane'd away.

"Ah-hah!" shouted Boyle, happy he'd journey homeward with an extra shilling in his pocket. "'Tis Anne Cecil!"

"Anne Cecil!" cried an astonished Lord Edward above. "I will not wed the girl!"

"Lord Edward," her majesty replied, "may we remind you of the great service the girl's father has been to us?"

"I shall not wed *him*, neither."

"Who raised you up as a second father."

"I had but one father," insisted the young man. "And a very great lord was he!"

"Indeed, he was. But now we ask you this favor."

"Never!" he said firm. "The girl is but a child."

"It is her station to which you object," said her majesty, quite awares that next to his beloved cuz, the Duke of Norfolk, young Edward held the highest title of all the nobles. "Rightly so. Thus, we shall entitle her father to be known from hence as Lord Burghley."

The young man could not believe his ears. Were titles so easily won as this?

"The grandson of a tapster made lord!" he spoke. "Her lowly state is not the reason nor the cause. I will not do it!" he spoke unmoved.

It was here that her majesty decided to trod a different path. For she knew the young man's affections toward her. Why, all at court had affections toward her. And so, with this in her wiles, she moved to him close.

"My dear Edward," she spoke soft. "You know the truth of this. My heart is yours." Her majesty took the young man's hand allgentle and placed it soft upon her breast. "This marriage shall be of today. And tomorrow, fate has ways to part what we now conjoin."

Milord was reluctant to give in, but a man does strange things when he hears words he has always longed to hear and feels things he has always longed to feel.

"You speak the truth?" he asked, with his face so near to hers that a breath betwixt them was all there be.

"I speak my heart, my heart."

And as he was about to plant his lordly lips upon her royal rosy mouth, a sparkle drew his eye. 'Twas the jewel 'round her porcelain neck. The pendant with Robert Dudley's portrait smiling back at him. And he pulled away rough.

"No! This is all Lord Robert's doing. To weaken the oldest and truest house of England."

"This is none of his doing!" she defended.

"Oh, you almost had me!"

"Do pay regard to whom you—"

"You almost had me gone!" he began to pace. "No, I'll none of it!" he swore, breathing hard 'round the room. "You wear Lord Robert's portrait 'round your neck and beg me kiss it!"

"Lord Oxford!" she was his ruler again.

"You do his bidding."

"I do no man's bidding!" said she, now truly angered. "I am ruled by no man!"

At this, they parted a step from each other, taking in some much-needed air. Lord Edward adjusted his silken hose and was full confused, whilst her majesty now knew 'twas time to thrust her fatal parry.

"Very well," she said calmly. "We shall move you in other ways."

"There is no wind wild enough," answered milord, now thinking of the great house of Vere. "I am the Lord Great Chamberlain."

"And *he* was the Duke of Norfolk," said she, staring out the window overlooking her courtyard below. "Now simply another traitor awaiting the hangman."

Oxford turned and raced to the window, shaken to see his dear cousin Norfolk below, dressed in heavy chains and held by her majesty's guard.

"Is your cousin, I believe."

"You know the rumors are unfounded!" he pleaded, now understanding the true power of this great woman. "You know he is innocent."

"That is impossible," the queen reasoned, "for the crown does not hang innocent men."

That word "hang" hung in milord's head, for are not condemned nobles always given the courtesy of the blade? *How cruel is her heart?* he wondered but dared not speak it.

"He plots to marry the Queen of Scots and replace me in this palace." She then turned to milord. "Marry the girl, Edward, and we shall look more closely at Norfolk's case."

CHAPTER TWENTY-THREE.

THE GRACE OF GOD.

The 1570s.

The bells knelled throughout the palace, and our glorious queen, together with Archbishop Parker, emerged from Whitehall. And nigh upon the Archbishop of Canterbury's tail was Lord Edward and his beaming bride of fifteen, Annie Cecil. Trailing in procession was the newly-made and nearly tearful Lord Burghley, followed by an awkward Robert Cecil and a satisfied Robert Dudley. One with a crooked back and t'other with a crippled soul.

The wedding celebration was all music and dance, but milord's mind was elsewheres, with ne'er a thought on the festivities. He couldn't tell you if they were playing *The Triumphs of Oriana* or *Happy Jack's Undrinkable Ale*. All he knew was that he was a married man who longed to breathe free. He would be found in the corner of the great hall with his fellows that day, and the sweet wines on the table supplied the merriment in his head that milord lacked in his heart.

"I heard your lordship made a run for Italy?" Lyly queried.

"I was full of drink and headed for the shore, but they fetched me back," replied the forlorn lord, who had tried an escape in a fit of confused last-moment desperation.

The earl and his men continued in conversation for many hours, but that day there were no rhyming contests, no tall tales, and no stories of glories to come. All milord could think on was the great fee paid to save the life of his dear cousin Norfolk. And whilst he paid that bill, he yearned for the time he would be free and clear of his burden, this young Cecil sister. The queen had made her bargain, and all Edward could hope was that she would keep it. A tittle did he know.

162

After many bottles were belched, milord took his young bride to the wedding chamber. He opened the door wide and gestured for her to enter. But rather than follow, he took the young girl's hand and kissed it gentle.

"Good night, sweet sister," was all he spoke, and then travelled to his own quarters down the passage, leaving a rather sorrowful young bride to find her own way to bed.

Days went by, and as sour as the notes of their wedding march daily played, a sourer sound milord heard within the dark passages at court. For 'twas going 'round that her majesty's heart was still hard as stone toward Norfolk, and milord could gain no access to her highness to argue his case.

Lord Edward knew his cousin was innocent. But as the dark clouds gathered over Norfolk's temporarily-affixt head, and as her majesty lay unmovable in her anger, milord knew only the grace of God could save his cousin now. Either that, or the grace of milord hisself.

A week later, the earl marched angry down the passage and approached the queen's chambers, guarded by her newly-invested captain of the bodyguard, Christopher Hatton. As Lord Edward stormed toward him, Hatton held tight his pike.

"Halt, my lord," said Hatton, throwing his stick 'cross the door.

"Stand aside, Mutton!" barked Oxford.

"'Tis *Hatton*, my lord," said Mutton.

Lord Edward looked the uneasy fellow in his cocked eye. "If a creature grovel as the queen's sheep, he is therefore a mutton." He thrust away the pike with his hand and kicked open the door with his foot, entering the chamber, where a startled majesty knew not what was happening.

Hatton followed with a timid bow and whimpered, "He was ordered halt, your majesty."

"We shall deal with him," said she, waving her useless mutton out. She turned to Edward. "What means this intrusion?"

163

"I was true to my word!" he said, holding his emotions as well as he could.

"Milord, do you know to whom you address?"

"Found guilty of treason. To be hanged."

"We may do him the kindness of the blade."

"I had your word!" he said, with a tear in his eye.

"A prince is not to be addressed in this manner."

"I had your word," he said and turned to leave.

"And my heart, true heart. But you broke it." This stopped him dead. And now her highness had a tear in her own eye. She went to the table and picked up a long bit of paper. "I know of the grace of God."

★

The rain whipped 'round as Lord Edward watched his prisoner, Peter Pygott, load the provisions. Pygott looked more than a little frighted that night, for what man in his right mind would attempt to sail in such weather?

"A bit soupy, milord!" Pygott shouted above the tempest, knowing not milord is the type of man that looks on tempests and is never shaken.

"I'll pay you fifty more," assured milord. "That shall make it three hundred in sum."

Three hundred! A weighty amount for any endeavor. I'd have been willing to attempt it myself, and I not able to row a raft to save my life.

"My wife shall be provided for," asked a worried Pygott, "should I end up in the drink?"

"She shall," vowed milord. "But you must deliver my man to the Duke of Spain and stop for no ship else."

"The Duke of Norfolk; is he not in royal chains?" asked the worried wherryman.

"Tonight, they remove him from the Tower to Charter House. My men shall intercept and bring him here."

Pygott then spied Lyly approaching. "Here comes your man."

Oxford turned anxious to Lyly. "Where is he?"

"They moved him not," said his fretted friend. "I think our motions discovered."

Milord turned to the sailor and handed him some coin. "Master Pygott, take these and hence away."

"We shall not sail?"

"Tomorrow's another day."

As Pygott rushed off in relief, milord and Lyly secured the bark to the mooring post. That ship with the very unapt name writ on its side: *THE GRACE OF GOD*.

★

"Saved by the Grace of God," said her majesty sadly. "How poetic, Edward. If only I knew a friend so loyal. The prison warder you paid is now under guard, your sailor's again been confined, and I have the confession of the man's wife under seal. Did you think you could get away with such a trick?"

Lord Edward felt lost. "I beg your majesty, my cousin is a man gulled by Dudley, Sir William, and the others. He is merely—"

"A traitor," she concluded. "And what of you, Lord Oxford?"

For the first time, milord felt defeated. He was sinking here at home, and ached to leave this place afore he would be too old to venture forth. Sidney and Hatton and all the lessers had leave to travel, but milord was trapped here. At a home he shared with a girl he could not bring hisself to much care for. A girl, thought he, controlled by her powerful father, the ambitious old Cecil.

"I beg you; I ask yet again for your majesty's permission to fight the wars. Or give me leave to travel far from here, so that I may see other men's lands before I die here in my own."

Now, a keen-witted fellow might think our dear queen would wish to award milord a jailcell and not a journey, but there was ne'er a thing she did that served not herself. And though she felt anger at her young boar, she also understood his true loyalty to the crown, for 'twas not a month earlier that milord alerted her highness to plots laid against her by his own Catholic cousin, Lord Howard, who now

165

languished in the Tower. Her highness also held secret designs for Edward that he alone could fulfill. Which would benefit both her majesty and her state. Because she knew the magic that milord could wield with a pen, for the plays he had begun to write for her court were so very persuasive, she knew him uniquely qualified for the employ she intended. And thus, she allowed her fool a bit of extra rope. Her answer would please both herself and milord.

"You may go," said she. "It shall do you good." And she approached the young man and stared into his eyes of brown and green. "Edward, find the songs you yearn to sing. The poetry of other tongues. But make this promise to England," she said, taking up his hand. "Bring back to our realm these new songs and conquered graces. And give them birth in our own tongue, for the betterment of our own peoples. But return you must, for God has destined you leave your imprint upon your own kith and kind. We shall see our nameless champion once more glory our blessed isle." She then let go his hand. "Now, take your leave."

And with the blessings of Gloriana, milord had his longed-for travels to many strange lands. 'Twas to be an adventure full of dukes, gondols, and a bit o' pilfering pirates.

CHAPTER TWENTY-FOUR.

TO ITALY, TO ROME.

First on his travels was the city of Paris, which many men say 'tis beautiful, but they be mostly men from Paris. 'Twas there milord was finally able to put to use the French mumbles he had wasted so many hours learning as a child. We find him dining with the man he called *Henri*, but the rest of us call his majesty, the king. 'Tis told they dined at the palace, most like because Paris lacks the many fine alehouses that we have in Cockfosters.

After his Parisian doings were done, 'tis no surprise milord's favorite place of travel was the heaven on earth of Italy, which I likeways always dreamt of. His first stop was the Republic of Venice, which so captured his heart that he decided, then and there, to build a house to his liking.

Now, milord never traveled alone. He had with him his serving man Adam, who had belonged to his Hedingham household ever since milord could remember. Adam was a true and faithful fellow who swore he'd follow young Edward to the end o' time, if such a trip should be required. A goodly servant indeed, unlike milord's other man, a whorson puttock by name of Yorke, whose task was to receive and dispense milord's traveling monies. And 'tis a pity he was there, for 'twould have been better had he stayed in England, for all the trouble he caused.

Milord soon found the best way 'round the Rialto was by its rivers, so he made use of the *gondols*, as they call them, which gives a man a smoother ride than a clanking over-priced Thames wherry, to be sure. Whilst in Venice, milord broke bread at the ducal palace with the *doge*, who is a sort of a king.

But as fast as flowing waters run under the Rialto, and afore you could say, "Bravo, Nunzio, now pass me another gorgonzola," milord bid farewell to his doge.

He dared not enter Milan, for fear of the Inquisition, so, in the stead, he turned 'round and journeyed to Genoa, Florence, Sienna, and Rome, which reminds me of a jest I told to a flap-mouthed lout at Dirty Nelly's in Deepditch. I says to this clod one may recall by name of Allen of Nilson on Pendle Hill, "You may *travel* anywheres about the world as you please, but you needs go to Italy to *roam*." And this foolish blockhead adversary o' mine laughed not a whit. He understood not the jest, nor probably never knew there was a city by name of Rome. Some suffer fools gladly; I simply poured my ale upon his noggin. At that, by the way, he laughed.

Not long after, milord returned to Venice to see how that house of his was coming. I suspect not well, as he ne'er moved into it. Perhaps 'twas too costly, for it was at about this time that milord became short of funds, and his no-good receiver Yorke was nowheres to be found that day. Luckily milord met two fellows by name of Baptista and Spinola, who supplied him the sum of five-hundred to keep him in gondols and gorgonzola 'til his own funds could arrive, shrewdly helping to tame milord's temporary bout of poverty.

Then, on one particular summer's day, one more lovely and more temperate than usual, Lord Edward paid visit to the eldest and most respected man of the city, painter Tiziano Vecelli, who called himself *Titian*, all three names of which I never before heard of. Milord was captivated by one of the old man's paintings of a young Adonis being draggled by the goddess Venus. 'Twas no *Madonna of the Yarnwinder*, to be sure, but I think 'twas a thing milord did oft remember.

Not long thereaft milord left Venice, and 'twas a good thing, for soon *la Pestilenza* crept in. And afore long, Master Titian was dead of it, rest his soul.

Milord arrived again in Paris, where the terrible events which would haunt his remaining marriage years began. He received that letter from Sir William. Oh, *Lord Burghley*, we should now call him. 'Twas a letter that would in normal days make a man merry and proud. Which was, in truth, the effect it first had upon milord. 'Til his man, that devious Yorke, put the worm in his ear. But I get atop my ladder here.

Your wife, my daughter, has happily delivered a child, wrote old Burghley to young Oxford, in the hopes to hasten him homeward. Now, this missive was writ and arrived to milord in September. I call attention to the month only because its great import shall be later noted. After hearing of the birth of a young girl they named Elizabeth (what other name dare they give her?), milord did intend to return home. But 'twas here that Yorke played his part, for into his master's ear he dribbled the poison of doubt about the child's parentage.

"He tells you she was birthed in July," whispers Yorke to his master, "but the court is all a-murmur the girl was just now birthed in September." And this is where the months come into play. Wherefore would the father of a child born in July not be alerted 'bout the birth 'til three months' time had passed? Since milord was gone from England for a year, this led him to believe that he had nothing to do with the fathering of the girl.

The court was also a-murmured with another story 'bout the child. For when word was announced of the babe's arrival, 'twas said by some that milord, who ofttimes claimed he had never bedded his wife, had been tricked into it. That he was brought to a chamber one night after a long bout of drinking, thinking he was bedding Mistress Nan Vavasor, when he was in truth topping his own bride. I dare say, if such a trick be played upon a stage, none would believe it.

"A scandal!" warned Yorke, knowing that such calumny would bring great disgrace upon the name Edward Vere. Milord did not then know that Yorke was also in the employ of his Catholic cousin, Lord Howard. The man who hated milord for revealing to her majesty the treasons he had plotted 'gainst her. The man rotting in the Tower whilst milord dinnered with kings and Titians.

Lord Edward thought he had become a stock to be laughed at in the court. And this he could not abide. So, after more months of roaming, he plotted his return. But a tittle did he know there would be battles to fight afore he could get back to England. For he may have expected the Inquisition, but he did not foresee the pirates.

169

CHAPTER TWENTY-FIVE.

BLOOTERS ABOARD.

At the Narrows 'twixt France and England, what appeared to be calm waters met Lord Edward and his men to carry them homeward. There was milord hisself, his faithful Adam, his troublesome Yorke, and a crew of Frenchmen.

Whilst his boat got underway with milord preoccupied, he noticed not the ship manned by Dutch pirates that came upon his vessel rather swift.

"Ho!" yelled an uninspired picaroon, saying exactly what a man would expect an uninspired picaroon to say, as he and his fellow blooters stormed uninvited onto milord's ship with a length o' daggers and a load o' swaggers, gathering all present, disarming them quick, and tying their hands. Lord Edward bravely stood in front of his men, though he could never protect them all, over-numbered as they was.

One by one, they pilfered milord's ship. Their leader was a lout by name of Penders van Portugal, which was a strange name for a tottering maggot-pie who only spoke Low Dutch and never set foot on the unsceptered isle of Portugal. Next came a dog-faced dewberry called Jolly Ned, who wasn't. Followed by a van Cheal, a van Chiljan, a van Geir and a van Grim, all raising their trusted but rusted swords high.

Penders approached my hands-tied lord and very quick-like plundered his silver dagger and embroidered velvet bag before attempting to wrench the new Italian garment off his back. I say *attempting* because it was then that milord, with hands bound, hit him an ungentle clout on the noggin that sent the man soaring down the deck. Van Portugal got up and applied a lucky blow to milord, which caused milord's likeways hand-bound but enbraven'd servant Adam, though unaccustomed to fisticuffs, to cuff a fist soundly onto the lout,

170

which brought my smiling lord back up, and the tossle continued to tassle 'til it was broke up by three more picaroons, the names of who I care not a whit.

By the end, it took all four of them to reave milord's new doublet and shirt from off his back. This done, left half-naked as if they were common criminals from Cockermouth, milord and his men stood tall. All but Yorke, who whimpered like the be-slubbering clotpole that he was.

'Twas then that the Scotsman appeared on the deck of the Dutch vessel, looking a bit pot-shotten. But he was steady enough to recognize who-all was what-all. Ole Mackie Mac-Somesuch, let us name him. At the time, he was a known enemy to her majesty, and had sense enough not to invite a great vengeance upon the whole stinking lot of them. Ole Mackie approached van Horn, captain of the Dutch ship, who was in deep conversation with his boatswain, Master Rodencrantz, standing by the gilded stern.

After a bunch of "Acchhs" and "Occhhs," Mac-Somesuch warned the pirate chief, "Ya dunna ne'er harm the man in the fare. He is England's Laird Chamberlain. I seen his face at cart. Acchh!"

And so, after van Horn worked out a good translation of what was just uttered, a signal was given, and the band of slovenous sea rats began to abandon ship and return to their own. But whilst this was done, milord crossed back to van Portugal, who was leaning 'gainst the side of milord's ship, clutching his booty.

"I shall have this back!" milord said sternly into the face of the stinking pirate, looking to his velvet bag.

"I think not!" said the pirate, as he drew the dagger he had pilfered from milord, believing the work he took in obtaining the ill-got gain meant it was his well-earnt.

"I think so!" answered milord, defiantly clutching the top of the bag, and then, of a sudden, pushing van Portugal over the side of the ship, causing great alarum and a splash so splitting it scared a school o' pilchards below. Even his fellow freebooters could not stop from laughing at the knotty-pated puttock flound'ring 'round the water.

A hero to his men, milord walked over to them, velvet bag in hand. Not wishing for a greater war with England, Captain van Horn let the prisoners sail away. And then considered throwing a rope to van Portugal below.

Thereaft, Lord Edward and his men came ashore at Dover, standing in their near nakedness. However, the earl had his bag, and in it were his gifts for Gloriana.

Widow Sears again took up the role of chronicler to Valentina, for what Master Munday was not privy to regarding the private life of milord, the old cook was happy to inform. Some say happy to *invent*, but what can be known for certain from such long-ago days as this, having been distilled through so many tittle-tattlers?

Milord refused to see his wife and babe when he arrived that night, and for the next five years afterways. But he would never be alone, for soon his heart returned to an earlier passion.

It was eighteen months since Lord Edward had been inside the queen's private chambers. And now he was entertaining Gloriana with tales of his travels. He opened his much-fought-for bag and presented her beaming majesty with a pair of fine bejeweled gloves.

Surprised at the scent, the queen took them to her nose. "Perfumed!" she cried.

None in England had ever heard of perfuming a glove ere this. Course not. Why would one perfume a glove?

"A pearl necklace from Venice, for the most beautiful pearl neck in all the realm," he charmed, as more tokens emerged from his bag.

"Tell me of your travels," she smiled, enjoying both the gifts and the visit, having truly missed the man.

"I dined with the duke your cousin, was awarded a spear for enchanting spells, and sailed down the old seacoast of Bohemia, where I met a beggar man.

Sweet Signore? pled the man.

My good man, quoth I.

I pray you, might I beg a sixpence for the mercy of God?

172

A sixpence? says I. *What wouldst thou say if I give you ten pound?*

Ten pound! the man near faints away. *Why, that would make a man of me.*

"And I handed him ten pounds, causing many a joyful tear. But fear not, for I always keep strict accounts and had my man write in his book: *Item. Ten pounds. For making a man!*" And milord laughed, and her majesty laughed with him.

"In Genoa, I mustered troops alongside the mighty Prospero Fattinanti." Her majesty gasped, feigning she knew the signore. "He was soon made Duke and is fighting hard to unite the two noble factions there. He has asked me if I, with her majesty's gracious permission, may be made Duke of Milan."

"No."

"I shall inform him so," said milord with a bow of the head, anticipating as much. "On the isle of Sicilia, I challenged all manner of man in defense of my great prince. Yet no man durst be so foolish to encounter me. 'Til the journey home."

"How I've missed you," the queen spoke, jumping up and running to her door. "I must show my ladies," she cried, as she left the chamber with her perfumed gloves in hand.

But, as she progressed down the passage, a sound stopped her halfway to her destination. It was a woman behind a door. And as her majesty peeped in, her heart sank, for she could see one of her ladies there being wooed. And the one doing the wooing from atop was no other than her favorite, Lord Dudley. There was no question about what was happening. And her majesty felt all a-flush, as the blood rushed from her heart to her head. She slowly backed away, and knowing not where to walk, she returned to her chamber where Lord Edward waited. He could see that all her happiness was gone.

"What is it?" he asked. Her majesty was for once unable to answer. "Do you not like them?"

Our good queen was on the very verge of royal tears, a state few had ever witnessed.

"Oh, my dearest," she finally uttered. "They are so beautiful." And with those words out her mouth, she sank onto the white ermine that lay next to her burning hearth. With her delicate hand, she motioned he sit down beside her. When he did, she softly said, "Tell me of your broken heart, my knight."

"What means her majesty?"

"With the one you love now gone."

"If you speak of my young bride," he said, "it is not my heart she has wounded but my name."

The queen knew that Edward had never warmed to the girl that had been thrown in his way. But she was always keen at reading the hearts of her courtiers.

"I know your eyes look to Montague." And Edward's soul stirred at the very sound of Mary's mention. "'Tis strange," the queen reflected, "so many souls now so solitary. Your Anne sits home and weeps. You dote on Mistress Mary, who is also alone."

"Alone?" For milord did not know about her husband's lot.

"Southampton's been arrested. More plots from Rome. And here we are," said she, as she faced him close, "together, but too far apart."

And here the queen pressed her lips to his. And he sure kissed her back, for what else was an obedient subject to do? Although, if any man would dare refuse her majesty, tongues would waggle that it would be milord. And now, milord's tongue did waggle a bit with her majesty's. And modesty forbids me tell more. Just to say, there was more waggling to tell, and I shall leave it at that.

Next morning, milord found hisself awaked by sounds of verbal combat. He crossed to the door and could see her majesty having it out with Dudley. They fought valiantly with words. At first came curses. Then pleas. Then forgiveness. And soon, milord could see them embrace and touch lips.

Lord Edward's horse was soon passing the palace gates, with milord pushing hard the reins. Traveling a good five mile per gallop, he raced both horse and mind, as thoughts came to him that he would, of course, later turn to verse.

174

If women could be fair and yet not fond,
Or that their love were firm not fickle still,
I would not marvel that they make men bond
By service long to purchase their good will;
But when I see how frail those creatures are,
I muse that men forget themselves so far.

Milord never stopped 'til he arrived at Southampton House. 'Cross town at Whitehall, her majesty and Dudley were playing the beast with two buttresses, as they say. Down the river at Cecil House, wife Anne sat holding tight her new babe Elizabeth. And over town with milord and Mistress Mary, these two were playing at the same game that the queen and Dudley had begun.

"And now…" told Widow Sears, as she leaned into Valentina and said almost in a hush, "…now begins the story of the babe."

CHAPTER TWENTY-SIX.

THE STORY OF THE BABE.

The widow's eyes opened wide, reflecting the candlelight. She spoke of Mary Montague, who stood many months later, looking out the door onto her lone Southampton Manor, caressing tight her newly-arrived and tender-hearted infant.

"At the very same time," the old cook continued, "'twas rumored our dear queen lay dying, refusing to see any of her court for near half a year," and she bedabbled her eyes once more.

The frail queen rest in her chair by the window, having lost much of the very little color her face ever held. Her ladies stood by in quiet prayer. Milord held conversation with her, and not long thereaft 'cross town, his men played a similar conversing upon the stage.

"Your majesty," Oxford approached his queen.

"Ill met by moonlight, proud Titania," Oberon approached.

"Fair maidens, away," Elizabeth waved them off.

"Fairies, skip hence," waved Titania.

"Your health?"

"Improved, dear Edward."

"Then all my prayers have been heard," said he.

"We understand Mistress Mary has birthed a child."

"You know I come to claim the boy," milord answered.

"I do but beg a little changeling boy," demands Oberon.

"Set your heart at rest," settles Titania. *"The fairy land buys not the child of me."*

"You shall claim him not," settles Elizabeth.

"Lord Southampton is his son!" Valentina concluded.

"A secret son," answered the widow, "Old Southampton being locked in the Tower and all."

And whilst Widow Sears knew it not, 'twas then, I am told, Lord Burghley altered the Treasons Act.

"Did Lord Edward never claim him?" asked the beauty.

"He could not," frowned the widow. "And soon, old Southampton died and young Henry become ward of the crown. Her majesty sent him far from Edward. Off to the wars, where he proved a right brave soldier. And I hear the king that now lives has sent Henry, now grown old, off to fight new battles." The widow sighed. "Shall these wars never end?"

Valentina sat in full fascination, whilst Master Munday went into the garden to tend to some flowers that had accidentally popped up betwixt a patch of weeds.

"No more can I say," she looked up to Valentina, "for no more do I know. How's the soup?" she smiled.

★

The 1580s.

If a fellow was to tell me about a boy whose very life was saved because he could not sing a song, I should find it a very unlikely stone to swallow. But true it was.

On Great Bartholomew lived the kindly gentleman from Norwich, Sir Hugh Clifton, who had always a smile on his face whenever he gave his young son Thomas the usual morning embrace and then sent him out the door. Sir Hugh was proud of his boy, who was good natured and witty. Thomas was a good son, and Sir Hugh was so glad to have him, especially as he came rather late in the man's life, as a joy that has been long waited on is all the more to cherish.

"'Tis the best day o' my life!" young Thomas had a habit of saying, near every day of his living, whether upon receipt of a new toy, or just a fine walk down Windmill Lane. This was how happy a lad he was.

A warm embrace and then out the door was the scene they played every morning. Into the dawn air, Thomas Clifton crept, making the short journey from their home on Great Bartholomew, down Cheapside, over Friday, up Paternoster, and into the grammar school at Christ Church. 'Twas a mere half-mile westward, but the cold that morning made the journey seem double by half.

This being a Thursday, 'twas only a half-day of Greek and arithmetics, so by noon he'd be traveling back. But a title did he know that on this Thursday, he'd not be making the trip home.

It appeared a usual day, and by that, I mean 'twas a dismal and over-peopled and boisterous day. But the moral of this telling is found in the great pity 'tis that lads of thirteen don't oft look 'round them as they traverse the busy streets of a city. I suppose country lads don't oft do the same neither. How many look left, whilst an angry tap-shackled bull is charging right?

Young Thomas' mind, rather than being watchful of his surrounds, was occupied in the stead on the Greek verse he was meant to memorize but hadn't, and on young Alice Aldebourne, with the pretty golden curls, who he would sometime spy at the front of Christ Church when she accompanied her brother, Ayland, Thomas' class-fellow. 'Tis a shame his eyes were not on the danger that lay in wait for him within the alley 'twixt Newgate and Fleet.

As the son of a Norwich gentleman, his future was fixed by fate for a life many boys his age merely dreamt on. But fate took not his side that morn, and the lad entered the alley, not knowing about the Welshman, Henry Evans, nor his muscle, James Robinson, who waited there for his approach.

★

1624.

Old Master Munday re-entered King's Place and handed the few wilted daffodils he'd rescued to Widow Sears, whose old wrinkles lit like a lantern. As she went into the kitchen to find a pot to put them in, Old Munday opened a window-board to let in the light.

178

"You knew Lord Edward well?" she asked.

"The Folly," said he, all-mysterious. He took a moment to look about the room, and then sat next to Valentina. "He was a great man," said Munday, with a watery eye. "Always revealing truth. Those were his family words, you know. *Vero nihil verius*. Nothing truer than truth," Munday looked up to the family crests that hung on the walls.

Through the particles of sunlit dust that magically flittered by, Valentina could now better see the tapestries on the walls, proudly proclaiming the blue boar and the golden star of the Veres. Her eyes then wandered to a small, feathered cap at the room's corner, held there by an iron nail. The cap that many a time made Master Munday water an eyeful of loss and guilt, which is why he oft avoided looking on it. He then pulled from his pocket a worn piece of metal star, touching it ginger-like.

"He was our star of England, we used to say. We wore 'em proud," he smiled. "And still each night, I look up to him in the sky."

"He was the star!" Valentina grasped and looked into Munday's eyes. "Tell me of the moon."

CHAPTER TWENTY-SEVEN.

THE SNATCHING OF THE SONGLESS BOY.

The 1580s.

Paternoster Alley was empty that morning, but for young Thomas Clifton entering from the east, old Henry Evans waiting at the west, and big James Robinson hiding in the midst. As Thomas passed, with eyes ne'er looking east nor west, and with a head full of tender words to give young Alice Aldebourne, the brutish Robinson jumped out and snatched the lad, keeping a gloved hand over the boy's cries, as he drug him to Master Evans and on to Blackfriars, not a cat's throw from the scene.

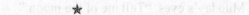

Young Munday was daily to be found at Fisher's Folly, where milord gathered his men to birth what they hoped would be a new English tongue. What was wrong with the old tongue, I never learnt. Who Master Fisher be, and what his folly was, I am likeways ignorant. But the names of places oft have never a thing to do with the place itself. Take the Drunken Duck on Dark Alley. Having spent the better part of three-and-thirty years there, I never once saw a duck present, let alone one that was besotted. A dizzy-eyed cat, yes, but a drunken duck, never.

At Fisher's Folly, milord cultivated his crop of Euphuistic scribblers to write their new plays. And to present them onstage, he assembled Oxford's Men at the Boar's Head and the Chamberlain's Men at The Globe. He even patron'd a gaggle o' youth called Oxford's Boys, which be the best lads with unbroke voices in all of Blackfriars.

But afore any play could be acted, words first had to be writ. And most was writ right here at Fisher's Folly. In addition to advice, milord furnished books, bottles, quills and inks. In attendance was always the ever-merry Tom Nashe, the soldier-turned-writer Thomas Churchyard, and the jolly Johnny Stubbes.

At the door, stood the serious-minded Marlowe, who for a time was a writer and for a time was a spy. Next to milord, quills ever in hand, were his two indispensables, Lyly and Munday. Lord Edward stood at table's end quoting aloud.

> *Fair and fair, and twice so fair,*
> *As fair as any may be;*
> *Thy love is fair for thee alone,*
> *And for no other lady.*

He turned with a grimace.

"Gentlemen, we can do better than this. We must create a new English language if we are ever to create a new English man. Our words can alter policy, encourage the doubtful, and lift the base-minded man to virtue. Munday, you fashion the new plays for the Boy's Company, Churchyard, the translations. Tom?"

"Pamphlets, milord," grinned Nashe.

"Hey-ho," smiled Edward, and the others laughed. "Stubbes, what you?"

"Anonymous tract, milord. On our queen's marriage proposal from the French duke."

"Careful with that one, Johnny," warned Oxford, knowing full-well the dangers that any opinions of her majesty could bring.

"Quite anonymous," said Stubbes.

"At what are you about, Master Marlowe?"

"Grand drama, milord," he answered. "Intrigue. Passion. Revenge." He bowed and exited the scene.

Nashe approached. "Speaks he of his writings or his life?"

Milord turned to face his men. "I have much hope for him, but for now be wary."

"Still in the spy game, they say," added Munday.

This troubled Stubbesy. "He would not betray us?"

"Afraid he'll tell the queen you think her advisors none but flatterers and her highness too old to marry?" poked Nashe.

Oxford turned quick. "You wrote that, Johnny?"

"I may have *suggested* it," Stubbes said.

"Excise those lines!" ordered milord. "She'll have your head."

And with that, Stubbes picked up his quill and, turning away so the others could not see, made a fatal error. For instead of crossing through the lines, he simply crossed under them. 'Tis the unfortunate flaw of all writers, as there's something in each scribbler's stubborn soul that tells him, no matter the danger, his every syllable is worth a pound of gold. 'Tis a pity these writers know not a pound of gold from a pound of flesh.

★

Once inside Blackfriars, Robinson dropped the lad onto the floor and went out for more, as Henry Evans barked an order, which the frightened boy took to be a command for silence. 'Twixt the lad's fright and the Welshman's thick tongue, 'twas hard to understand the man. Young Clifton looked 'round, and to his surprise, the chamber where he lie was no pirate's den nor putrid prison, but a playhouse. There was a stage at one end, benches 'round the sides, and a dozen boys within.

"By Got, be quiet, boy!" commanded Evans to the shallow-breathing lad. He grabbed a small book of musical scratchings and held it out. "You can read this?" demanded the man.

"N-No, sir," said the scared boy.

"You can sing?" the Welshman became concerned.

"N-No, sir," repeated Thomas, which caused the frowning Welshman, who thought the boy a singing boy, to think quick, and then take from his doublet some other pages.

"Then you're a player now, boy," he said, tossing the papers to him. "Learn it, by Got!" And he stormed off.

It wasn't long afore Henry Evans approached the scared Thomas. Now, this Henry Evans wasn't the old man who had snatched

182

him, but a young lad of about the same age as Thomas. And truth be told, it was never clear why he went by the name of Henry Evans, for he was not the son of the boy-snatcher, and 'twas not the name he was birthed with neither. Thomas learnt that young Henry lived in the house of the snatcher but could get little else out of the lad. 'Twas not the first time this boy had a changed name, and 'twould not be the last, but I get ahead of my turkey-quill here.

Thomas learnt more from Henry, once the ice 'twixt them melted a bit. Old Master Evans, as I shall call the boy-snatcher, was not your usual nabber, for he was also tutor to the boys that lived here. And that meant he was now Thomas' tutor. But what he taught them was never Greek nor arithmetics, but pronouncing and presenting. He was manager of the Children of the Chapel Royal, where some children were meant to sing in the choir and others to perform in the plays. And as young Thomas was taken to sing, but could not sing, he would then join the company of boy players and not boy singers. He was to act in their next masque. Course, like Henry the younger, the Children of the Chapel had a second name. For they were also called Oxford's Boys.

★

"Milord," said Munday, turning to the business of the day. "'Tis going about that Lord Burghley shall retire as secretary, and in his stead, her majesty wishes to appoint his son Robert."

"Heaven help us!" cried Churchyard.

"She would not do this, would she?" feared Munday.

"We're all done for!" fretted Nashe. "He's a sworn enemy to the stage."

"Calm yourselves, men," assured milord. "As long as the nobles have her majesty's ear, she shall rule temperately. And there are many good men who advise her against such an act."

"You'll tell her for us, milord?" worried Stubbesy.

"I give you my name on it," answered Lord Edward. And satisfied with such an oath, the men returned to their work.

There were only so many streets that his dear son could have traversed, Sir Hugh thought, as he tread with heavy heart, to and fro, from Great Bartholomew to Christ Church. Over and over, he walked, since the time he discovered his precious son had not returned from school.

After the noontime meal, milord returned to the Folly to find constables unceremoniously evicting his writers and throwing a heavy chain across the door. In front stood Baron Horatio, milord's cousin. Course his real name was Horace, but ever since milord returned from Italy, he was called by his Italian moniker. He turned to see milord arrive with Lyly and Munday and approached.

"What do they want?" enquired Edward.

"The rent," said Horatio. "And the playhouses are closed." He then moved closer to speak in confidence with milord. "Cousin, her majesty desires histories. She does not want private confessions nor court intrigue to be played upon the stage. Given your last show of *Midsummer*, I fear this is a personal message to you: rein in your men."

"MILORD!" came Churchyard's cry, as the old soldier was being draggled away by the constables.

"What mean you men?"

"Beg pardon, milord," the officer answered. "But this one is being taken to debtor's prison."

"What is his debt?" asked Oxford.

"You'd 'ave to speak to the warder, your grace."

Oxford turned to Churchyard. "I'll get you out, Thomas," he assured him.

And they draggled the poor man off, with him yelling, "Thank your worship!"

184

Oxford turned to Lyly and Munday. "Have the men gather at my rooms at the Savoy." He then spoke to Horatio. "I am in desperate straits, dear cousin."

★

Sometime, *who* a man knows is much more of import than *what* a man knows. Not that from mine own life I can attest to either, for most of the bum-baileys what I knew did me very little good. And the things what I learnt commonly caused me more mischief. But so the river runs.

What happened next could only be described as a twist o' fine fate, a bit o' good luck, or a semblance o' divine intervention. You choose. For as the broke-hearted Sir Hugh trod that path for the fifth time that afternoon, he spied a young lass with golden curls standing a-front of Blackfriars. And if one's smelling nose is fastened on a-right, one might sniff out that this be young Alice Aldebourne, sister to Thomas' class-fellow. And as to the whys and the wherefors that caused her to be standing at the very place where young Thomas was held, 'twould take a story as long as a book to explain. Leave it to be said, she was standing there.

Sir Hugh was about to approach the girl when, of a sudden, he heard angels sing, which caused him to turn 'round and approach the window. There, off to the side where the boy players waited, he spied his son! Relief rushed to his heart, and he burst inside and embraced the boy like he had never done before. With their joyful reunion done, father asked son and son told father all he knew. 'Twas right in the midst of *If Ye Love Me* that the crooked eye of old Evans caught sight of this reuniting and, whilst giving signal for the boys to keep singing, he marched over to them afore they could get out the door.

"By Got, what means this intrusion?" demanded the Welshman.

"By God, what means you taking my boy?"

"This boy is now member of the Children of the Chapel. He shall be a player before her majesty and, from now, he be in my care."

And with that, Evans took hold of the boy, which caused his father to break between them.

"A player! Do you have any idea..." he fumbled for the words. "To take the only son... I shall get a constable forthwith!"

As Sir Hugh went to take his son, Evans stopped him. "I have an impress from her royal majesty!"

"What's this?"

From within his dirtied doublet, Evans pulled out a worn paper. "By Got, 'tis true. This boy is here by order of Queen Elizabeth."

Knowing much about the law, Sir Hugh viewed the page.

"I am merely doing my duty, by Got!" barked Evans.

Clifton looked over the impress careful and saw many words that threw his heart into a sea of deep despair. Her majesty, in truth, did have the power to have any boy of the realm took into service of the crown, whether to sail seas or sing songs. But, alas, as Sir Hugh perused the page, there was but one lone word that caught his eye, and he hoped it might be the ship to rescue them both. He gave the paper back to Evans and knew that something must be done fast.

Reluctant, he took his son aside and told him never fear, as he would soon come back for him. With an embrace, and a *God b'uy you*, and a promise of quick return, Sir Hugh left Blackfriars, feeling like he left half hisself behind. He was now determined as ever.

As his father left him, the boy knew not what to think, for he loved his father, and he loved his home, and he never felt anything but happiness for his life. He did not wish to act upon the stage. And, truth be told, he was no Henry Condell.

For the rest of the day, he was made to learn speeches and walk the stage alongside the other boys. And as he did so, he wondered how many of them had been took from their streets. Were they orphaned or snatched? He never dared ask.

Whilst this was done, his father marched straight to Wardrobe Place. But his mind was never on a visit to his tailor to fit him a new pair of buskins, biggins and slops. For this is where the saying about *who* a man knows comes in. His feet were swiftly taking him to find the Master of the Great Wardrobe, who also happed to be Chancellor

186

of the Exchequer. Sir John Fortescue. And a man with many titles should have great power, one would think. Power which Sir Hugh hoped could be used to free his son.

That night, within his soundless house, Sir Hugh sat in one, at his table for two, and could not bring hisself to eat nor drink nor do any but think upon his lone son.

CHAPTER TWENTY-EIGHT.

AND THE SERPENT DIED.

Sweet music filled the air of her majesty's gardens. On the platform, Master Lyly and the afore-met Welshman Evans, by Got, were giving their last-minute guidance to Oxford's chapel singers, whilst the chapel players were there to provide audience. Thomas Clifton sat there, too, most confused about the turns his life had took these last two days, and full of apprehension of what was to come. A tittle did he know that what was to come was about to come.

The gardens were well-peopled, with our good queen seated betwixt a Dudley and a Burghley. Lord Edward stood on t'other side of the bushes in secret conference with Munday. And all manner of lords and ladies filled in from the lilies to the lilac. The ministers of the wine cabinet, Masters Mutt and Boyle, enjoyed the pageantry perhaps more than the nobles, as they stood there holding (and emptying) their wine trays afore them.

Soon, Munday left milord to find his fellow conspirator and discuss their recent march upon a mutton. Horatio approached milord, who was busy glaring upon the serpent, who looked rather sickly this day. More so than was usual. Near her highness, her lovely ladies sat, with the beautiful Knyvet niece, Nan Vavasor, holding the full attention of all men who had eyes. Yet, her own gaze was given to Lord Edward alone.

Boyle made good view of them. "Milord looks rather cross today."

Mutt asked, "Which lord is that?"

"Lord Edward, the Italianate earl," said Boyle.

"The Italian et what?" said Mutt.

"They call Lord Oxford the Italianate earl."

"Who do?"

"The court do. Since his travels."

"Travels to Italy?"

"Of course, travels to Italy. Why, you wouldn't call a man the Italianate earl for his travels to Ingleby Barwick, would you?"

Mutt made good view of Knyvet, who shot his angry visage toward Lord Edward, who had just thrown a secret kiss to Lady Nan.

"Not half as cross as that Knyvet fellow," he observed.

"Is that Knyvet's cousin Lord Oxford just puckered?" asked Boyle.

"Mistress Nan," said Mutt. "'Tis why the Knyvet is vexed, and I can sure tell you a tale."

"Then tell it, man."

"First, I am told she had a child by Lord Oxford."

Stupefied, Boyle nearly dropped the tray of wines he was drinking from.

"Who told you thus?" he asked.

"I have it on good account," answered Mutt.

"Then account for it, man," demanded Boyle.

"'Tis true," Mutt asserted. "Master Ricketts told me."

"Master *Robert* Ricketts?"

"How many Master Ricketts dost thou know?"

"I know a Master Robert Ricketts, a Master Ralph Ricketts, a Master Roger Ricketts, and a Master Rafe Ricketts."

"I knew not there were so many Ricketts 'round."

"There you have it."

"Hold on. Master Ralph Ricketts and Master Rafe Ricketts are the same Ricketts."

"Are you sure?"

"'Tis the same name, my Boyle."

"I never knew, good Mutt. I never knew. So, which was it told you?"

"Told me what?"

"'Bout what you were speaking of."

"What *was* I speaking of?"

"I do not remember," said Boyle. And then, neither of them remembered. And so, both of them returned to the listening of the music. And the adjusting of the silver cups upon the silver trays. And the peering at the peers that peeped by 'til, of a sudden, Boyle recalled.

"Oh!" shouted he all excited, nearly tippling over his tumblers. "The fellow who told you Mistress Nan had a child by Lord Oxford!" he said too loud, as some nearby nobs turned and gave him the look.

"Oh yes. Master Ricketts told me."

"I *know* Master Ricketts told you. We've been 'round this rosy."

"Right."

"Master *Robert* Ricketts?"

"The same."

"The queen's one-leg'd shoemaker?"

"One and only."

"Go on."

"Seems a boy was birthed by Lady Nan, and Lord Edward claimed him rightly. And at that, our queen threw plate and dish all over the chamber. The good plate, mind you. The breakable plate. And when she had done throwing plate, she threw all three of them to rot in the Tower."

"The Tower. What three?"

"Are you listening, man?"

"I thought I be."

"Milord Oxford, Mistress Nan, and the babe."

"'Zounds!"

"Christ's wounds!"

"And they shall rot there?" asked Boyle, foolishly.

"You see them here, do you not?" Mutt turned to the fool.

"Oh, yes," said he, putting down his cup.

"Then, her majesty run Lord Edward out of court 'til the time he promised to return to his own wife, Anne. The one that had her own babe without milord's assistance, whilst he was busy enjoying the wines of Italy."

"Oh, I enjoy those wines," interjected Boyle, picking up his cup again.

190

"As do I," intersperse'd Mutt. "And now that Lord Edward is back with Countess Anne, the queen has allowed him back to our royal gardens," Mutt finished his tale.

And Boyle stared him on.

"And it is indeed nice to have him back with us."

And Boyle waited still.

"What?" asked Mutt.

"And?" asked Boyle.

"And what?" asked Mutt.

"And the Knyvet?" asked Boyle.

"Oh!" said Master Mutt, now, of a sudden, remembering why this river began to flow in the first place. "Her cuz, the Knyvet, made a terrible stir, and promised to be revenged upon Lord Edward for the disgracing of his family honor."

"I knew not his family had any honor."

"'Tis here nor there."

"Lord a mercy!" said Boyle, grabbing a goblet.

"And some of the Knyvet men have been battling in the alleyways with some of the Oxford men, as if these be the unruly streets of ancient Italy."

"I wondered why the streets were unruly of late."

"'Tis the reason."

"And what do they say the Knyvet said?"

"*Better she was a murderer,* they said he said, *than a punk strumpetty waggle-tail!*" concluded Master Mutt.

Mister Boyle could say not a word after that. He just looked upon the serpent.

Now, a man may wonder why this Knyvet fellow was given the title of serpent, so, to satisfy the undersatisfied, the tale has it that when he was a young ruffian, he was bit in the Butts Field by a serpent.

And the serpent died.

"Oh, Horatio," Lord Edward moaned, "the howling hounds of hell do haunt me still."

And Horatio turned to him. "That's a bit flowery, is it not?"

"I fear I now have troubles with the printers, who have orders not to publish my works."

Just then, a lone Dagenham dog howl'd loud as the crooked Robert Cecil approached.

"Even the curs show taste," whispered milord.

'Twas here Lyly and Munday ran up. Their smiles revealed that the secret play milord had writ 'gainst an enemy was about to begin.

"He comes, milord!"

"Did you put it in his ear?" he asked Lyly. "'Tis her majesty's favorite fashion?"

"This morning, just as you instructed."

"You did not tell him direct?"

"No, for we knew he would suspect. So we made certain he was nigh-by, and Munday and I spoke loud, so he may overhear the conversation."

"Good work, boys," milord was pleased. "I must remember that trick."

And without much ado, each head turned to the path, where their unknowing clown now entered the stage. 'Twas Hatton. And as he neared, all lords and ladies stood a-shock'd.

"My dear Hatton," smiled milord, "never troubled with any substance of wit."

Horatio could not believe his eyes. "You told him wear *yellow* hose?"

"But 'tis the criss-cross of the garters completes the man, methinks" said milord, as he approached Hatton.

"May I ask, Sir Mutton, the meaning of the hose?"

"The hose, milord?"

"The yellow hose."

"They are but hose."

"Have you a dog, then?"

"What dog, my lord?"

"A dog that makes water."

"Water, my lord?"

"I wonder, did a dog make water 'gainst your hose?" And the men laughed.

"Why, really, my lord!"

"And why do your legs show anger?" Oxford persisted.

"Anger?" cried the man.

"Why your garters, they appear quite cross." And they laughed more.

"'Tis the fashion," said Hatton, near to tears.

"Is this so, Sir Mutton?"

"The name's *Hatt*—"

And as if to spare this mutton, a lone hautboy signaled the performance was at hand.

"Go thy ways, good mutton, go thy ways," and Hatton walked over to join the queen. "Was he not warned that the boar tusk may both raze and tear?" Milord then turned to watch her highness. "Now, see her majesty's face."

They all spied her highness, who appeared outraged.

"Master Lyly?" enquired milord all innocent. "Did we neglect to tell this poor fellow that this was the very look King Henry wore the day he chopped off the head of our dear queen's mother?"

"Dear me," Lyly acted his part. "We may have forgot that small detail, milord."

"You throw daggers," turned Horatio to his cuz.

CHAPTER TWENTY-NINE.
THE BOY WITH A BORROWED NAME.

The boys began to sing some Tom Tallis, who made famous such buskin-tappers as *Ave* something and *Salve* something else. 'Twas a beautiful sound, to be sure, but not at all like what I preferred to sing as a lad, such as the ever-pleasing *Two Maidens Went A-Milking*. I never knew who writ that ditty, as the best works oft lay unclaimed, I have learnt. And I admit, earthy songs as these might not be fit for such a noble crowd, but one man's rose garden is another man's rumple-room, so they say.

Now, the name Oxford's Boys must not lead a country tinker to think the four-and-twenty lads were all of Lord Edward's making. Industrious he was, but every bowstring has its limits, and these limits may be stretched only so far. These were the boys Lord Oxford lent his name and coin to. But the official record states milord was father to only three living daughters from the deceased Anne Cecil. As for the rest, *it is silenced*, as one great poet once writ.

I fear I may have spilt the beer here by calling poor Anne Cecil deceased. And since I cannot take back what has already been dribbled, I shall simply say that if milord's life was a book, we would be a mere three chapters away from the touching death of his poor wife Anne.

Returning now to the number of branches sprouting off milord's tree, his unofficial numbers of offsprings is much open to debate, depending upon whose lies you believe. There was the base-born son of Nan Vavasor, name of Edward, which milord rightfully acknowledged. There was a son grown up at Southampton House, name of Henry, which milord was never allowed to acknowledge. There will be another boy, also named Henry (milord must have liked that name), who is yet to come, which would spring-off from his second marriage to the countess. And who knows what-else from where-else, for milord dipped his quill into many an ink pot. And the nobles keep tight lips when they have a mind to.

After the boys had done with their first song, her majesty led Lord Edward down the long garden path. He had hoped for this conference, and now it was begun.

"What is it troubles you, Edward?"

"I am a poor creature," he began, "who cannot help my own men."

"You wish relief?" she asked. "Tell us your terms." Ever the bargainer, her majesty knew that if she could give one thing, she would get tenfold back.

"Open the playhouses and the coffers. That is my request, your majesty."

The queen thought on this for a moment, for there were, in truth, things she wanted from milord. She was about to bring her Scottish cousin Mary to trial and needed his vote. She also needed something else.

"We can open the playhouses. And finance them. But what in return, dear Edward?"

"Merely ask," said milord, his heart for the first time in a long time rising with the promise of hope.

"We now pretend to woo France to buy time. While Spain is arming against us," she began, "we want you and your men to write the histories of our past. To prepare our subjects for the battles to come, the fight against Rome, and the sacrifices that must be made."

This idea excited milord, who thought back to the days of his invisible knighthood.

"That we can do."

"And we shall fund it," said she. "But one thing else."

"Simply name it."

"We want your loyalty."

"I have always been loyal to the crown."

"No," said she, and his new-rising heart now started to fall like Icarus, for he knew what she intended. "We want your public loyalty."

Milord was caught betwixt a rock and a Hardington riverbed. He knew that, to get his men free and supported proper, free to create a new England even, he had to make this bargain, no matter what others may think.

"Agreed," said he.

"You have our word," she said.

"And your majesty has mine."

Of a sudden, there was a commotion upon the stage as two corpulent constables were dragging off of it a very irate Welshman.

The queen looked to Edward. "Interesting epilogue, milord. Is't new?" she asked, as she dismissed him to see what was the matter.

"What means this?" Lord Burghley approached the officers.

"We've a warrant for this man's arrest, milord."

'Twas then that Sir Hugh snatched up his very perplexed and now joyful son Thomas into his arms. Together with his boy, he approached Burghley and explained all, including that one word from the impressment that so saved his son.

For he had learnt that the paper Evans held was very specified, as it gave him the royal right to obtain boys to sing as — and this be the most important word on that document — *choristers.* The queen's consent was strict for boy choristers only, and not boy players. But Thomas was being held as a player and *not* a chorister. And since he could not sing a song to save his life, it appeared that it did, in truth, save his very life.

Evans was being hauled away with a few strong "By Gots!" shouted out alta voce, as many onlookers looked on. Lord Edward arrived and just then learnt, for the first time, of how his choirmaster procured young Thomas and some of the other boys. As the wild Welshman pleaded for his help, the irate earl had a few strong *By Gots!* of his own, which ended in Evans' dismissal.

And it should be noted that once milord had been made aware of the soliciting practices undertook for his Oxford's Boys, and after all those taken lads were took back from whence they had been took, he ordered his new-hired chapel manager, a Dr. Rafe Ricketts, to follow the new no child-snatch policy.

Not remaining to indulge in what was, in normal days, the social event of the year, a tearful and joyous Hugh Clifton departed with his tearful and thankful son Thomas. A boy who could now truly say 'twas the best day of his life. And so they left, but not afore Sir Hugh once more took his grateful lad within his strong arms, from whence he would never let go.

And it may have been that very day that Henry Evans the younger, the boy with a borrowed name, decided to change it once more. For not long after, and from every day forth, he would be known as Henry Oxford. And don't think some tongues ne'er waggled about the why-fors of this new name.

I'm happy to report that both young lads of this story's leg led happy ever-endings. Whilst Thomas Clifton grew to become one of London's top lawyers, a noted member of the Parliament, and the happy husband to a lovely lady with pretty golden curls, forgetting all about his two-day role as a chapel boy, Henry Oxford grew to one day become manager of the chapel boys hisself. And would later find fame as one of London's greatest players of the viol da gamba. Such was the destiny of Henry Evans the younger.

As for Henry Evans the elder, some say he died in a jailcell in Milford-Haven. Some say he lost everything and became mayor of Milford-Haven. And some say he could later be found 'twixt the tales of two merry wives. In Windsor.

Nearby, the queen spoke confidential with her Burghley.

"Why has he changed so? Never before thought he so highly of these writings."

"I think, my good mistress," regretted old William, "it is because he has become so good at it."

"We shall now address our subjects."

The old man stroked his white beard and then called out as strong as he could, which was not very strong, "Lords and ladies!" The nobles turned to face majesty and minister. And Burghley began to speak. And after what seemed like a half-day of preamble, as the man was never one to use three words when three hundred would serve the turn, her majesty, hoping to give her speech sometime afore the twelfth night of Christmas, gave a stern look, and the old man stepped aside as the nobles clappered their queen.

"Loyal subjects," she began, with all eyes set upon her beauty. "We first wish to thank Lord Edward for the lovely performance of his boys." Her majesty led the claps toward Oxford, who gave a slight bow of his head, daring not to stretch it out too far for fear her majesty might next chop it off, as he suspected what was to follow. "And on this glorious day, we think it most fitting to announce our new appointment."

This was the moment the men had dread, but at least they knew that milord and Horatio had done their best to dissuade her highness.

Her majesty continued. "After careful consideration, and much consultation with Lord Edward," she turned to milord, causing his heart to halt, "we take great pleasure in naming Robert Cecil to the post of principal secretary."

There was applause, more polite than enthused, as the crookback stepped forwards. Though, given the man's strange shape, one never really knew whether he was stepping forwards nor backwards.

"We are also pleased to announce," continued her majesty, "a lifelong grant to Lord Edward, in recognition of his devoted services to the crown, of one thousand pound per annum."

All eyes fell to milord. The nobles looked surprised, Horatio looked confused, Lyly looked shocked, and Munday looked crushed.

To make bad matters worse, the queen persisted. "Have we your approval, milord?" she asked, for she was eager to receive his very public surrender.

Lord Edward stood there, but his throat was nowheres to be found. Finally, a feeble, "I serve for your glory, my Gloriana, and not mine own," at the last left his lips.

The queen herself led the applause. Robert Cecil took his place next the queen. We think. He nodded his odd nod to the musicians, who began to play a pavane in his honor. Milord walked awkward through the congregation, finding many a face full of wonder.

198

Framed in the front of forlorn hope past all recovery,
I stayless stand t'abide the shock of shame and infamy.

★

The door to Fisher's Folly was again open. And Master Munday spoke serious with milord out front.

My sprites, my heart, my wit and force, in deep distress are drowned;
The only loss of my good name is of these griefs the ground.

Munday walked away, looking wounded by the man he had come to love. Good Horatio approached.

"What is it?" he asked, suspecting full-well the cause of milord's distress.

"Munday has left us."

"But why?"

"I cannot say," was all milord could say.

CHAPTER THIRTY.

ON EVERY TREE AND LIMB IN CHRISTENDOM.

The 1580s.

'Twould not be long before the violent attack on the Edward. But afore that happed, Master Munday sent word 'round town that he was not pleased with his position with milord, and in short time he found a place elsewheres.

Lord Edward entered the Folly, where his men were there assembled.

"In return for our stage at the Boar's Head," milord addressed them, "her majesty demands works that will ready her subjects for war. Johnny?"

Lyly took up his quill, ready to write down the words as fast as his master could muster.

"It will not be long, gentlemen. We will soon be at battle, and we are her majesty's front line. With our sharpened quills, we shall move the English spirit, harden the English heart, and braven the English soldier." He walked from man to man, inspiring each, as Lyly took down every pentameter.

> *Once more unto the breach, dear friends, once more,*
> *Or close the wall up with our English dead.*
> *In peace, there's nothing so becomes a man*
> *As modest stillness and humility.*

Soon after, the players were reciting these very lines in the playhouses, rousing the people for what was to come.

> *But when the blast of war blows in our ears,*
> *Then imitate the action of the tiger.*

And a short time later, the true battle began. At sea, Lord Edward led his own ship 'twixt two Spanish galleons that were firing hard upon them, as he shouted encouragements to his men.

For there is none of you so mean and base
That hath not noble luster in your eyes!

The Spaniards boarded.

I see you stand like greyhounds in the slips,
Straining upon the start. The game's afoot!

And the fight began.

Follow your spirit, and upon this charge
Cry 'God for Harry, England and Saint George!'

At dusk, Lord Edward and his valiant soldiers removed their prisoners from his ship and handed over their captives. Milord glanced back at his *Edward Bonaventure*. 'Twas a magnificent vessel, and he was glad she had taken only small damage that day. 'Tis a pity she would later be tempest-wracked off the Bermudas, wherever that may be.

Young Toby, now a lad of thirteen, ran up to assist in the removing of Lord Edward's drenched vestments.

Anxious to learn of his master's exploits, "Milord?" he asked. "Prithee, tell all."

"We are victorious, my boy" said the exhausted earl.

"Would I could fight alongside you, milord. I yearn for such glory!" said the lad, not understanding the cost such glory often asks.

"There will be wars enough for you, lad."

"Oh!" said the excited boy. "To run my dagger through the enemy. To draw his blood and hear him cry for life."

Milord turned to Toby, watching him act out a bloody battle in his mind.

"Did you scourge them, milord, then make them walk a plank?"

"We did not. They cried for mercy," Oxford said, but he could see the boy understood not. "We gave it them." The lad seemed disappointed, and so milord sat him down.

"They were already defeated, lad," said he softly, of a sudden remembering the picture from atop Garrowby Hill. And he knew 'twas finally fit to charge up that hill one last time to set his boy aright. And maybe rid his nightmares evermore.

"I was not much older than you, Toby, when rebellion rang through the north. I fought beside the great Sussex and saw many days of blood-letting. When all was done, we rounded our captives. Boys and men. But mostly the young and the yearning. Entire counties. Seven-hundred hard-breathing boys. Then word was sent from London. And then and there..." milord stopped, unable to speak the words he wished to tell the boy. But he looked into Toby's eyes and knew he must go on. "Then and there, beyond the hill, we hanged them all. Hundreds upon hundreds. So many boys. From every town and shire. On every tree and limb in Christendom, it seemed. Nothing but death hanging off every bark, as far as a man could see. On every lifeless limb lay the futures of Cumbria, Durham, Cheshire, Lancashire and Yorkshire. All forever lost."

Toby was rapt withal.

"I wondered then if mercy might be better spent than the dread of kings." Milord rose with his boy. "Come, lad."

And milord put a fatherly arm 'round Toby as they walked away. A tittle did the boy know that he would very soon be fighting England's next battle alongside his hero.

The November wind ran cold when the Lord Great Chamberlain, in celebration of the recent victory, was given the honor of holding high the golden canopy over the head of her royal majesty upon her entrance into London.

Were't aught to me, I bore the canopy.

"Fine work, Thomas," milord said to his new man, handing him a score of pages. "Here are my corrections."

Welcome to Fisher's Folly, Thomas! Tom Bedingfield was a friend of Master Churchyard's and was hired by milord to translate the book of *Cardanus Comforte*, which was previous only in the Latin. For some reason, milord liked well the book's passages on death, of all things.

> *If thou compare death to long travel, there is nothing that doth better prophecy the end of life than when a man dreameth that he doth wander into far countries unknown, without hope of return. We are assured not only to sleep, but also to die.*

Now I myself admit I might pass up this *Cardanus Comforte* should I spy it in a book shoppe, seeing how 'tis a melancholy tale about death as a sleep and a dream and a travel to a far-off unknown country, whilst never touching on the *Comforte* part of the title. I myself enjoy cheerier tomes about love and daffodils and even mine own intended book, a fanciful fiction I had always hoped to finish called *The Troublesome Adventures of Ole Agnes of Aylesbury, a joyful romp 'round the gardens of Cheapside with a beautiful ale-keep named Agnes, and her noble, courageous, and comely knight, Sir Arthur Drink-well, accompanied by his young page, Bantickle Prickling of Stickleback.* Howe'er, I am sorry to say that such a book never made it to print. I began it aright and got me as far as the title page and the dedication afore I quit it. But Lord Edward saw something in this *Cardanus* that might smell of a small success, and I would wish him well with that tricky biscuit.

Back at the Folly, milord was a great guide to his men. Unless it was a specially asked-for translation, such as this dying and dreaming and unknown-countrying book, he never told them what to write, but helped them along their way to it. His own works he thought up by hisself, preferring to stand or fall by his own petard, as milord liked to say. And though I don't know what a *petard* is, I suppose 'tis always better to stand by one than to fall by it.

Course, after he left this world, his unfinished writings were give to other hands to complete. I heard that Fletcher filched a few and Middleton meddled with more. Better 'twas to give these papers over to others, for 'tis oft said, though I never actually heard it said, that "A full play by two on the stage is better than a half play by one in the grave." Except for that *Titus Andronicus*, o' course, but we'll let that one go for now.

Milord approached Lyly, who happed to be holding a new pamphlet in hand.

"What's this?" he asked his secretary.

"Someone has printed an answer to your poem, milord. And there's also a new work from the great *Fortunatus Infoelix*," replied Lyly.

"Fortunatus Infoelix?" said Bedingfield, never having heard that moniker before.

"'Tis the new name Hatton writes under," smiled milord.

"Why on earth choose a cock-stupid name like *Happy Unhappy?* Could he not make up his mind?"

"'Cause he was *happy* to write it," said milord, "and we are *unhappy* to read it!" And he sat for a good listen. "Recite us Master Joyous Unjoyous, would you please, Master Lyly?"

And Lyly began to read.

> *Beauty shut up thy shop, and truss up all thy trash,*
> *My Nell hath stolen thy finest stuff and left thee in the lash.*

"Enough!" milord raised his white scarf. "We surrender. What was the other?"

"Someone has printed an answer to your poem."

"Which one, milord?" asked Bedingfield.

And milord obliged him.

> *Were I a King, I might command content;*
> *Were I obscure, unknown would be my cares;*

And were I dead, no thoughts should me torment,
Nor words, nor wrongs, nor love, nor hate, nor fears;
A doubtful choice, of these things which to crave,
A kingdom or a cottage or a grave.

Milord turned to Lyly, "Who was it writ the answer?"

"'Tis unnamed but sounds of Sidney's wit." And he read it out.

Wert thou a King, yet not command content,
Since empire none thy mind could yet suffice;
Wert thou obscure, still cares would thee torment;
But wert thou dead, all care and sorrow dies;
An easy choice of these things which to crave,
No kingdom, nor a cottage, but a grave.

"Admirably answered it is," he smiled broad, thinking on his many bouts with his worthy opponent, whether spear to shield, poem to page, or ball to face.

'Twas then sad Churchyard entered the room.

"'Tis time we renew our war of the poets, methinks."

"'Tis too late, milord," spoke soft old Churchyard.

"What means you?"

"Philip Sidney is dead. Killed in battle," Churchyard said. "They now return him for a hero's funeral."

A silence fell over the room like a heavy shroud, removing all the air beneath it.

"He is a hero sure," milord said at the last.

"And there's quite a stir about," Churchyard went on. "Marlowe's gone missing, Nashe is being sought, and there's again talk of closing the playhouses."

"More Puritans!" shouted an angry John Lyly.

"More Robert Cecil, more like," chimed Churchyard.

Milord took a breath. "I fear a new war coming," was all he said.

And no truer words were spoke that day.

CHAPTER THIRTY-ONE.

A YOUNG BOY DOWNED, A POET CROWNED.

There was only one man fit to be appointed general, and that man be Edward Vere. But as the battle began, none suspected that milord would abandon the field early, deserting his own troops afore the final skirmish.

'Twas sundown. Their ships were small and their armor doubly strong. As the fight commenced, they jumped out their boats and into the mire, crying queen and country. Oxford's men rushed the small island fort, as the screams of the watered and the wearied filled the darkening sky. And this time, alongside his hero, young Toby ran. He thought on none but the victory ahead, soon to learn that sometimes fate is of a different mind.

At Vere's command, his men flew flaming spears over the fortress walls. But atop the battlements were the enemy, flinging fired munitions of their own. Fireballs flied hither and yon, whilst wailing soldiers fled yon and hither.

With Lord Edward holding left and Toby on the right, the two fought hard. But just then, milord heard the unmistakable sound. 'Twas the whish of an arrow, which passed by his right side. His heart jumped high in his throat, for he knew his young page stood there beside him.

He turned to throw his dear Toby out of the way, but alas, he was too late. For milord, all battle sounds ceased. He saw his boy was hit. They both stood still. Time fled not. Milord looked into the lad's stunned eyes, as the boy stared upon hisself, eyeing the small shaft of the arrow jutting from out his chest-plate. Milord rushed to face him. He stopped. He spoke.

"'Tis a pity, lad, you're dead."

Milord's men were near to taking command of the fort, as a good part of one wall had begun to flame. Some ran with buckets to quench the beast, whilst others returned with fire to feed it anew. Great confusion reigned all 'round. As General Vere's men seemed near victorious, with hell and havoc breaking every whichways, none saw the fireballs that overshot the fort and landed onto the peasant thatches in the village beyond.

Oxford pulled the blunted and bated-tipped arrow from out the boy's doubly fortified armor, patted him on the pate, and told him to join the other dead men off the field. Disappointed, Toby marched off to the side where he sat next to the dead others, who watched on all-eager, hoping their band of brothers would win the challenge. Behind them, and not far from the battle's edge, sat good Queen Bess herself, in front of Castle Warwick, very much enjoying the exciting entertainment milord had arranged for her.

Above the battle cries and shouts, milord was first to sense the situation in the village. Weaving past flying fireballs and bobbing boats, he saw the smoke over the castle walls and knew he must abandon the fight. He jumped into the Avon and swam ashore. Milord could swim near as good as I. Horatio eyed him as he called through the commotion. Milord jumped onto his horse and Horatio followed. They raced toward the burning village, yelling as they fled. And when the eye of the queen herself now followed this unplanned exeunt of her warrior-actor-noblemen, all heads turned toward the cottages, and then others abandoned the battle and rode off to help in this unrehearsed actus secundus.

There were four homes ablaze'd, and many villagers were shouting and scurrying. Water pails were fetched as milord jumped off his frightened steed. He could hear cries within a burning thatch and 'rounded the side, smashing the bolted window-boards. Through the smoke, he saw an old woman kneeling over an ancient fellow, who was collapsed onto the rushes. He leapt in and took up the woman, carrying her to the window, all the while she screaming for her poor husband Andrew. Horatio grabbed her from without, and she fainted dead away.

Milord turned to collect the husband, but black smoke blocked his every turn. With eyes that were of no use to him, he trusted his feet to get him back to the ancient. Once there, he bent o'er and picked up his charge, speaking to him calm, telling him he was aright, not knowing if he be heard nor unheard, but talking to him none-the-same. He somehow made his way to the window and handed the man over to Horatio, who took him from the fire. Milord escaped, and the fiery thatch fell. His heart was pounding hard, and he hoped the same for the old man and his wife.

More courtiers arrived and assisted in the pulling out of goats and the putting out of fires. Any flame that could be smoted, they smited, and all hell was quelled and vanquished.

The morning arrived to find two distinct worlds laying side-to-side. Those of the court and those of the village, with no true difference 'twixt them, if truth be told. For both were bone-wearied and dead-tired, and don't each man put on his slops one leg at a time the same as any other? Why, if you happed upon them in the blackest of night, you'd ne'er know which folk was what folk by the similar snortlings of the slumbers they both shared.

As the goats bleated a waking call, milord walked 'round to each noble with his hat in his hand, and man after man put in whatever coins lined his purse. And if the events of the night were not unexpected enough, the villagers witnessed a sight they had never thought possible, for the royal carriage now approached.

Full of love and fear, each weary subject bowed low as her royal groomsman helped Queen Elizabeth out of the carriage. She surveyed the scene and approached old Jane and Andrew Fyngland, the couple that milord had rescued. They were both both terrified and thrilled with the surprising visit.

"Our dear subjects," her majesty spoke to them. "You are unharmed?"

"We... we are..." said the ancient husband, "thanks to you, your majesty, and your men."

"Each day we pray for the welfare of our people," said she in truth, as their eyes welled with tears. These were like all of her majesty's subjects. They loved their queen, for it was said she did love them.

Her majesty then walked over to milord, still holding his hat.

"Must all your performances, dear Edward, end in chaos?" smiled she, dropping a handful of gold coins into his hat afore walking away.

Milord handed his cap to the old couple, and for the first time that day, he took a breath.

★

It seemed for every moment the queen would provide sustenance to milord, there was also a day he would be royally scrutinized by her. This was such a day, when he heard about the events at the palace and ran breathless to Horatio at the hall.

"Is't true?"

But he could see now that it was true. Through the passage, he spied Gascoigne kneeling before the queen, who placed a wreath upon his head.

"How could she crown Dudley's man Royal Poet?" Horatio asked.

Milord and his cousin left Whitehall in silence. They walked the length of the lane a long while with never a word, 'til they came upon the bookseller's at the Charing cross. The new book in the window caught milord's eye, *Astophel*. But 'twasn't the title that halted milord, 'twas the words betwixt the two lines at the bottom: *by Sir Philip Sidney*.

"To think a man must die to sign his name upon a poem," said milord. And then his eyes flashed fire. "Have Lyly speak to Creede."

"The printer? What do you intend?" worried his cousin.

"To claim my own words before I die."

"By printing your play?" Horatio worried more.

"I have a thousand pound a year, I have a rope."

Horatio looked at him blank.

"Good cuz, think you a blessing may be truly a curse in disguise?"

And milord walked off, leaving a perplexed Horace behind. It would not be long afore he prepared the manuscript of his self-lived *All's Well* and handed it to printer Creede. Even a blockhead with a brain full o 'milk 'n mush can imagine how well her highness took to that.

"A ward of the crown, an escape to Italy, an elevated title, a forced marriage, and a reluctant groom!" The queen held high the copy of milord's scribbled manuscript, given her by printer Creede, a wise man who well-knew on which side of the loaf his bread was honey'd. "And last, an ugly portrait of a bellowing monarch!" bellowed the monarch, as she thrust the papers hard across the floor.

"He writes too bold," said the ever-astute Dudley.

"I want this printed," said Gloriana, astounding the astute.

"Your majesty?"

"With a name attached. Any name shall do, as long as it is not *Vere*."

Then Dudley understood and smiled. For as these plays continued to be printed anonymous, people were starting to wonder who writ the things. And if people began to wonder if a courtier writ the things, might they not begin to wonder about the identity of those portrayed within the things, resulting in the very public airing of some rather besmirched royal breeches?

"It shall be done," smiled the earl, as her angry majesty left, leaving the poor Dud to bend his knee and take up the pages.

Later that evening, he approached his new man in darkness and held out the manuscript.

"See to it it's printed," he said. And as his new man reached to take the pages, Lord Robert held tight. "But," said he, "use a name. Any name not associated with our court."

"Yes, milord," bowed the man, who now had the play in hand.

Dudley walked away into the dark. And his new man walked on into the light. The play would soon be on its way to the printer, safe in the hands of Dudley's new man. This new Anthony Munday.

CHAPTER THIRTY-TWO.

A NAME NEW-MADE AND A VIOLET IN HER HAND.
The 1580s.

There are many chapters within a man's life. Some are penned with joy and light. And others are spelt with heaviness and doom. What lies ahead are not the days of light.

The Boar's Head was crowded that night. Drinks were full and spirits merry. Horatio, Lyly, and milord were busy at capering and carousing, a tittle knowing that servant Adam was racing 'cross town with news of terrible import.

At the same time, Munday walked down Friday, manuscript in hand. He crossed High and neared the Boar. He stopped and saw milord sitting there with his men, and with a pounding heart, he entered on cue. And though he seemed no longer a servant to milord, things are never as they seem.

Munday advanced and milord turned.

"Et tu, Brutè!" was milord's roar, as all sounds in the place ceased. 'Twas now quiet enough to hear a dizzy-eyed cat drop. "Stand ho!" he continued. "Who is there?"

"Friend to this ground, and liegemen to the boar!" quoth Munday, bearing high the manuscript and beaming wide a grin.

Milord raced to embrace his man, and all cheered.

"Our device is successful?" grinned milord.

"Here is your manuscript," beamed Munday, "now sanctioned for printing."

The others made way for him at the table, there to celebrate their victory. And just then, a lone hautboy was heard playing a Tom Tallis, which was the music sung at her majesty's garden celebration the day Munday and milord plotted their designs on t'other side of the bushes. And Munday smiled to think on it.

"We shall find pretense for you to leave my service," milord had instructed Munday that day. "And you must find some way to seek favor with Dudley, who can get my plays printed."

"We will march one step ahead of their boots, milord," said Munday.

He rejoined his friends, and in no time at all, all was as 'twas, as if 'twas only yesterday 'twasn't. Milord was ever so glad to have his Munday back, who then informed milord of the mission Dudley had devised.

"But how can you ever hope to claim these works with another's name attached?" argued Horatio.

"That is her majesty's stratagem," said milord. "We must therefore create a counter-stratagem." He raised his glass and pronounced, "Gentlemen, we shall think on't. Drink on't. And invent a name that is no name at all."

From the huswife's window above, a chamber pot was emptied onto High Street just as Adam flew under, causing the fellow to near take a tumble. But it never tripped him up, and he continued his race, well-knowing where he could find his master. And time was fleeting.

In the mean, milord's men considered various false names to attach to his plays, my favorites being *Cornelius Codpiece, Barnaby Bulge-hose* and *Will Scribble-shittel*. But they finally hit upon one most fitting.

"*Will Shake-Spear*?" laughed Horatio.

"None would ever believe it, milord!" cried Lyly.

"Precisely!" answered Lord Edward. "We satisfy the queen's demand, yet for all who read and think, 'tis a tale told by de Vere. Why, my life is scattered throughout. Each word tells my name. And one day, I shall reclaim them properly."

"It sounds like our company man, Will Shaksper!" laughed Lyly.

212

"I not long ago made him our new play-broker," answered milord. "Munday here shall task him to deliver this and all other manuscripts to the printer under the new name. 'Tis fitting. For who shakes spears at court?" he laughed.

"No enemy will deny it," marked Horatio.

"'Tis Pleasant Willy, Old Minerva and the Invisible Knight all bound within one quiver," smiled milord. "Have him tell the printer to place a hyphen within the name, to make clear 'tis a jest," instructed milord to Munday, raising his glass to all. "To Will Shake-speare. The sweet bard of the Boar's Head!" laughed he. And all did laugh with him.

But then Munday worried, "What if our man Shaksper should slip a tongue?"

"We must send him back home," milord thought. "What is the man's passion?"

"Money," answered Munday quick.

"So, we shall feed the beast," smiled milord. "Buy his name with a bag of coin, a horse headed homeward, and a rich estate. What more?"

"Why not a coat of arms while you're about it?" jested Horatio.

"Munday, visit my friend Dethick on Tuesday."

"The herald of arms?" Horatio looked to him doubtful.

"A man who also loves money!" And they all did laugh hard.

But then Adam ran in.

"My lord!" he cried with tears. "'Tis Countess Anne. Come quick."

At one-and-thirty years, the Countess Anne Cecil Vere lay dead in her bed from a heated fever that none but death could cool. Having given milord three children alive, and two who were not, she had no more life to give. Lord Edward sat at the side of her bed, holding onto her small hand. And only now he wondered, after 'twas too late in life to alter a thing, if he had been too hard on the girl. He was terrible sad, milord.

Yet, he also knew he had reason to be thankful. For the last few years had brought Anne and he to a happier time. Where they would walk the gardens together and sing the songs that others sang. Where they learnt to love the slow pavane as they danced to sorrowful lutes, now sounding in his mind all the more sorrowful. 'Twas the touch of her warm hand as they danced that he contemplated now, as he held her small cold fingers. There was a love that had grown out of the comfort he had begun to feel with her. After all these years. And with the cheer of their children.

Whilst milord could teach hawking and jousting to his youthful page, he was for a very long time at a loss with his three young girls. But through the years, he had learnt even that. And he had begun to enjoy his days with them. The songs he'd sing to them in French, the stories he'd tell them at night, the lessons he would o'ersee for their education. And the flowers they'd gather for him each day. He loved nothing more than the gift of those flowers. He had even come to accept the eldest, Elizabeth, as his own. After all, she possessed a strong mind and a stubborn will, so she must have been milord's, thought he. 'Twas the beginnings of a good time. And he was thankful he knew such days. But now those days were done.

After a prayer of protection for her soul, he delicately placed her hand alongside her still body and moved toward the door to Horatio. Milord watched old Burghley sitting sadly alone in his chair 'cross the room.

'Twas then the crooked Robert came in, followed by a woman unknown to milord. Behind them were Edward's daughters. Elizabeth stood tall and somber, all of thirteen. In one hand, she held a sad lone violet, and he wondered if she had picked it for him. In t'other, she held onto her little sister Bridget's hand, who was a small lass of four. A good and quiet lass. The strange woman held the youngest, Susan, in her arms, still in her first year of life.

"What means you this?" Lord Edward said to the younger Cecil. But it was William who rose to answer.

"Milord, without my sweet child, your wife, her majesty thinks it best the three young ones reside at Cecil House."

214

Milord's heart sank anew. "You mean to take my children from me?"

"Milord," answered the crookback. "You're hardly in a state to raise them up. Your fortunes have been squandered on your men. You've no official position at court. You are barely welcome there since the birth of your base-born son with Mistress Vavasor. You live by her majesty's graces alone. You have nothing. And nothing will come of nothing." Each of these pronouncements was a dagger into the heart of Edward, for he knew each to be true.

"'Tis well this way," the old Cecil tried to calm milord.

"Think on the girls," said crookback. "They must be schooled."

Lord Edward tried hard to rein in his anger, and it was only his heartbreak that made this possible.

"I shall speak with her majesty at once," he said. "I'll demand she cease the withholding of my forest at Essex, which I will sell to support my own children."

"You may appeal to her majesty's new Lord Chancellor."

"Who is he?" asked milord.

"I believe you are well acquainted with the man," smirked the crooked one. "Sir Christopher Hatton." He then nodded to the woman, who escorted the young girls out of the house. Robert then crossed to the door and turned back. "After all, milord, it is not like you have been a father to them yet."

Milord looked at the man and wondered why there was so much bitterness in him. I think 'twould have been different had his father, just once, give him the treacle he so sought after as a boy.

The Cecils left the home.

"They have the power, cousin," warned good Horace.

"And they shall poison the hearts of mine own three daughters against me. While I am useless against such new-made men."

Milord held no hope at all. And then he saw it upon the table by the door. The lone violet that young Elizabeth had left for him. He crossed and picked it up, holding it gentle in his hand. 'Twas a flower of sorrow and death, thought he, but 'twas also a promise of faithfulness.

Break heart, prithee break.

Milord ran frantic. Past Poultry he flew. 'Cross Christopher and Carol Lanes he leaped. 'Round carts and o'er cats. All to save poor John's life.

Over at the Cross, the scaffold stood. The axe-man held high his weapon as a frightened John Stubbes was led forward. The crowd howled.

"Pray for me now, my calamity is at hand," pled Poor John.

"Off with the offender!" barked the crier.

The axe came down hard and hit its mark, as the rabble cheered and milord arrived. Poor John atop the scaffold, whose writing hand had been chopped off, stood a-shocked. With precious life rushing out his wrist, he removed his hat with his left hand, and in softest voice announced, "God save the queen."

With that, he swooned over cold. The guards approached to take Stubbesy away, and milord gave them all the coins he had with him.

"See to it his wound is dressed, will you?" And they took him away.

Milord's breathless men approached.

"'Tis another one of us gone," said Lyly.

"They'll return him after he is cared for," answered milord.

"I don't mean Stubbesy," said Lyly.

"Who else?" asked Edward, afraid to hear more.

"Marlowe," was the reply. "Killed last even in Deptford."

Milord was shaken, for all he had held dear was crumbling afore him. And so, of a sudden, he became quite resolute.

"Johnny," he ordered. "I want you to secure a new lease at Blackfriars."

"For the boys?" asked Lyly.

"For my men."

"Blackfriars?" asked Horatio.

216

Desperate, milord turned to face his cuz. "Invisible or no, truth is truth, though never so old. England shall have a true chronicle, so all will know the tale of this court. But should I not live to see that dawn, promise me this."

"Milord?"

"Tell my story."

★

1624.

Old Munday looked into Valentina's bright eyes and saw she was rapt withal, a sight he had not known in many a year.

"And so, the war began in earnest," he told Beauty. "With words. But also, with daggers." And here Munday's eye could not help but wander to the iron nail on the wall. The one that held the feathered cap and a sad tale. "He had his revenges. But they came at a cost."

CHAPTER THIRTY-THREE.

A FEATHER THROUGH THE DARKNESS FLEW.

The 1580s.

A few years before young Toby was made page, that employ belonged to his brother Robin, the lad who so loved pranks. He always looked up to milord, oft musing that the next best job after being the great Lord Oxford is to be page to the great Lord Oxford.

In exchange for Robin's daily duties to run messages, spit-clean bodkins, and care for milord's quills, quillets and quiddities (whate'er they may be), Lord Edward would teach his charge archery, hawking and humility. And the lad did excel in all, they say.

With milord's guidance and love, Robin had matured in many ways and was on the road to becoming a goodly young man, tempered with mercy and kindness. In the addition, the lad's preference for ancient books over new oft made milord think the lad had and old mind stuffed into a young noggin.

"You're an old soul," Lord Edward used to tell him with a smile. An old soul, he'd say.

Young Robin was an important coggle within milord's wheel of playmaking. Lord Edward would scribble up a play, and then Robin would run it to the scribe, who would pen it in a clear hand and then deliver it to the printer.

'Twas just such a day when milord called Robin into his book chamber.

"My boy," said milord, handing him a new bundle o' blots. "See to it these are delivered to Scribe Quealy."

"Yes, milord," said Robin, proudly taking the papers in hand. And, as was his usual custom, he made a deep bow, touched a finger for good luck to the quill-tips on the desk, and scurried off. This always made milord smile, as he thought this habit a humorous one.

And he noted the boy's favorite, for 'twas always the colorful phoenix rooster that he went for. Which gave milord an idea.

Three hours later, the box was waiting for Robin when he returned.

"Milord?" asked the boy.

"For you," said Lord Edward, with a grin the size of happiness.

"For me?" the boy could not believe his ears, as milord told him to open the box.

From its confines, the lad took out the most handsome cap a fellow could imagine. 'Twas made of the finest tawny silk, with a proud gold star at one side and a most wondrous bunch of phoenix feathers on t'other, which made young Robin touch the soft feathers and jump for joy.

"For me?" the boy repeated, afraid 'twas meant for him to deliver to another of higher state.

"For you to wear," laughed milord, as he placed it atop Robin's small head and sent him off to display his new plumage to the others of the household. A fine old soul, indeed.

When Oxford's Boys were not *in occupato* at the Blackfriars, it was occupato'd by Oxford's Men. 'Twas a playhouse like none other, I can tell you, though I never patron'd the place myself. For this was a theatre not for the common clods to stand, but at half a crown per bum, 'twas meant for gentlemen to sit. All to glimpse an inside cat's-eyed view of her majesty's court.

Sir Christopher Hatton was in attendance on the first night. Some laughed in hystericals, whilst others fumed in anger. You may guess into which camp Sir Christopher fell.

Afore I carry on, I would like to alert those who have not yet seen this play that, (like milord), I intend to reveal all. So, if you wish the ending not to be spoilt, you may want to pass o'er the next passage.

The stage was now a mirror glass to the court. Center, stood an ill-willed fool named Malvolio, dressed in a turd-green doublet and a cap much too tall for his head, the very spit of Hatton hisself! He read a letter from *The Fortunate Unhappy*, which will remind a fellow of Hatton's cock-stupid pen-name, and he's later gulled into wearing the fool-happy yellow hose and cross-garters we have likeways seen in the flesh 'n bone. And since all the nobs in the know knew, they laughed all the harder at the gull sitting amongst them.

Night after night, milord continued to pen more of his life's secrets, whether about an evil humpback that dogs bark at, or a wrongfully jealous husband who learns all too late, or a father heartbroke at the loss of his three daughters.

Then came the time milord was most daring. The stage was peopled with the most familiar. A friend called Horatio. A winded, white-bearded minister. And a forlorn Prince of Denmark, orphaned at youth, pursued by the minister's daughter, kidnapped by pirates, and played by the very person of Lord Edward hisself! When Hamlet called the white-beard a "fishmonger," old Burghley in the audience flinched. When he questioned his daughter's loyalties, the old man winced. And when Hamlet thrust his dagger into the man's heart, one of them fell, and t'other did not like it well.

And for the rest of his days, Lord Edward continued to scratch out his heart and his secrets with his pen, the only weapon left to him now.

★

Her majesty's mood was most unpleasant when Robert Cecil brought Knyvet into her chamber. Furious with the recent strife fought on the streets by the Vere and Knyvet servants, she demanded an end. And the men left, deciding what to do.

Two households, both alike in dignity,
In fair Verona, where we lay our scene,
From ancient grudge break to new mutiny,
Where civil blood makes civil hands unclean.

220

The serpent, whose thoughts were ever-fixed on the honor of his niece and a vengeance on milord, ordered his men to ready their swords and end this grudge forever.

From forth the fatal loins of these two foes
A pair of star-cross'd lovers take their life.

Young Robin, feathered cap proudly cock'd, came out the Boar's Head first. And as milord and his men emerged after him, the final fight began. The serpent pounced, and his apes followed suit, cutting and slashing as wild as they could.

Whose misadventur'd piteous overthrows
Doth with their death bury their parents' strife.

A cry rang out from the alley, and a feather through the darkness flew. Milord immediately knew the sound. Knyvet's men kept busy Lyly and Munday, as milord ran to the alley. And lying there in his blood, lay sweet young Robin. *You cannot be dead!* was milord's only thought. *You must be alive! A lad so innocent.* But motionless, he lay. And milord looked up to the stars. *Oh, God!* his heart anguished to the heavens. *You have mistaken, taken my young boy for an old soul!*

Lord Edward cradled his dear boy in his arms. He took up the lad and the cap and carried them out of the alleyway. But as he walked toward High Street, heavy with double burdens weighing down both arms and soul, two hellhounds pounced upon him. The lifeless body of the boy again fell to the ground, as Knyvet's demons slashed out wild with their broadswords. Milord did best he could, armed with his rapier, but he was soon wore out by the savage pummels he received. As he was knocked to the stones below, the two brutes weighed him down, and let their master fell the final blow. All the while, more armed fiends came to occupy milord's men 'round the front.

With his great broadsword in hand, and his men restraining arms and legs, Knyvet stood above his hated victim and thrust his blade down and into the wore-out object of his revenge, drawing it slow across his thighs, whilst howls of pain rang through the heavy air. This done, smiling their brown smiles, the villains heard milord's men approach and left Lord Edward for dead, as the steam of life slowly 'scaped his body, which lay in a new-made pool of blood.

"In answer, the queen's swift sword would soon come down on Knyvet," continued old Munday to the breath-took Valentina, who now held a tear in her eye. "And then it glistened as it was raised from his shoulder, making him her newest knight of the realm. Rewarded for saving the sanctity of her majesty's ladies. Yet Lord Edward barely survived. He had not the heart to write for a long time thereafter. But his men needed him, and 'twas perhaps one year more when he could answer the call. Took his troop to the country. 'Twas this that made him whole, I think. For a time, at least."

Valentina was engrossed in his every word.

"What can you tell me of his boy?" she asked.

"The son?"

"I know that he and Lady Montague had a child."

"Then you are like the dog got too close the bear," said he mysterious, "with only half a tail 'twixt his legs." For Munday knew he could tell her some, but to tell her all was still a danger in the time of our King James. Yet Valentina's eyes begged him to continue, and so he carried on cautious. "He did write to his son," said the old secretary.

As a decrepit father takes delight
To see his active child do deeds of youth,
So I, made lame by fortune's dearest spite,
Take all my comfort of thy worth and truth.

"It was after the gypsy left us, he wrote to his love. Before he found his happiness and marriage with the Countess Elizabeth. It was the end of the gypsy. The day Dudley died that he began to woo his last and greatest prize. The woman he had always loved."

Now Valentina's head was full of confusion, for she thought 'twas Mistress Mary that was closest to his heart. But Munday knew. It was never she.

Our dear queen stood alone. And pity her I do, for it must be remembered that, unlike every other soul in Christendom, she was the only one of us who had no queen to look to.

'Twas then milord saw the chance to help his dear Southampton and save England from the fate of having a foreign monarch occupy the throne. For talk was about that cousin James of Scotland would take the reign, and what man with good English blood running through him could endure such a fate as that? This was the spark that fired milord to forward the cause of Southampton for the crown.

"Lord Edward sat in this very room," told Munday. "His final hope was to wed his great mistress. To make certain the succession was secured for the house of Tudor. It obsessed his mind and pen. And he wrote daily to her."

Who lets so fair a house fall to decay,
Which husbandry in honor might uphold
Against the stormy gusts of winter's day,
And barren rage of death's eternal cold?

He carried his marriage proposals to her, and waited outside in the cold snow-hinted morn below her window as she read them. He looked up for her response, and the gentle flakes fell soft onto his face. And then her answer flowed from her window above, as the hands of the queen, made wet by snow-fluffs and tears, let fall the pages. They fluttered down atop the mighty earl, who finally understood it was now too late in the year. Yet, he could ne'er stop thinking on her majesty, his all-powerful heaven-sent regent, who had took from him his dear son.

Even so my sunne one early morn did shine

With all-triumphant splendor on my brow.
But out, alack! he was but one hour mine;
The region cloud hath mask'd him from me now.

"But among all the other nobles," Valentina asked, "why would *his* son be in line for the throne?"

Munday smiled sadly. "Matters not. She refused him. And he refused to leave this home until that late winter's day, when called upon to save the boy's very life."

CHAPTER THIRTY-FOUR.

THINGS ARE NEVER AS THEY SEEM.

1624.

Three days passed without event for Martin and his men. Of course, there was event, they just did not know it then. For 'twas in that time that Nick and I stood face to face in my cell. And whilst Valentina learnt much about Lord Edward, she was beside herself not knowing where to find Nick.

The young lady told Martin's men all she had discovered, which helped them collect the final pieces to their puzzle. Well, I should say to *part* of their puzzle, for there were still a few more surprises to uncover. The day draggled by slow, and the talk was all about Nicholas. *Where was he?* they pondered. *Have you heard a thing?* they enquired. None knew. They never thought to seek him in a jailcell. Though, truth be told, he was no longer there. But where he was would remain a mystery 'til that messenger came the next morning.

Valentina arrived at the law office and was met by Horatio's man Cuddy, who handed her a letter promising news of old Arthur. She read it fast and ran up to the men, who had just finished unshelving their books. They all soon followed Cuddy to the Thames.

Horatio Vere stood at river's edge. And whilst he spoke with the magistrate, his first mate Whittemore questioned the new seaman coming aboard the ship.

"Your papers?" he demanded, giving both the papers and this fellow his once 'round. Whittemore was never a man at ease when such an important endeavor as this had to be manned by a new sailor. But, as he had lost his own man in the rough seas off Sicilia, and as this new recruit had been sent to fill the part, he had little choice.

Funny, he didn't look the sea-faring type, the first mate told hisself. But his papers were in order, and Whittemore was quite short-handed. As was this new fellow, as bad luck would have it, for he was missing a few of the fingers of his right hand.

Back ashore, Horatio gave assurance to the excruciated magistrate, who was painfully wringing his hands at his side.

"The body is aboard and shall be buried at sea."

"I do pray this puts an end to the matter, milord," winced the magistrate.

"It shall," answered the baron.

Horatio could see that the ship's captain was leading the confused researchers aboard and handed the magistrate a purse full of coins.

"For your pains," said Horatio to the man, who sure looked to be in considerable pains at the moment.

"You are most kind, milord," bowed the official, who proceeded to turn his already twisted body and totter away.

As the ship sailed from the smells of London, Martin approached the commander.

"Good Captain," he said. "Now will you please tell us why we have been sent for?"

"That is milord's right, sir," was all the captain could say.

"Who is your lord?" persisted Martin.

"I'm afraid I am," came the noble voice behind him.

Martin and the others turned to see Horace Vere appear from the cabin.

"Baron Tilbury," Horatio bowed his head, "at your service, gentlemen."

"My Lord," Martin spoke, "We have been told that you know of the fate of my brother, Arthur Taverner. And of Nicholas North."

"Now that we are away from the ears of London, your questions shall have answers. But perhaps you'll want to ask them directly," said the nobleman, as he opened the cabin door behind him, and, much to the surprise of every man present, and the one woman too, there emerged Nicholas North.

226

Valentina abandoned all care and ran to embrace her friend she had thought lost forever.

"Nick!" said she with so much happiness, "you are unhurt."

"I am," he said, as he was sure glad to look into Beauty's eyes once more, and quite unashamed to hold her, too. Peals of joy rang 'round the deck.

Then Martin's smile left him as quick as it came. "What has happened to my brother?" he asked Nicholas quite somber. And then all got quiet. Baron Horatio nodded to the captain to join him in the cabin as Nick began to tell of my strange and wondrous fate.

"How long before we meet up with *The Venture*?"

"With the present wind, milord, I'd tell an hour."

"They'll be waiting for us?"

"Yes, milord."

"God's speed, then," said Horatio.

"Thank you, milord," bowed the captain, as he left to perform his duties, not eyeing the man in the shadows with secret ears upon them. Not eyeing that shadowy Master Digges.

Horatio looked out the cabin window as Nicholas recounted the adventure of Old Arthur Taverner. After the which, he spoke the story of Master Shake-speare. 'Twas near an hour when the baron emerged to reveal one final surprising turn. Now that they were far from the banks of England, it was time that all could be confessed. For there is often many a good twist and turn within a good tale. And things are never as they seem.

"It is now time for farewells," said the baron, as the ship pulled alongside *The Venture*, and the two crews began the mooring.

And here our drama peaks. What happened next was never expected by any of them, leastways most by my dear brother. The captain called. The door opened wide. And there I stood!

"Martin!" I called and held my hand way out. My brother turned and his face lit up.

"Brother!" he shouted and ran to embrace me. I must admit, that took me by surprise, too, for I can't recall a time he called me brother. Nor embraced me neither. But it was good, and I liked it well.

All the others clapped my back whilst Valentina kissed my cheek, which turned quite red, I'm sure of that.

"Your brother shall be safer on the Continent," Horatio explained.

"Retired, shall I be," says I, "to tramp the grapes of Italy, and write sweet poetry to me wifee."

"Wifee?" says brother, still in shock from my arrival. And then, as on cue, my sweet Peg emerged from the cabin behind me.

"She has finally understood the errors of her ways," says I.

"Now don't you start," smiles she, "or I'll change my mind and swim home."

I grabbed her close and pointed to the blue seas beyond. "There, my dear Mistress Taverner, is our home."

I was thankful for good Horatio for bringing me both my Peg and my Italy. And to be reunited with Martin, who would now deign call me brother. It was a glad day, and I owed the noble Horatio everything. For 'twas he who discovered my presence in that stinking cell. 'Twas he who knew I was put there by that Knyvet snake for enquiring after the poet. And 'twas he that arranged the deceit which was to set me free. For he showed Nick that stage trick at the Boar's Head. The players with the bladder full o' blood and vinegar. He demonstrated the process to Nick, and then to me in my cell.

"You are to place this goat's bladder under your waistcoat," says he.

"And why would I do such a thing?" says I.

"It is filled with blood," notes he.

"All the more reason not to do it," notes I.

And then he explained. "The only way to take you out of here is to take you out a dead man."

"I see," says I, in fact not seeing at all. But as the hours wore 'round, I quickly learnt the plot. Nick was to kill me dead. Lord Horace was to purchase my body with the promise to throw me o'erboard to the angelfishes. Then, to rescue Nick, he'd place another dagger at the scene.

"This dagger!" said Horatio to the jailer. "Why, I could have your life for allowing a prisoner to keep such a thing!"

228

"Oh, your grace!" sweat the jailer, "I had no idea 'twas there!" shook the jailer.

"Well, don't you see," said swift Horatio, "this man was acting *se defendendo*?"

"Yes, your worship!" sobbed the jailer." What all you say, your worship!" blubbered the jailer.

And for a few coins more, Lord Horace had Nick released into his custody, and the jailer kept his sweet employment. A goodly smart man, that Horatio Vere.

A shame it was that all the while we had our teary talk, none thought to watch the two crews at the mooring. As five men from our ship brought provisions aboard *The Venture*, only four men returned. It was that fatal fifth that we shall later come to. That fatal Master Digges.

"Gentlemen, it is now time," said the baron. "As you have been informed, the answers you have sought have brought to others grave consequences. Therefore, any of you who desires to accompany good Arthur to the Italian shores may do so now, and you shall be well-provided for. If you choose to return with us, then I can offer you my protection with no surety, as our enemies are powerful."

"Well," says I, "who shall join us in our venture?" I looked first to Nicholas and Valentina.

"You know my thoughts, old friend," said Nick, as we had spoke all this before.

"I'm with Nick," smiled the beauty, and the young man smiled back at her.

I then looked to brother as he addressed his men.

"Any of you will go, I shall wish you well." He turned to me. "As for me, brother, I am too old for such a shift." And although I was hoping I'd see him once more afore I die, I knew 'twas true. He was too old for such a journey. Of course, I was still three years his senior, but in a way, he has always been older than me. He then embraced me one last time.

"And let these angels accompany you," said he, thrusting into my palm a bit of coin. I thought to refuse but did not wish to offend.

"You are a good brother," I said, wiping a bit of sea mist from mine eye.

"Well?" said Martin, as he turned to his men. Turning, I think, to wipe some sea water from his own eyeball, too.

Simonds walked over to my brother. "I stand with the Major," said he.

"And I," said the scoundrel Long Tom.

"Professor?" asked my brother.

After a bit of a think, he too stepped over to Martin. "I have a wife awaits me," says he.

"More reason to get aboard, then!" says Tom.

And we all had a good laugh. Of course, 'twas I that laughed the hardest, 'til my Peg gave me the once 'round, and I thought it wise to stop right quick.

"I'm afraid," continued the professor, "that I shall visit Italy only in my books." I knew what he meant and I sadly smiled, for I had also traveled for so long likeways.

Looking a bit sea-sick'd, Master Rollett wobbled to the others, leaving young Loney as the last man standing where they all had stood afore.

"Master Loney?" Martin enquired.

After a pause, the quiet little man simply said, "I should like to see for myself that mosaic at Sienna Cathedral, sir."

"Then, God's speed, my boys," wished Martin, full of hope.

Master Loney joined my side as the captain proclaimed it was time to board.

"Ay-ay, Cappy," says I, and then I turned to my fine friend Nicholas. But afore I could think of a way to thank him, he said, "I thank thee, my friend."

He held open his arms for one last embrace, and I approached, stopping for just half a wink to see that he held no dagger. For after all, a dog that bites a man twice bites a foolish knave indeed! It was a warm embrace, and then I held my brother's hand, and soon I was standing on the plank with my dearest Peg and my good Loney. But as I neared the new ship, I stopped of a sudden, remembering my forgetfulness, and turned 'round to look at Nicholas. I took the papers

230

from inside my doublet and yelled, "My book, lad! My book of poems!" as I tossed them into his hands.

"I'll see they're printed!" shouted he. And I knew he would be true to his word.

I then helped my sweet bride onto the deck of *The Venture*. The two ships were now parting, and I yelled "God's speed, my boys! God's speed!"

And with that, my final *Addio*, I waved. And from my sight they vanished, in the winkle of a salty eye, as I thought to myself, this is the last I will ever see of them.

CHAPTER THIRTY-FIVE.

DAYS OF JOY AND LIGHT.

Back on the banks of London, it was time for farewells. The usual silent Long Tom was first to approach Valentina and Nick, and surprisingly declared, "*I have too grieved a heart to take a tedious leave.*" And then he left.

Player Rollett neared next. "All this has heightened my desire to tread the boards once more. I shall invite you both when I return to the stage at Barton-upon-Humber." And he bowed, showing all that he must be a fantastical actor, for he truly had a fantastical bow. He then made room for the tidy clerk.

"*There is no darkness but ignorance,*" quoth'd sweet Simonds. "Thank you both for sharing the light."

Quite unexpected, the goodly professor stepped up, took Valentina's soft hand, and with trembling lip, he sadly spake. "*Good night, good night. Parting is such sweet sorrow, that I shall say good night 'til it be morrow.*" And with that, he dared kiss the fair maiden's hand. "*Thus with a kiss, I die.*"

Valentina kissed the dear man's cheek. He then made way for Martin, who stepped close to them, with one last adjust to his crooked collar.

"And when you go, walk like new poetry. In couplets, always." And he smiled.

Puffed with the pride of solving this great mystery, and with earnest anticipation of a new day and perhaps a new puzzle to unlock, into the night Martin and his sequel of learnéd gentlemen journey'd.

Johnny Rollett, player of the stage, strolled to meet friends at the nearby Ye New Tavern. The wiry Long Tom headed dockside to chase wild geese, as some call them. Whilst Professor Charles Ogburn, Master of English letters, Simon Simonds, well-abled clerk and assistant, and Martin Taverner, Master at the Law, walked to his office, there to open a very costly and well-deserved bottle of wine. 'Twas the Rhenish, I think.

Horatio stood at the riverbank awaiting news. Nick and Valentina stood a short distance away. Both now understood many of the scenes of this drama. But there was one important side-story they did not know, though Nick, unbeknownst to hisself, be a leading player. They understood that Lord Edward had hid under the false name of Shake-a-Spear. And Valentina knew that milord had fathered the boy Southampton with Mistress Mary. What she did not understand was why milord would fight so hard to sit his boy upon the throne of England. But Nicholas knew.

As they strolled the bankside, she spoke her part first.

"What'll you do now?" asked she.

"Now?" said he.

"You cannot return to the print trade."

"True," said he. And after a bit of a think, he added, "Perhaps I'll farm."

"Oh?" smiles she.

"Yes," smiles he. "I have a friend in the north who's been left more land than she has hands to work it."

"I see," says she coyly.

It was then that the terrible news was delivered. Whilst Nick knew much, he did not know of the recent events in the Dutch Republic. A messenger ran up to Horatio, and Nick could see the great man shaken. He left the beauty for a moment to learn the cause, and after a brief talk with the baron, he returned to Valentina's side.

"What is it?"

"Lord Southampton is dead," said the lad sadly.

"But how?" asked the beauty. And then she spoke what had remained in her mind from the moment old Munday told his tale. "I know there is more to this than you have said. And I'm not leaving until you tell me."

Nicholas could see by her face that she was speaking true.

"This is a story that can never be told aloud," he warned. "For it is a tale not of a book, but of a kingdom."

He looked at Horatio standing at the river and began his tale there.

"Lord Horatio has awaited the return of Southampton and his boy. And this is as much Lord Southampton's story as any man's. It began on the night that my dear father was taken and Southampton arrested. The night Lord Edward died. The baron went to the palace to recover what had been taken from Lord Edward's home."

★

1604.

"We desire his will," demanded Horatio.

"We desire the manuscripts," croaked the crookback.

"Manuscripts?" asked Horatio, as if he had never heard the word.

"The unprinted plays," the treasurer clarified.

"There is no will," said Horatio plainly, "there are no manuscripts."

"That will be all!" said the king, ending this meeting.

The baron, now seething hot, was shown the way out.

"The nobles will never allow us to keep Southampton, your majesty," warned Cecil.

"We have the will, we need not the man," answered the king.

"And so, the king freed him?" asked Valentina.

"After assurances. No attempts to usurp the crown nor publish new plays."

And what Nick said was true. That was the agreement young Southampton signed and sealed that morning. No new plays. But no one ne'er said a word about poems. So, someone, and to this day I'll ne'er know who 'twas, printed that sonnets book with the cipher'd dedication and the poems that told more of Southampton's birth than the king wished known, for he feared this Southampton. And it also seemed he wasn't jumping for joyousness 'bout anyone enquiring after the earl of Oxford, neither.

234

"What became of Lord Edward?" Valentina asked.

The 1590s.

Elizabeth Trentham was both beautiful and clever. She was a lady well-placed, for her place was at the palace where she was maiden to the queen.

'Twas four years after milord's first wife departed us that he entered into marriage with Mistress Elizabeth. But unlike past dalliances, this jointure with one of her majesty's maidens was met with the approval of the queen, perhaps thinking that milord finally needed a wise soul to save him from his ever-lasting impoverishments.

Lord Edward, nearing two score years, had finally found a Venus to match his Mars. I'd say a Juliet to match his Romeo, but we all know how that drink was drunk. Milord and his new lady were about the happiest couple at court. And the proof 'twas in the pottage, for not five years later their son Henry was born, and to avoid confusion with all the other Henrys in their life, they nick'd him *Harry*. And whilst milord delighted in his other sons, at this time in his life he reveled in young Harry best, as this was the lad he could embrace and share his days with. And as we have come to know, the greater the years in a father, the greater the love for the boy, though 'twas not a long time they shared together.

Seeing his lantern was ever dimming, her majesty finally gave Lord Edward the right to his Forest of Essex, and his shrewd new bride saw to it that, together with Castle Hedingham, it would provide for the benefit of their young son and heir, now that milord at last had one.

Young Harry was a joy to the man who was now nearing the end of a much-traveled life. The times he held the boy in his arms were the very best times for Edward Vere. They hawked and they hunted. They fenced and they feasted. And the boy was taught to love books. The ones he most preferred was the ones his old man writ, which gave milord great happiness. And he would never forget his last contest with the boy, who was 'round the age of ten at the time.

'Twas the day Lord Edward welcomed his guest inside, whilst outside, young Harry ran through his secret path, the one that led from behind King's Place and through the gardens, past the south mill field to the moor, and back again, where he could gallop his feet in muck and bramble, unseen and unheard.

A merry meeting was had 'twixt milord and Ben Jonson when young Harry peeped his pate 'round the door.

"Ah!" opened milord's arms wide, which was always the sign for the boy to run to his dear father and embrace him tight.

"You remember Master Jonson, Harry?"

"'Tis my pleasure," said the boy all-polite, with a bow and a smile.

"'Tis mine, my young viscount," Ben bowed his head and returned the smile. "And how go your studies, may I enquire?"

"I am happily done for the day," quipped the lad.

"We shall see about that," said milord, eager to parade the boy's skills before his friend. He put his face to young Harry's. "Know you the time?"

"Time for a turnip tart?" hoped the boy. And his eyes gleamed.

"After a rhyme!" smiled milord.

And with that, Lord Edward sat the lad down opposite him.

"I shall begin, and you will answer the tale."

"And then the tart?" gleamed the persistent youth.

"And then the tart!" laughed my goodly lord. "And to start you dancing upon the right foot, my dear son, I might suggest your first answer be *Hey-ho holiday.*"

"Thank you, dear father," smiled back the boy, with a bit o' the Puck upon his face, as this bright lad had always a song of his own to sing. And off they went.

"*To fell upon a holy eve,*" milord began.

"*Hey-ho Harry Vere!*" laughed the boy, making milord laugh with him.

"*When holy fathers wont to shrieve.*"

236

"The time for a tart is near."
"Sitting upon a hill so high."
"A long way to the top."
"The while my flock did feed thereby."
"My hunger I could not stop."
"I saw the bouncing Bellibone."
"What be a Bellibone?"
"Tripping over the dale alone."
"We tripped into a hole."
"My sheep did their wonted feed."
"And climbed back with a start."
"That ever since my heart did grieve."
"'Tis time to eat the tart!"

Milord laughed at this, and held onto his boy, who was sure declared the victor. And all with a good eye could see that, thanks to this young lad, these were the final days of joy and light for milord. 'Til the visitation. But that is the saddest part of our tale, and I cannot now put down into words such a sorrow as this. So, I'll sail over the years, and try to turn this ship 'round when I have the courage to speak it.

CHAPTER THIRTY-SIX.

LIKE THE OCEAN CRADLES A KINGDOM.

1621.

The Two Fighting Henries they were called. Harry Vere, the tart-loving lad who grew to become the eighteenth earl of Oxford, and Henry Southampton. They fought on the fields and they battled in the Parliament, where their opposition 'gainst the king's party, who wished his son to marry the infant of Spain and place our nation under the boot of Rome, soon booted both of them into the Tower where Horatio paid them a visit.

"It's seventeen years since the great earl died. Perhaps now is time to give over the manuscripts."

"Never!" exclaimed Southampton at the window, eyeing the king walking his dogged Spanish ambassador below.

"Until his majesty is satisfied, you both shall stay in here to rot!" said Horatio.

"Then rot we shall!" answered the defiant Harry, so much like the father of the son he was.

"Look at him," Southampton said, as he ripped off his gloves and slapped them 'cross the window. "His majesty, selling our English souls to the Spanish devil. You wish to save us. Then save all of England, too. Have you read the new books they print? *Nero Caesar*? Telling the tale of when our England was never more grand than when it was ruled by Rome! Is that what we should give them? Instead of handing over our glorious history to the king's party, hand it to the people. Remind them of what England is. Go to Pembroke and Montgomery. They've offered their help. With the king aligned with Spain, print milord's works before the papists take stronger control of the presses. Print them all. Tell his story, Horatio."

1624.

"And so they printed the complete folio," Nicholas concluded.

"But why did the king so hate Southampton?" asked the beauty. And Nicholas understood he must now tell all he knew.

★

'Twas only weeks earlier that King James had perused the red-covered book laid in his way. "The heirs lie heavy still, after all these years!" he roared. He walked a bit and thought on how he should handle this Southampton threat, and then it struck him. "He wishes to wear our crown? Then let him prove the hero. We shall send him to the wars. And send his own heir with him. This young Southampton. To end this forever," and he crossed to his wine chest. "'Tis time to send the Rhenish!"

★

Both father and son fought valiant in the Low Countries, bravely leading their troops. After days of battle, the twenty-year old James arrived at his tent to find his majesty's gift. The lad tasted the new-arrived Rhenish and by morning he was dead.

The heart-broke Southampton, after finding his dear son, and after finding the Rhenish, took the lad's body to the shore, where, by dawn, they were both aboard the small boat ferrying them to their ship, which would sail them home.

The light was sharp and low. Two soldiers held firm their oars, which would propel the small bark from shore to ship. The body of Henry's young James had been wrapped in his cloak, with his brave sword placed in his lifeless limbs. Lord Southampton sat holding the boy tight in his arms. Cradling him like the ocean cradles a kingdom. And the rowers began.

It was a sad morning, and few gulls cared to sing. The broken Southampton said not a word. He leant over his silent son, speechless, motionless, the whole of the way. It was a sore sight to be sure. A sight to make a mermaid weep. Where any soul could see, they rowed not on the water, but on the tears of the oars themselves. The mighty lord shielded his dearest boy. A boy who had meant the world to him. Now broken. Quiet. And the morning wind ran cold.

As they neared the waiting ship, the soldiers stood for their grieving lord's command. None came. He just sat there. They waited for their instruction. There was none.

"He too was dead," said Nicholas, who had learnt this sad tale from Horatio just moments before. "Cradling his kingdom."

"Poisoned," whispered Valentina.

And Horatio stood at the shore voiceless. For if he dared speak, he would but cry out. The ship arrived with the Lords Southampton aboard, and Nick and Valentina watched as they brought the two bodies off. Nick rose and reverently removed his cap.

"They are now returned home," was all he could say.

Horatio knelt to view his kin. He looked upon young James, whose life had only begun. And then upon dear Henry. Soldier, poet, jouster. A lot like another he knew. Such a kind soul this Henry was. Seeing his well-worn gloves folded within Southampton's doublet, Horatio sadly smiled. He reverently removed them and placed them into his pocket, knowing where they should finally have a fitting rest.

"Why was Lord Southampton more of a threat than any other English noble?" Valentina needed to know.

"You have read Lord Edward's sonnets. They repeatedly speak of a young man for whom the poet wishes marriage and an heir." Nick looked into her eyes. "Why?"

From fairest creatures we desire increase,
That thereby beauty's rose might never die.

240

"Why should he care so?" asked Nick.

"Because he was his father. And only a father would care so much to want his son to produce heirs. But if he were the child of Lord Edward and Mary Montague, why would that give him right to the crown?"

"What was it that threatened the king so?" asked Nick. "What of this strange tale in the *Midsummer's Dream*?"

I do but beg a little changeling boy to be my henchman.

"He was the boy," said the beauty.

"But why is he a *changeling boy*?" Nick asked. "The rumors name his father Edward Vere."

"But his mother—" Valentina edged nearer.

Whilst I, my sovereign, watch the clock for you.
And all those beauties whereof now he's king.

"If he were sovereign and king, his mother could only be—"

"The queen!" Valentina's lip shook, and then she quickly set her brain to thinking.

That thereby beauty's rose might never die.

"The queen is the rose!" said she. "The Tudor rose. She fell ill at the same time Mistress Mary was bearing her babe," and then she understood. "They were both with child! And they thought the queen was dying."

"She was not losing life, she was giving life."

"So, there is truth to such stories?"

"These poems are printed rumors," said Nick shrewdly. "But if a son was born, and the queen was wooing France to save her own kingdom, she could not have such rumors around. A home would need to be found for the child. A noble home. Where a child already existed. Where a child could be replaced by another."

"As a changeling!" said she. "As in the *Dream*! But is it true?"

"Why did Lord Burghley call upon the Privy Council to change the wording of the Treasons Act?" asked Nick. "In order to secure the line of succession, they removed the requirement for the next king of England to be a legal *heir* and simply allowed for him to be *her natural issue*. Why?"

"To allow a bastard child to reign," Valentina reasoned.

Nick then took out the scribbled page Millington had given him before he died. "Sometimes the truth lies beneath our very eyes," he continued. "Millington's note to me. I was so occupied with his scribbled numbers that I neglected the text beneath it. *Albion's England*. The line reads, *Hence England's heirs-apparent have of Wales been Princes, till our Queen deceased concealed her heir.*" He looked at Valentina. "He is telling us that she died with a hidden heir."

CHAPTER THIRTY-SEVEN.

A NAME FOR A SON.

In the addition to that *Albion* scribbler, there was Sanford and Peele and Nashe. Some called them fools, and others called them traitors. But there were many who considered them the bravest of all. Writers who dared to publicly paint forth a forbidden scene. The friends of milord who touched upon treasonous gossips, much like the songs sung at the Bull and Spectacles. Oh, the uproar it caused the queen. How it touched off her hot temper, which was never known to have a cool side anyways. But touched, she was.

Her majesty threw the papers 'cross the floor, which was beginning to become a bit of a habit with the queen ever since milord learnt to write.

"Who is it claims authorship of that first libel?" she demanded of the crookback, who was forced to scurry 'bout on all fours like a mad cur to find the demanded poem.

"Uh… George Peele, your majesty," he huffed as he found the thing.

"Ha!" she barked. "Yet we know the true author behind it. Read it again!"

Her cur obediently obliged. "Yes, your highness. *Gentle Henry, Southampton's star, I wish all fortune that in Cynthia's eye, Cynthia, the glory of the Western world—*"

"'Tis *us* he speaks of!" she interrupted. "A fool would know it. Only a muddle-minded fool would read such a libel. Go on. Read it!"

"Your majesty…" the scared cur pleaded.

"Read it!" she insisted.

And all-reluctant, he went on. "*With all the stars in her fair firmament, bright may he rise and shine immortally.*"

"He means to place that boy atop our throne while 'tis still warm!" shouted the enraged queen. "What is the Latin at the end? Placed next our Tudor rose, which is us, yet again, in thin disguise!"

Robert Cecil feared to read such words again but had no choice in the matter. He took a breath and pronounced, "*Stay far away from here, hateful disorder. While the nettle produces only course weeds, the offspring of the rose is noble.*" And with fear, Cecil looked to her majesty.

"*Offspring of the rose,*" she repeated. "Does he think he can disguise such a lie by hiding it in the Latin? Who is meant by this rose?" asked the queen all-gentle, trying to keep her fire within.

A drop of perspire crookedly ran down the crookback's forehead. "Why, your majesty is generally called by such—"

"And so!" she interrupted, "he claims there is an offspring, does he not? Who is *Cynthia*? *Beauty*? *The rose*?" And afore she could get an answer back, she supplied her own. "*We* are! Means he to suggest to the world that this boy is an offspring of *ours*!?"

"I will see to it he is drawn and quartered," came Cecil's reply. "And boiled."

"I would have Peele's head did I not know the true voice behind this gossip!" She then stooped to look the crookback in the eye, which was never an easy task. "My dwarf," said she, "read me the next. By that grammarian."

Cecil was on all fours again searching for the piece writ by milord's friend, Sanford.

"Tell me, my pygmy, what says he about this boy Southampton?" she demanded, knowing full-well the libels he had writ.

"He speaks first of your beloved father, our great King Henry," croaked the crookback, hoping this should suffice. One look to her majesty told him it did not, and so he went on. "He then speaks of the boy. *There follows a Dynasta—*"

"*Dynasta!*" exploded the queen. "A hereditary prince of our lineage, if my Latin does not deceive me." It did not. "Of this boy! This is treason of the highest degree!" her majesty cried. And looking for more heads to roll, she persisted. "Where's the poem by Oxford's man Nashe, dedicated to Southampton?"

It took a moment for Cecil to find that one, but find it he finally did. "*Pardon, sweet flower of matchless poetry, the fairest bud that red rose ever bore.*"

The queen's fury flamed hot. "And now we are painted even more plainly," said she, "with the red rose of our family giving birth!"

"He claims to *paint forth the things that hidden are.*"

"And we shall paint forth a beheading portrait for all concerned!" fumed her highness.

But alas, none were beheaded. Nor even Stubb'd. Poor Tom Nashe did leave London, never to write again. Hey-ho. Peele would have been punished, but afore they could ready the rack, he perished from the pox. Sanford was delivered a far worse fate, for the queen draggled him from his beautiful Canterbury home and sent him to live out the rest of his days… in Snave! Lord Edward, perhaps as a result of his high state, was spared his life, but ne'er could he raise his boy nor marry his queen nor see his lad rule England.

But out alack, he was but one hour mine.

"If this be true," Valentina posed cautiously, "then revealing the identity of the Shake-speare author would have revealed the identity of the changeling boy. And the young man of the sonnets."

"And that being done," added Nick, "there might have been many an Englishman who would have preferred a popular English noble on our throne, a noble who was possibly of the queen's own blood, rather than a Scotsman, whose ties are with our Spanish enemies."

Nick again looked at Horatio, and at the two warriors that lay at rest on the shore. "Such is the myth of the changeling boy. The son, whose father was the shining star, and his mother the virginal moon."

"The star and the moon and the son," Valentina spoke. And then she wondered. "Why would the queen not wish to place her own son on the throne after her life was done?"

"Lord Edward had hoped for such a time. And it might have come to pass, had it not been for the day Southampton made a fateful mistake."

And Nick went on to describe that terrible morn when Lord Southampton, as rash as he was, met with his friend, Lord Essex.

'Twas the year 1601 when Southampton had been persuaded by Essex to demand in her majesty's final years that she name her heir. But this was a queen who feared that choosing a successor would cause a war to displace her early. So, the two young nobles entered the city with three-hundred men in arms. And that, of certain, was against the laws of this sceptered isle. Son or no son.

They passed the gates of the palace. Open up, they did, the royal chamber. Barge in, they did, upon her majesty. And arrest them, they done, sending them to the Tower. For this was treason sure. And by month's end, Lord Essex lost his head.

However, Southampton waited in prison, with never a visitor to see nor a cat to stroke, as her majesty weighed his final fate. And there was not a man at court who never wondered why she didn't have his head upon a pike, like she had done with Essex. It seemed she could not quite bear the killing of this boy. And many say it was due to Lord Edward, for 'twas he who held up the proceedings after they called him to head the jury of peers.

As highest earl of the realm, 'twas his signature they needed to see that justice was done. But it seemed that Lady Justice had a bit of a turn up her smock sleeve. For all the nobles, but one, had signed their names onto the *Guilty* side of the parchment, and it's my thinking that even a muddle-minded apple-john could guess who the *but one* was.

Robert Cecil ran to milord's chair at the back to ask for his signature.

"We must have your name, milord," he said, reaching his deformed face close to the earl's. "You must vote him guilty."

Lord Edward looked up at him, heart all broke, but mind still strong.

"'Tis your duty, milord," added the crookback.

246

And after a breath, milord gave his answer. "I shall."

And Cecil smiled.

"On condition," added milord, extinguishing the smile on the crookback's face, for the words *on condition* were the last he ever wanted to hear from milord.

"Her majesty will name no successor to remove her early from her throne!"

"His life must be spared," said milord.

"You know the law," breathed Cecil.

"And I know her heart."

Cecil looked back at the lords waiting at the front. He dismissed hisself with the promise to return with her majesty's answer. And all waited silent in the chamber, not knowing on which side of the page milord would write his name. Cecil finally came back huffing.

"She has agreed," he barked, and milord breathed his first full breath in a fortnight. "*On condition!*" came the words from the crooked man, joyfully throwing back the very dagger that milord had flung at him. Edward looked into Cecil's eyes as the crookback spoke. "You fight no more to claim your writings."

"My writings? What are they to her?"

"You must choose, Lord Edward. Your name upon a book, or the boy upon a block."

Milord answered swift. He rose, propping hisself onto that gold-topped stick of his, and stepped to the front of the hall, where the paper was held for him. Cecil was glad, for he knew that if the works remained untied to milord, then the many privy stories of the court revealed therein, and the tale of the secret son, true or no, would remain likeways hid. With quill in hand, Lord Edward signed under the *Guilty*.

And true to her word, the queen tore up Southampton's death warrant and kept him locked in the Tower 'til that day, two short years later, that was to be her last on this earth. And when James was made king, milord vowed his support for the new monarch with a bargain. He agreed to keep the reins tight on Southampton, who he'd make certain would never claim the throne, in exchange for his release from the Tower.

James knew he was never popular with the English peoples. He feared a man like Southampton could rally forces enough to take the crown. But he kept his vow and released Southampton as his first royal act, only to have him brought back the next year when Lord Edward hisself joined our good queen in heaven. And once he was assured Southampton was yet reined in, and held no royal ambitions, and would print no more inciting plays of milord, he was let go again that next morning. The morning of Nathaniel North's execution.

This was a lot for Valentina to take in.

"But the king has reigned safely now for twenty years," said the beauty. "He is old. Why should it matter now?"

"He is a king, but he is also a father. A new succession dawns. And again, Southampton's star would seem to shine over the legitimacy of a Scottish prince. The Spanish match is threatened. The new Shakespeare book just printed. So, his majesty dispatched his rival." Nick looked to the cloaked bodies at shore. "And now he is returned."

"This is the story your own father intended to tell?"

"As he saw our good queen fading with no named successor, and the dark clouds of Scotland forming, he began to write this tale. After the new king arrived, he knew the story must still be known."

"And the printer's son?"

"Will keep his head."

She smiled. And desperately yearned to know how all had ended for milord on his last night of life, which was the first night of our tale. And so, I shall try to relate it as best I can, without the breaking of my heart.

248

CHAPTER THIRTY-EIGHT.

THE HEARTACHE IS IN THE NEVER KNOWING.

1604.

'Twas mid-June at King's Place when milord felt the spot upon his neck that caused the achings in his body. The countess and young Harry, who had just begun his eleventh year, would soon be on their way home from Hedingham when the pains shot through him.

He crossed to his wall-glass and observed as best he could, given the tiredness of his eyes, the purpled protrusion upon the right side of his neck, and he now knew that what had spread throughout the city was now spreading throughout his body.

He understood at once the deadly visitation was upon him. But his first thoughts were not of the poems he had yet to write nor the dreams of countries yet to be discovered. His first thoughts be of his son, for the life the young lad would soon be forced to lead alone. *I know I cannot get on without him,* thought milord. *So how will he get on without me?* Looking within the glass, milord saw the phoenix quills upon his desk behind him. And he thought on another lost boy of his. *Will my dear Harry's fate be that of young Robin or young Toby?* The heartache, he knew, was in the never knowing. He crossed to his chair where he had laid his silken scarf and wrapped it tight 'round his nape and approached the door.

'Tis hard for a fellow now to really understand how strong the Pest reigned over our world at the time. The countless dear souls it touched. The lives it took were of such high numbers (near half our world, they say), that the only way to comprehend the truth about it is to put a face to each name writ into the many parish records. For a man must look into the sparkle of an eye and hear the whisper of a voice to understand 'tis not a name buried in a book, but a beautiful breath within a being. These be dearest living souls of sons and fathers, daughters and mothers, grandsires and widows. For just in our own small tale, before the end is told, amongst the dead from the plague we will find:

Captain Titus Addicock, old servant Adam, Big Jack Kole, dear Martin Taverner, Barnaby Brodnax, Ole Hopkins Hughes, Professor Charles Ogburn, Simon Simonds, Johnny Rollett, Francis Langley, Johnny Clayton, Anne Hathaway, the Whatley woman, John Heminges, Henry Condell, Doctor Luck, Master Godsgift Goode, the lovely Lettyce, Master Willowaugh, a besottedly wobbling pottle-pot, sweet Sexton Edmunds, he who writ *Guy of Warwick*, sweet Master Strittmaster, Anthony Munday, Giles Allen, mean old Master Mugge, Professor Joseppi Magri, ale-keep Agnes, young Ginger, the Archbishop of Canterbury, one Herbert brother, Countess Susan Vere, Gabriel Harvey, Mistress Margaret's mistake, the messiah Willy Hackett, Widow Sears, Mistress Mary Montague, nuncle Arthur Golding, Sir Thomas Smith, Catherine, Countess Palatine of Kleeburg, Master Bantickle Prickling of Stickleback, Master Mickel Mutt, Mister Geoffrey Boyle, old Thomas Churchyard, drunken Tom Nashe, Sir Christopher Mutton, the palsied Willard Hesterfield, the deaf Master Gooch, the single-eyed Mistress Green, prisoner Peter Pygott, the Pygott wife, a clod named Allen of Nilson on Pendle Hill, Tiziano Vecelli, Penders van Portugal, ole Mackie Mac-Somesuch, the mighty Prospero Fattinanti, Dudley's trollop, Alice Aldebourne, Poor John Stubbes, Henry Evans Oxford, Sir John Fortescue, Master *Robert* Ricketts, Thomas Bedingfield, first mate Whittemore, old Jane Fyngland, the infant of Spain, Thomas Middleton, and alas my lord Edward Vere.

"Adam," milord called out to the only other being within the house. As his faithful man approached, he yelled, "Stop!" And the man did so. "I pray you, my dear friend, find us Dr. Forman."

Adam's heart at once sunk, for he knew what Dr. Forman's speciality was. And after the good doctor came and went, Adam was once again summoned.

"Stand not so near," came the command, as milord filled a purse with coins and cast it to his servant. "Take this, and with it my ever-living love," and Adam's eye began to wet. "My dear Adam, you know, you must leave this place now, and never return for forty days."

"My dear master," spoke Adam, understanding now the Pest was the ruler of King's Place, "I have served you since your great father lived. Let me be your servant still."

Milord had feared this would be the man's answer. He also feared for this good man, who had been like an uncle to him for all his life. But he was now old, and Lord Edward was afraid such an ancient body as his was far too frail to fight this enemy. 'Twas perhaps the hardest thing he could do, but milord was forced to play the villain.

"I do not wish you here, is the truth, Adam," and he looked straight into the man's tearing eyes. "I do not *want* you here, old man."

Adam's tears were not for the hurt these words inflicted, but for the love he bore his lord who spoke them, knowing them unsincere. Adam moved not, and milord was forced into drawing another wicked arrow.

"You're a noisome fellow. I sit here to write and hear nothing but your boots above as if dancing a Morris." He could see Adam was having none of it. "You chew your beef like a Coleford cow."

"I'm from Colyton, milord."

"Like a *Colyton* cow, then. I want you gone!"

"Begging your pardon, master" said Adam, "Milord was ever a great writer, but I fear, never a good actor."

And milord looked upon his sweet man.

"I shall do you the service of a younger man. For know you," and he cast back the purse, "wherever you go, I will follow thee."

Milord smiled sadly. And Adam smiled sadly. And from then, old Adam followed milord to the end o' time. Lord Edward felt hisself fortunate that his countess and boy had been to the country that month. But they were close upon their return, and he knew he must act fast.

"See to it we have provisions for two score days," he spoke soft, "as the doctor is now sending for the watchmen, and we will soon be unable to leave."

"Yes, my master," he said, as he made his way to the house behind the house and gathered all they would need for the time prescribed.

'Twas only an hour 'til the warder came with his men. One fellow took a brush and painted the red cross onto the door. A second man nailed it shut so that none but Dr. Forman may enter. The warder then instructed them to stand at each end of Morning Lane to ensure as much.

Whilst all this happed, milord raced 'gainst time to make certain all that needed sorting would be set. He opened the box that held his legal testament and saw to it that it was signed aright. Once done, he placed it atop his bible and then collected his other life's testament, all the pages of his plays and poems, and tied them together.

"Adam," called milord, who placed the bundle just outside his door and then shut it tight. "Dear Adam," he spoke, when he heard his man near. "These papers are to be given to any friend who comes for them."

"Yes, milord."

The 24th night of June was upon them when the carriage that carried the Countess Elizabeth and young Harry was stopped at Morning Lane, and they were given the cruel news that they may go no farther. The countess began to weep, and her first thought was to insist that they proceed. But one look at Harry and she knew 'twould be his young life in danger if they entered King's Place. But she could not abandon her dear Edward, neither, 'specially in this time when he must need them most. Though confused, it was Harry who thought up a device.

"Dear mother," he whispered, looking into her wet eyes. "I know a way to father."

And the boy told the coachman to drive them to the south mill field. They were headed to the lad's secret path.

Inside his chamber, milord struggled with his breath, for 'twas a difficult thing to draw in the air he needed. 'Twas also the pain 'round his neck, as the purple mark had grown blacker. There was no cure, and milord knew it. But his thoughts were more of wife and child than of hisself. And so, he tied his scarf all the tighter and sat at his table to do the one thing he must needs do. He writ.

252

A letter to his sweet wife told that which he ne'er had time to tell her in the past. And a letter to his dear son told that which he ne'er would be able to say in the future. 'Twas only a short time for some of it to be told, for there were ne'er enough seconds to tell all. Milord understood that Time was the villain now.

The most important of tasks done, to occupy his mind, he then writ more. Invisible knights and tales of nuncles and frogless heaths traveled their way from milord's mind onto rivers of ink atop the pages in front of him. He was lost in a world of fancy and truth, 'til of a sudden, his head became heavy and fell onto his desk. He ceased to write. His goblet overturned. His quill still in hand. And the Sherborne bled onto the page.

'Twas then came the tap at the back window, the one far from the eyes and ears of his watchmen. After a moment, another knock followed. And another, until Edward finally heard the sound. His ears became alive before his body could awake. He struggled to open his eyes and lift his head, but he could not. Hearing knock upon knock, he knew he must try. He knew he must succeed in this, his final battle. And he slowly did.

He turned and saw his beautiful countess and his lovely boy, as if in a dream. And his heart shook. He took up his walking stick and made it to the window, he knew not how. With a tear in his eye, he reached out to them, knowing he could never touch them again. And in one final irony of life, in the life of the man who gave the world its words, his own were now of no use to him, since they could not be heard.

He held his left hand high to match his wife's hand on t'other side of the glazed glass, and his right hand low to shadow the lad's small fingers. His whole body ached with the longing of touch, as he cursed the atomies of the glass that kept him from sensing his beloved family. From embracing the only things upon this earth he desired to touch and hold and feel. 'Twas a sorrowful sight to see, 'tis true. But milord was brave, which made his son as brave as a boy in his boots could be. 'Twas not words that passed between them, but looks that told all. For this was the picture that the Countess Elizabeth would recall, whenever she thought on her husband. This was the image young Harry would carry when oft he thought about his father. 'Twas that last twinkle from his green-and-tawny eyes. 'Twas the old silken doublet and the sullied scarf.

But the agony of not a final word, nor a last touch, was their unbearable punishment. At a time when a warm whisper and a loving embrace was needed most. 'Twas not the piercing pain of his self-attacking body that stung him so, but the bursting of his breaking heart. He intended to speak with them awhile, in silent words and in feeble fingertops, but life doesn't always live up to our intents. 'Twas not milord's heart that was giving up, but his breath. And afore he knew what was happening, the glisten on the cheek of his bride was fading away. The gleam in the eye of his boy was turning black.

And he was gone.

As you from crimes would pardon'd be,
Let your indulgence set me free.

Romeo is poisoned. Hamlet vanquished. Lear forgiven. Prospero drowns his book. And Oberon, at the last, walks off with his sons.

CHAPTER THIRTY-NINE.
A MIDNIGHT BURIAL AND A BLASTING ABOARD.
1624.

Valentina had a thought perhaps none had ever wondered.

"Whatever became of the first Southampton child taken from Mary Montague? The one replaced by the changeling?"

Nick had never thought on that. "Raised, I suppose, by another. Or worse. I doubt there is any who knows for certain."

"There must be some way to learn," she pondered, her appetite for adventure whetted still.

"Look for a man 'round London wearing an old chain and cross of Southampton," he mused. For he knew the symbol well, as it adorned the entry of Southampton House. The cross with the four falcons. They were the family crest and would have decked the chain the countess placed upon her babe on that stormy eve, as they sadly pulled him from her.

"So Lord Southampton knew this fable?" asked Valentina.

"That's his ship," Nick gestured. "He named it."

Valentina turned and looked at the ship's stern, where painted in bold letters read its royal name: *THE PRINCE*. And then she smiled.

Nick told her, now that she knew all, she must leave for the country come dawn. The longer she tarried, the more danger awaited.

"Let us go together," she suggested. "You need a farm, after all, if you are to become a farmer."

He liked the idea well and had been about to suggest the same. "There is one thing more I must do."

"I will wait for you," she vowed.

"If I am not at your side by morning," he said, "you must go alone, and I will follow."

Valentina anxiously took his hand. "'Til then," she said.

"'Til nothing else," he answered.

And of a sudden, for some reason, they both shared the single thought that they might never see each other again. And they kissed lips. And all was well.

She walked away, reflecting on their future, not suspecting that what awaited her at her lodgings would be a deadly villain. Nick slowly walked to Horatio and they spoke. He knew that something was devised for that night. One final blow to enemies. One lasting tribute to their ever-living poet. But before he could ask, Horatio invited him to join them in their crowning triumph over death.

★

As I peeped out the portal o' the poop, I could see the distant shore ahead. Far from the land we left, a brave new world beckoned us. A land to bring us hope. A tittle did I know that the shady Master Digges was at that very instant stealing off our ship and onto a small rowing boat. Not my dear Peg nor I could see that fellow, and we could neither see the rope which he joined to the barrel of whatever mischief he had brought aboard there. But he soon lit that rope afire and rowed away.

Which rather brings me back to where I began. For though 'tis the strange tale of mine own death, there is also a report of a birth that ends the telling. But I sail ahead of my ship here, for that was yet to come. And there was trouble back home that must be met afore any good news be told.

★

Valentina had embarked upon a terrible mistake. She walked to Martin's office one last time, unawares that Knyvet and his two men, Skeres and Poley, lay in wait 'cross the lane. She went in to bid again her farewells, and they wished her all happiness as she ventured away that night, sending her off with their blessings. But unbeknownst to them, they also sent her off with a vulture at her heels. For as she traveled back to the sign of the White Dove, Mister Skeres followed.

She entered the inn as the vulture watched. He waited and could see no other figure, since, as oft would hap, and as an astute soul may well remember I mentioned previous, she was alone in that place. Skeres removed his dagger and slowly approached the inn.

Nicholas also passed by Martin's, as it was halfway 'twixt his start and his finish. And watching him pass, Knyvet and Poley set to work.

It wasn't long that Nick reached the Hackney churchyard of Saint Augustine. The mourners must have counted two hundred or more. Many wore the golden star of Vere on their shoulders. Mostly nobles and gents, but Nick was quite welcomed. He approached the marble tomb, which stands no longer, but at that time read:

Edward de Vere, Earl of Oxenford,
Lord Great Chamberlain of England d. 1604.

The tomb had been opened and the coffin placed atop, draped with the great earl's banner and a sprig of rue and rosemary. For now, it was time to right a wrong, and rebury the great Edward where he belonged, amongst his poet friends at Westminster's Abbey.

Horatio asked for all to take their place, and a group of boys began to sing like seraphim. Horatio and Pembroke and Montgomery joined the side of Harry de Vere, the eighteenth earl, who led the way. Six noblemen bore the funeral bier that held Lord Edward, as all moved from the church to the yard and down the lane. Nicholas' heart at first felt heavy as he marched, 'til ahead of him he spied three ladies. *Could these be his daughters?* he mused. And of a sudden he thought on his own dear father, and of the life's work he had created. The beautiful books. The timeless words. He was proud of his father, and he knew sure his father was proud of him. Nick then thought on this march, which seemed a song to sing from all children to all fathers. And then he felt light.

The procession turned a corner, and people stood on streets to see. Nick's spirits lifted more, knowing he was a part of it. Hearing the angels sweetly singing, and seeing the mourners' glistening tears and glittering stars twinkled by torchlights, he felt no longer in London but in heaven. In the sky, a million stars shimmered above them. In the fields, a million glow-flies fired about them. All for this man who had given so much. Most greatly lived. This star of England. A night had never been so magical nor so beautiful. And Nick was reminded of the feeling he knew when he read the poet's verse. A feeling that made him grasp that man too was made of star-dust and dreams. This was a thing he felt. This was a thing called joy.

Lord Edward's army approached the playhouses, where the players, old and young, stood, doffing their caps as their great lord passed.

As they neared the finest tavern in Whitechapel, the gentlemen of the Boar's Head shook high their spears whilst the ladies lifted candles. Old Anthony Munday stood tearful, as he waved his worn star high above his head. His streak of ginger glistened from the torchlights. Beside him old Widow Sears wept. She was glad, and she wept.

Old Munday patted the back of their companion, a fellow of loyal cheer, who then left their side and joined the walk toward Westminster. He marched all-proud, adjusting his cap and touching his feather for good luck. The old phoenix feather. *One last errand to run for milord*, thought he. *For my brother and for milord*.

The marchers strode into the city's center and many others joined in. They passed Blackfriars, where a kind and tearful fellow with a borrowed name followed in step, playing the smallest and sweetest-sounding viol da gamba as he went.

Finally arriving at their sacred destination, the funeral procession entered the abbey at Westminster in the dead of night. 'Cross the street, overlooking the place, a man looked down from his window above. He knew exactly what they were doing, and he raised his drink to the memory of *his* Shake-speare. A final farewell to his sweet swan of Avon. From Ben Jonson.

The procession slowly marched down the south cross aisle. At the corner of the poets, betwixt the resting place of the great writer Chaucer and milord's old friend, Ed Spenser, the floor stone had been removed to receive its new and noble tenant. And again, and forever, milord could now rest long beside Ole Chaucer! As his coffin was lowered into the hole, Nick could smell the sweet and holy frankincense lit to honor the great poet. They readied the slab to place above it, but Horatio asked them to halt. Milord's three daughters approached, and each placed a lone violet atop milord's coffin. One final gift to father. Then Horatio took from his cloak the pair of soft leather gloves with the black ribbons and laid them reverently atop, nearest milord's heart, where they would remain for ever.

After a prayer was spoke, the scriptless slab was then placed above it. A slab without a name.

My name be buried where my body is.

And far away, aboard *The Venture*, we could just make out the shoreline of the continent. An old land new to us, that would bring us hope. 'Twas about then that our ship burst from the explosion.

CHAPTER FORTY.

ONE FINAL BATTLE, ONE ULTIMATE UNCOVERING.

The mourning song had ended.

Nicholas was amongst the last to leave the abbey. After a prayer, as he turned to retrace his steps, noble Horatio called him back. He took from his pocket a magic token and pierced it onto Nick's doublet. A golden star. A glittering wish. And Nick was proud. He thanked this gentle man and soon was off to start his new life.

Of course, Horatio had not read Nicholas the full folio. For when the very throne of England is at stake, there are chapters that a fellow must never know. He quietly called to his man Cuddy and pointed out the printer at the door. He gave his man a dagger and bade him follow.

Nick walked the desolate streets toward Valentina. Most good citizens were in their beds as the late hours turned into early ones. Master Cuddy kept his distance and was quiet in his pursuit. He was an able man and good at what he did. But it did not take Nick long afore he heard another pair of boots upon the ground. He began to quicken his own, but those behind him likeways picked up. The faster Nick tread, the faster he was pursued. Through alleyways and falling fog, the pace increased.

As he came upon Pleasant Street a bit befuddled, instead of turning left, he veered right, leading him into a walled courtyard. He had made a deadly error. With nowhere to go, the feet were swift upon him. And the attacker too, who pulled out his dagger and swung his deadly arm back. Nicholas turned and looked the man in the eyes. The eyes of evil about to end his life. But the man did not attack. Instead, his eyes turned dead. He fell onto the confused Nicholas, clutching him as he made his way down to the dirty ground below.

Nick then saw Master Cuddy standing there, behind Poley, wiping his dagger clean. Saved by Horatio's man! Cuddy handed him the dagger and, with a wink and a wish, he vanished into the fog. Nicholas took a breath and sheathed tight the new weapon into his doublet. Thinking all was safe, he stood for a moment. But all was not safe, and would I were there to tell him so.

As I said, 'twas about then that our ship burst from the explosion. And I give thanks I was not on it at the time. For having always been blessed with the knack of a nose for smelling fires, whilst I could not see it, I could sure smell the fiery mischief that Master Digges had ignited. So, I presently alerted my dear Peg and our new Loney, and together the three of us ran to that barrel ole Digges had brought aboard. With a *heave* and a *ho*, we managed to lift it up and o'er the ship's rail just as the thing exploded, blasting a fine but harmless hole into either the starboard or the stern or whatever they call that part of the ship. But save it we did, and heroes we were. Leastways, that's what the good captain called us.

Now, a fellow may remember me saying I was not on the ship as it blew, and rightly speaking, 'twas true, as I had the good misfortune of falling off with the barrel as we pushed it o'erboard, p'raps slip-sliding on the wetness of the deck below my buskins. One moment, I was *heave-ho'ing* a barrel of fire powder off the ship, and the next, I was swimming 'mongst the angelfishes as good Horatio had promised the magistrate he'd see to. And I don't know what happed in the between. But 'tis only one thing I can say for certain, and that is, I am sure thankful I missed all those schooldays to become such a fine swimmer.

'Twas then, they say, that Master Loney fell o'er-board. How that happed, I'll never know. But soon a small rowing boat was dropped to us and we got in. Since we was close to shore, they thought it best we join up with *The Venture* at port. Which is what we did. And this is when I learnt 'twas a good thing Master Loney was a cook's swain at his college, for in fact, 'twasn't a cook's swain at all, but a *cock's swain* that he be. And that was a great thing here and now, for a cock's swain is the fellow on a boat that guides the thing. And that was Master Loney's speciality. A cock's swain! You know, the man what gets the ship from *A* to *B* without falling into the *sea*! So, guide us he did, right to shore, where I finally grabbed hold of my loved-for Peg and my longed-for Italy!

Back in London, Nick saw past the stable yard of the White Dove, and his breath now caught in his throat. The door to Valentina's inn was open. He ran in calling her name. No one in the front chamber! He turned a corner. No one in the next! He vaulted the stair, all the while calling "Valentina!"

And there she was at the room atop, being held by that serpent, with dagger to her throat. Old Knyvet had waited 'til Nick returned, for what good is a show that plays to an empty house? As Nick entered the room, from behind the door jumped out Skeres. He ran at Nick, who reached for his new-given dagger. The two men struggled, each with blade in hand. Using the heavy end of his dagger, Skeres pummeled his pommel onto Nick's poor skull as Knyvet watched and cackled. Valentina shook to free herself but could not loose the serpent. Nick got up and swung his dagger as a scythe. Left and right and left again. Skeres laughed and charged in on the printer. Nick took one last look at Beauty and then charged forward. The two men met, each dagger into flesh. Neither would let go, and both fell hard.

Then they both lie stilled.

Knyvet released the girl. She ran to Nick and her tears began to fall. She kissed his face, all bloodied from the fight. Knyvet kicked the bulk of Skeres and saw there was no more fight left in him. He crossed over to the quiet body of Nicholas, thrust Valentina aside, and stuck his head low to see. That's when Nick swung up and took the serpent down. Valentina screamed and thumped at Knyvet as Nick wrestled the knight onto the floor. He thrust his dagger into the evil creature's heart, and it may have been the darkness of the room, but Valentina would swear his blood ran black.

Brave Nick took Valentina in his arms, and there she would still be found ten long years after.

★

262

TEN YEARS LATER.

1634.

They walked there, hand in hand, the beauty and her boy. Then, little Nate let go his mother's grasp and ran to greet his dear father. A noble lad of nine, with the cleverness of his mother and the gentleness of his father. And when his small hand, clenched tight as a trapped wish, opened wide, the golden star of Oxford shone its light.

"What be this, father?" asked the inquisitive lad, looking up to his hero, as his eyes gleamed bright. They always gleam in these days. With a smile and a winkle 'twixt Nick and Valentina, she left the two men to have their talk, as she approached the lovely cottage of their farm.

A farm that had grown and prospered, as had their family. Their house sat upon a rolling hill, surrounded by many miles of mulberries 'twixt them and London. It was a home for Valentina and Nicholas and little Nate. It was a home where Uncle Ned could raise his chickens and where a smiling Auntie stood a-front, proudly snipping her beautiful roses from her many miles of glorious rosebushes, whilst Kit had grown to merry young manhood, writing cheery ditties to play on his pipes.

The proud father took his boy within his book chamber. It was a private place, where all the memories of days gone by were celebrated. Though the printer could no longer ply his trade, he never neglected his love of books. Upon his shelves lay hundreds for the reading. A very fine library 'twas, for here you'll find Shakespeares and Sidneys and Dantes a-plenty, but never one play by Webster nor one copy of *Guy of Warwick*!

Next to his newly-bought magnification glass on the table was the well-worn, red-covered Shakespeare. The sonnet book and early quartos were neatly stacked nearby. Upon the wall hung the old portrait of his parents and engravings of the great Lords Oxford and Southampton. And last, but not at all the least, was the most cherished book to Nick's heart, which sat upon his table, and meant the most to him: *POEMS BY ARTHUR DRINK-WELL*. Hyphen firmly placed.

Young Nate picked up a book as Nicholas peered out the window. And although the sky shone with a blessed light, he had no way of telling that lightning was about to strike. One last bolt of enlightenment for the end, for what's a tale told that brings no muse of fire for the finish?

"What's this one, father?"

"The sonnets, boy."

"This is grandmother and grandfather," the lad pointed to old Nathaniel and his dear lost wife. "May I see?" asked the boy, and father Nicholas obliged. He handed him the engraving and the boy began to investigate. "It's dirty."

"I saved it from the fire. 'Tis very old."

"Very old," the little one repeated, as he held it under the new magnification glass.

"Careful with that glass, son. Father just got it," he cautioned.

"His clothes are strange." And then something caught the young lad's eye. "What does he hold?"

"Hold?" said the father, not paying the lad much mind, as he was sorting out some new books 'cross the room.

"A chain," said the lad.

"Oh," said Nick.

"Yes. A chain. With birds on it."

Nick dropped the book he was holding.

"What did you say?" he crossed quick to his boy and looked at the old engraving beneath the new glass.

"Just birds, father," said the lad, "Grandfather has a chain with birds." And with that, the boy's mind wandered off to the sonnet book.

Despite years of gazing upon that worn portrait, there was indeed something new to see. For the first time, and with the aid of this new glass, Nick could spy something in his father's hand. A chain. An emblem! He moved the engraving to place it in the sunlight. He moved the glass a bit closer to the image. And then he saw what just may well have been there. A cross with birds! Which may well have been falcons. A chain which might have held the cross of

Southampton. A man who might have been the missing child. The changeling boy. The child that was removed so long ago!

A lightning bolt had hit. And as he stood staring thus, the eyes of Lord Edward smiled back at Nicholas from the wall. The printer now imagined his own father's role in this great tale of fathers and sons. A part he played, albeit unwilling at first. To think, his own father could have been the true third earl of Southampton, who had been taken away to create a space for the queen's own child. Then making a new life as the printer North. This gave Nicholas a shudder. For his father's role set the poet free to sing of his own taken boy. And to see his own son live on in immortal lines. Leaving the printed page as his only last will and testament that we shall ever find. For South had in truth become North!

And little Nate held the sonnet book in his hands.

"The son lives in this book, father?"

"Hm?" Nicholas was fixed upon the portrait.

"You say the son shall live forever?"

Nicholas turned to his son and was for some reason moved to pick the boy up and hold him in his arms as tight as he ever did.

"Yes, son. He shall live forever!" said he, holding on with… holding on *to* his very life. "And fathers, too. Sons and fathers, too!"

> *Or I shall live your epitaph to make,*
> *Or you survive when I in earth am rotten,*
> *From hence your memory death cannot take,*
> *Although in me each part will be forgotten.*
> *Your name from hence immortal life shall have,*
> *Though I, once gone, to all the world must die.*
> *The earth can yield me but a common grave*
> *When you entombéd in men's eyes shall lie.*
> *Your monument shall be my gentle verse,*
> *Which eyes not yet created shall o'er-read,*
> *And tongues to be, your being shall rehearse,*
> *When all the breathers of this world are dead.*
> *You still shall live, such virtue hath my pen,*
> *Where breath most breathes, even in the mouths of men.*

The End.

Acknowledgements

My dearest thanks to Siqing Song and Nicholas Destro for their love and support, Malcolm McKay for his invaluable advice, Kristin Linklater for setting me off on this quest for the truth, my publisher Fiona Smith, for believing in this book, Sir Derek Jacobi for his wonderful audiobook narration, Jon Sayles for the beautiful music, and all of those intrepid Shakespeare authorship researchers upon whose shoulders I stand.

About Ron Destro

Ron Destro is a proud father and a Kennedy Center award-winning writer, actor and director. His works include THE SHAKESPEARE MASTERCLASSES (Routledge, 2020) and the play HIROSHIMA, with an original score by Yoko Ono. He has staged more than 50 Shakespeare productions in Stratford-upon-Avon, Birnam Wood, Elsinore, Agincourt and Venice, and is the founding director of the New York and London-based Oxford Shakespeare Company.
For more information, go to www.rondestro.com

Next Arthur Taverner Mystery...

The Troublesome Adventures of Ole Agnes of Aylesbury, a joyful romp 'round the gardens of Cheapside with a beautiful ale-keep named Agnes, and her noble, courageous and comely knight, Sir Arthur Drink-well, accompanied by his young page, Bantickle Prickling of Stickleback.

The Starre, the Moone, the Sunne.

Also available as an unabridged audiobook
narrated by award-winning actor, Sir Derek Jacobi.

Printed in the USA
CPSIA information can be obtained
at www.ICGtesting.com
BVHW030706200823
668707BV00005B/17